T0305946

The Fundamentals of Tabletop Miniatures Game Design

This book presents a much-needed framework for the critical examination of miniatures games and their design. It provides the reader with both a conceptual model for understanding how these games work as well as a toolbox of mechanical approaches to achieving a range of design outcomes and assessing the fit of any given approach within a specific design.

Though dating back to the 1820s, tabletop miniatures games have been little explored critically and lack a conceptual vocabulary for their discussion. Active practitioners in the miniature games design community, Glenn Ford and Mike Hutchinson explore what defines these games, proposing the term 'non-discrete miniatures games' to encapsulate the essence of these open and immersive hobby gaming experiences. Discarding the term 'wargame', they argue against limiting conceptions of these games to direct armed conflict and champion their diverse narrative potential.

The book provides a fresh conceptual framework for miniatures games, abstracting the concepts of positioning and moving markers non-discretely across scale-modelled environments into inclusive and generalised terminology, untethering them from their roots as military simulations and providing the foundations for a fresh consideration of miniatures games design.

Written for game designers and with a foreword by Gav Thorpe, *The Fundamentals of Tabletop Miniatures Game Design* is a handbook for those who wish to design better miniatures games.

The Fundamentals of Tabletop Miniatures Game Design
A Designer's Handbook

Glenn Ford and Mike Hutchinson

CRC Press
Taylor & Francis Group
Boca Raton London New York

CRC Press is an imprint of the
Taylor & Francis Group, an **informa** business

Designed cover image: Sean Sutter

First edition published 2025
by CRC Press
2385 NW Executive Center Drive, Suite 320, Boca Raton FL 33431

and by CRC Press
4 Park Square, Milton Park, Abingdon, Oxon, OX14 4RN

CRC Press is an imprint of Taylor & Francis Group, LLC

ISBN: 978-1-032-32402-9 (hbk)
ISBN: 978-1-032-32401-2 (pbk)
ISBN: 978-1-003-31482-0 (ebk)

DOI: 10.1201/9781003314820

Typeset in Times
by KnowledgeWorks Global Ltd.

Contents

SECTION 1   Miniatures as Medium

SECTION 2   The Raw Materials

SECTION 3   *Miniatures Rules Systems*

Foreword

Games are Serious Business.

At the time of writing, I have been working in games design and related employ-ment for just over thirty years. Directly and indirectly, games have put food on the plate and a roof over my head for three decades, which is pretty remarkable for a life spent writing about small metal and plastic toy soldiers, and the (sometimes fictional) worlds they occupy. Over that time tabletop games have both increased in popularity by orders of magnitude, and become a highly lucrative industry that shows no signs of slowing.

Games design is one of those disciplines that traverses the entire spectrum of art to science, depending upon the game and the designer. Understanding the probabili-ties of something happening and the importance of that occurrence are two different but interwoven necessities when making games. Miniatures specifically demand a kind of interaction from players that spans the creative to the analytical, requiring the designer to understand the woolly but nevertheless real rules of narrative as much as basic principles of mathematics. Blending the two successfully is the alchemy of games design.

So we have here the *Principia Ludus* for toy soldier games, setting out the founda-tions of miniatures games design so that we can examine not only our own decisions and processes, but engage with other designers within a similar framework of refer-ence and nomenclature. It is a work that does a job not tackled yet. Previous volumes of games have focused either on high theory of human interaction and psychology, or approach from the bottom-up of writing and presenting a game as a set of rules. This book serves as an excellent study for those that want to not just design a game, but make a career out of designing a lot of games.

I came to this via Mike Hutchinson, who I met years ago when he was first dem-onstrating his splendid *Gaslands* game; a game that showcases the best of modern design mechanics to create a tactical experience with plenty of narrative moments. Having worked with Mike on *Gaslands* and *A Billion Suns*, Glenn Ford has been busy breaking ground with Man O' Kent games. Together Mike and Glenn have recorded two hundred episodes of their games design podcast, Rule Of Carnage, and continue to gather knowledge and experience across multiple projects, but remain inquisitive and analytical about some of the decades-old baggage and assumptions that have shaped miniatures games design since the time of luminaries in the 50s to 70s like Donald Featherstone and Charles S Grant, and the rise of the behemoth Games Workshop from the late 80s.

Combining experience and innovation, Mike and Glenn are among the most exciting and relevant creators of the current and next generation of tabletop games. This book should be studied by those that want to join them.

– **Gav Thorpe**

Preface

Glenn

Games are the art of inscription of agency with mechanics as a medium (Thi Nguyen, 2020). I believe that one of the ways that art can be defined is as the inscription of the experience of the artist in one or another form. A painter inscribes the experience of vision, a musician inscribes the experience of hearing, and so on. The game designer inscribes the experience of agency, the experience of having a series of choices, and the results of those choices. That means that while a novel can make a reader feel anger over the betrayal of one character by another, only a game can make a player feel *guilt* over betrayal, because *they* were the betrayer. There are certain emotions that can only be engendered by our making decisions ourselves, not via empathy for others being put in the position to make them. As such I believe that games have a unique and important voice within art, a voice that I love and value.

What excites me about games is that despite their being a popular and unique art form, their artistic aspect has been barely brushed upon. Games number among the oldest physical artefacts of various civilisations, play itself is possibly the oldest and most widespread of all aspects of civilisation (Huizinga, 2016), and yet they have little critical examination and are rarely pushed forward in what they can do as a form. It is as though we had invented the film camera and then spent the best part of two thousand years using it to capture the image of a train pulling into a station. That potential excites and drives me in my investigation and designing of games.

On a personal level, I love games. I mean that in a very deep and intense way, increasingly so as years pass and I find that the idea of putting away childish things is a fundamentally and personally destructive activity. Life is, at its best, a search for joy, for the moments that bring happiness, and the magic circle of games is a shared environment for the hunting of fun, where an agreement to engage in savage competition can shape our most aggressive instincts into something mutual and constructive.

On a social level, I love that games offer an intervening mechanism to allow total strangers to engage with each other. I have long been a tournament gamer and, increasingly, a frequenter of tabletop clubs and conventions. I have repeatedly seen people who struggle to hold a conversation with a stranger come alive when the game steps in to offer them a set of frameworks and agreed structures to communicate through. Games are a place where people who struggle to understand the motivations of others can find common ground to interact and find understanding. Games are engines for fun, but they are just as often engines for empathy, channels for connections with others. Alexis Kennedy in *The Snare of the Tree, and Other Perilous Seductions* (2021) writes that designers should 'make games that embody an ideal experience of the contact of human souls'. I slightly disagree, I think the word 'ideal' should be replaced by the word 'actual'.

Glenn Ford

Mike

As independent designers, Glenn and I have spent a fair amount of time dragging our games to and from UK games conventions to share our enthusiasm and excitement with others. When we travel together, we spend all of our time dissecting the games we make, discussing other games we feel strongly about and brainstorming how to improve our own current projects.

When lockdown hit in 2020, we lacked a forum to continue our conversations, and so we started Rule of Carnage[1], a podcast and YouTube channel that initially existed only as an excuse to meet up regularly over video and continue our ceaseless mastication of tabletop miniatures games. We had both been writing on this topic on our own websites[2] for some time, examining our own design processes and sharing the challenges we encountered along the way. These articles had received positive feedback from other designers who found them interesting and useful, and that gave us the confidence to record our conversations and post them online.

About a year later we received an email asking if we might be interested in proposing a book on the topics we were discussing. There was no question in either of our minds. We'd already agreed that there appeared to be no single volume that attempted to define the sort of tabletop miniatures games we have spent most of our lives obsessing over, and if the opportunity had arisen for us to correct that omission, well, we'd give it our best shot.

For me, the creation of miniature games rules has always been inextricably entangled with the hands-on nature of the miniature gaming hobby in general. The freedom to create your own miniature worlds to play in always seemed to me united with the freedom to create the systems governing such play. As a teenager, I designed arcane miniature games to enjoy with my school friends, filling ring-binders with graph-paper incantations for spaceship games, racing games and grandly conceived generic all-purpose miniature game rules to suit all periods and technology levels. As an adult, I have had the opportunity to share my games with a wider audience, and I have found a deep joy in the strange alchemy of writing simple text that yet somehow ignites in other adults a joyous form of imaginative play that is at once structured and free, abstract and tactile, competitive and collaborative. We are playing serious, difficult, complex games, so we can remain confident that we are behaving as adults... yet our inner child's eyes are aglow with the simple pleasure of playing with toys. I do not take this alchemy lightly.

Glenn and I are passionate and curious practitioners. What you have in your hands is the result of many hundreds of hours of debate, discussion, research and gaming, and we truly hope you find something in it to inspire your own game designs and your own gaming.

Mike Hutchinson

NOTES

1 http://ruleofcarnage.com
2 Find Glenn's writings at https://www.manokentgames.com and Mike's at https://planetsmashergames.com

REFERENCES

Huizinga, J. (2016) *Homo Ludens. New York*: Angelico Press.
Kennedy, A. (2021) *The Snare of the Tree, and Other Perilous Seductions*. London: Amazon.
Thi Nguyen, C. (2020) *Games: Agency As Art*. Oxford: Oxford University Press.

Acknowledgements

Thank you to the hundreds of designers whose work has inspired and informed this book. Thank you to the Rule Of Carnage community for their endless curiosity and enthusiasm about the craft of table miniature games design. Thank you to our friends that have shared in our enthusiasm for toy soldiers and to our families who lovingly support our pursuit of this odd craft. Thank you to Sean Sutter for the cover illustration.

Author Biographies

Glenn Ford is the designer of miniatures games including *Pukeapocolypse* and *Boarders and Black Flags* as well as the regular developer of the games of his friend and Rule of Carnage podcast collaborator Mike Hutchinson. He runs an independent games publishing company, Man O' Kent Games, and has successfully funded six Kickstarter campaigns so far. Glenn lives in Deal, a small town with far too many castles in Kent in the United Kingdom, with his wife, son and a disturbingly high number of games and toy soldiers.

Mike Hutchinson is an award-winning designer of miniatures games, including *Gaslands*, *A Billion Suns* and *Hobgoblin,* and runs an independent game design studio called Planet Smasher Games. He is the co-host of the Rule of Carnage podcast, a weekly series examining tabletop miniatures game design. Mike lives in the inexplicably named village of Old Wives Lees in Kent, UK, with his wife, Vanessa, and two daughters.

Introduction

Our goal with this book is to provide a definition of tabletop miniatures games as an artistic medium and to offer a guide to the design of any given ruleset. We intend it as a learning resource for new designers and a source of inspiration for more experienced creators. We do not intend this book as a guide to the preparation of a game for either pitching or publication nor will it make a specific examination of player psychology (although we will examine how certain rules can be used to elicit player responses or motivate player activity in a particular direction). It is our hope that, by defining and then examining the nature of tabletop miniatures games and offering an in-depth examination of their component parts, we can help you design better miniature games.

DEFINING OUR TERMS

While we have sought to avoid jargon and explain any that is used, there are certain terms we will be using frequently that are worth mentioning before we begin.

A completed and pre-existing game is, well, a **Game**. A game that is still in the process of being created is a **Design**. A **Mechanic** is the concept behind a particular rule or combination of rules intended to create a given effect; they are the medium by which a game designer achieves their art. The sum of a game's mechanics is its **System**. A game is played by **Players**. A particular instance of a game being played is a **Session**.

A **Miniature** is a small-scale model, most usually a humanoid creature or scale vehicle but not always, directly manipulated by players to achieve their intentions within the game world (Figure I.1). A group of miniatures arrayed in a formation with ranks, files, flanks and rears is a **Ranked Unit**; a group lacking these features is a **Squad**. A single miniature in a unit or squad is a **Trooper**; one that operates independently is a **Character**. Where a player's intentions may be realised by a miniature, token or standee, they will be referred to by the collective term **Marker**. Where Characters, Squads and Ranked Units are referred to collectively or interchangeably, they will be referred to as **Units**.

FIGURE I.1   A character, a ranked unit and a squad. Photograph by the author.

DOI: 10.1201/9781003314820-1

A Piece of **Terrain** or **Scenery** is a small-scale model representing hills, trees, buildings or any of a range of stationary features representing the world in which a set of miniatures exists.

THE STRUCTURE OF THIS BOOK

This book is divided into three sections. In 'Miniatures as Medium', we attempt to define these particular games as discrete from all other forms and examine their key features in broad terms isolated from their specific mechanical implementations. In 'Raw Materials', we look more closely at the common components, both physical and conceptual, that these games rely upon as their foundations. In 'Miniatures Rules Systems', we examine the areas that these games most often have to consider, mechanically, and provide a range of examples and explanations for their possible structures and implementations.

Throughout, we make reference to existing miniature games that either demonstrate the conventions or provide examples of interesting departures from the norm. You will find that we make reference to our games with regularity. We apologise for this bias, but it is somewhat unavoidable, given the depth with which we have considered and discussed those particular games among ourselves.

HOW TO USE THIS BOOK

Whether you read the chapters in order or dip into specific ones that apply to a particular area you are currently curious about or engaged with in a design of your own, we hope that you are able to extract fresh ideas and perspectives on common areas of tabletop miniature games design.

At the end of each chapter, you will find first a summary of the topics covered and then an 'Experiments' section, which will offer some suggestions for changes you might experimentally apply to a design as an exercise.

If you are currently working on your own design, we hope you will consider performing some of these experiments on your current project, altering your rules and then playtesting them with an open and curious mind, using them as an opportunity to push yourself into unfamiliar or uncomfortable territory in order to better understand where the boundaries for a successful design might lie.

If you don't have a game of your own that you could apply it to, we suggest that you pick an existing rules system that you're familiar with and perform the experiment using that game. It doesn't matter if it's a massed battle game or a narrative skirmish one, so long as it's something you know really well: create some house rules and then playtest the new version of the game to see what impact the changes have.

As you explore the exercises at the end of each chapter, it can be valuable to have another curious designer to discuss your findings with: why did a particular rules change feel off, or how did it lead to a change in the game's pacing or complexity? If you are looking for a community to discuss these matters with, consider joining the Rule of Carnage discord (linked from http://ruleofcarnage.com), where you will find a friendly community of miniatures game designers wrestling with these very same questions.

Section 1

Miniatures as Medium

Rules are for the obedience of fools and the guidance of wise men.

Douglas Bader

In the first section, we define what we mean by a tabletop miniatures game and what its fundamental characteristics are. We propose a number of frameworks for conceptualising how they create both enjoyment and meaning for players, and explore what they can offer that other types of games cannot.

DOI: 10.1201/9781003314820-2

1 What Are Tabletop Miniatures Games?

There is no name for the games we love. Having played them for 30 years and designed them for almost as long, we still don't know what they are called. As this book will define what they are and give our opinions on how to approach their design, we need a name for them.

They are certainly *tabletop games*, as they are not played on a computer, but board games are played on a tabletop, and they are not what this book is about. They are certainly *miniatures games*, but there are plenty of board and role-playing games played with miniatures, and those aren't what we're talking about either. Some call them *miniatures wargames*, but we don't agree that they have to be about war. Some call them skirmish or mass battle games, but those are just categories of scope. Games Workshop called them '3D-roleplay hobby games' in the 1980s, which is delightfully descriptive but didn't catch on. When talking to the uninitiated, we describe these games as 'like Warhammer'.

We want to talk in depth about those games that are played on a tabletop, which probably use miniatures, feature scale-modelled scenery and likely don't use a preset board. This will be hard if we don't have a name for them.

WHY DOES IT MATTER WHAT THEY ARE CALLED?

Without a name for something, it becomes difficult to think about it clearly or talk about it clearly with others. Describing something as 'like' something else limits your conception of it; it bounds the definition in terms of comparison.

When thinking about any concept, the words we use to frame it shape and define our initial approaches. Without effective and crystalised language, we struggle to grasp and shape concepts effectively. Without shared and agreed-upon language for common concepts, we cannot communicate effectively as designers and build on each other's work.

By describing the entire genre of tabletop miniatures games as 'like Warhammer', we limit our conception of the medium. This form of game is not inherently about war, high fantasy or space opera. These assumptions cramp the creative and conceptual space of the medium and limit its potential. By describing them in these terms, we risk creating them in the same mould over and over again.

By comparison, think of the transformation of pen-and-paper roleplaying games over the last 50 years. What began as a medium for small-scale mediaeval combat against fantasy foes in *Dungeons & Dragons* (Gygax and Arneson, 1974) grew to a diverse and experimental medium, including games as varied as *Star Crossed* (Roberts, 2019), where players create a simmering romance disapproved of by their society, or *Thousand Year Old Vampire* (Hutchings, 2018), a solo journaling game of ethically complex choices.

DOI: 10.1201/9781003314820-3

Over the same period, video games advanced from simplistic physical simulations such as *Pong* (Alcorn, 1972) to sophisticated interactive stories such as *The Last of Us* (Minkoff, 2013), which received critical acclaim for its powerful emotional narrative and its depiction of female characters, or *The Stanley Parable* (Wreden and Pugh, 2011), a game about driving players to question their relationship with the medium of video games themselves.

Boxed tabletop games too have enjoyed diversity in subject matter, from the gentle family-friendly critique of capitalism in *Monopoly* (Darrow, 1935) to recent games such as *Holding On; The Troubled Life of Billy Kerr* (Fox and O'Conner, 2018), which puts players in the position of nurses working on a terminal care ward trying to unearth the regrets of a patient to ease their passing, or *Train* (Romero, 2009), a game designed to ask players to question their reactions to rules and authority by making them complicit in the holocaust.

Conversely, tabletop miniatures games have spent a hundred years moving from *Little Wars* (Wells, 1913), a game about combatants trying to kill each other with a range of weaponry, to *Marvel Crisis Protocol* (Pagani and Shick, 2019), a game about combatants trying to kill each other with a range of weaponry, by way of *Chainmail* (Gygax and Perren, 1971), *Warhammer* (Ansell *et al.*, 1983), *Warmachine* (McVey, Snoddy and Wilson, 2003) and *Infinity* (Liste, Rodríguez and Torres, 2005), all games about combatants trying to kill each other with a range of weaponry.

Direct conflict, while currently ubiquitous in the medium, is ultimately a narrative framing choice of the designer and not an inherent characteristic of the form. To be clear, we play many 'wargames', and have no problem with direct armed conflict as a subject. While there are many subtle and intelligent tabletop miniatures games based around direct armed conflict, it is our hope that by presenting an abstract conceptual framework for these types of games, we might inspire the design of some that are not.

NON-DISCRETE MINIATURES GAMES

So, if 'tabletop miniatures game' is an inexact term and having a specific and accurate term is important, what else could we call these games? What defines them? We believe it is their inherently non-discrete nature: they are non-discrete miniatures games. We intend 'non-discrete' to suggest both analogue placement and movement of markers in physical space (non-discrete positioning) and a lack of concrete definitions for required components and markers (non-discrete components).

In tabletop miniatures games, players position and move markers, usually representative scale models, around a scale-modelled environment to play out tactically interesting interactions between those markers, constrained by a set of rules governing those interactions.

In most board- and card-based games, markers exist in discrete states. In *Monopoly*, a player's marker can be on 'Go' or the space next to it, but it cannot be between the two. Conversely, in tabletop miniatures games, markers are moved in a non-discrete manner. In *Warhammer: Age of Sigmar* (2015), as in Tony Bath's Ancient Warfare rules found in *War Games* (Featherstone, 1962), troopers within an infantry unit are moved individually, each up to six inches, measured with a tape measure and turned as they choose during this movement. A unit in *Warhammer* can move to an infinite range of positions since it moves through an analogue space with the ability to stop at any point through that movement. This method of non-discrete movement originates from an intention to simulate the infinite configurations of terrain, landscapes and soldiers in the 'real' world. This freedom is one of the unique strengths of the form and provides players with much of the hobby game loop we will explore in Chapter 5. Thanks to this freedom, it is possible and indeed common for tabletop miniatures games to be presented simply as a set of text-based rules that ask players to provide their own miniatures, terrain features, buildings and topographical features.

In some instances, the required components for a sprawling and non-discrete miniatures game are gathered into a single box for retail, such as with Games Workshop's 1988 release of *Adeptus Titanicus* (Johnson, 1988). Crucially, while a box may provide sufficient components to play the game, it cannot provide all the components that *could* be used to play the game. Rather than providing an exhaustive game experience, they are instead offered as a starting point, an indication of the direction you might choose to follow.

Conversely, a boxed board game provides the complete components for its play, and anything not included within the box cannot be considered acceptable as a game component. Such games have no method of understanding or referring to anything not provided with them. Should you and I be preparing to play a tabletop miniatures game and I place my shoe into the play area, we can reasonably expect the tabletop miniatures game at hand to provide mechanisms to define and interact with my shoe as a rational (if potentially un-thematic) game element. I expect our soldiers may take cover behind it, and that it blocks line of sight, and that it impedes movement of models. Should I perform the same action while we are playing *Monopoly*, the game is destroyed. There are no mechanisms within the rules to define or interact with this alien object; it simply disrupts the game.

The infinite flexibility in the playing area, markers and interactions gives rise to our chosen name for this type of game: **non-discrete miniatures games**.

SUMMARY

These games will be called **non-discrete miniatures** games because:

- They are not necessarily games about war.
- They operate within analogue spaces.
- They are accepting of an infinite range of objects.

We intend 'non-discrete' to suggest both:

- Analogue placement and movement of markers in physical space (non-discrete positioning)
- Lack of concrete definitions for required components and markers (non-discrete components)

We make this definition because it allows us to re-frame our thinking.

REFERENCES

Alcorn, A. (1972) *Pong.* [Video game]. Arcade Cabinet. Sunnyvale, CA: Atari.

Ansell, B., Halliwell, R., Johnson, J. and Priestley, R. (1983) *Warhammer: The Mass Combat Fantasy Roleplaying Game.* Nottingham: Citadel UK.

Darrow, C. (1935) *Monopoly.* [Board game] Beverly, MA: Parker Brothers.

Featherstone, D.F. (1962) *War Games.* London: Stanley Paul & Co. Ltd.

Fox, M. and O'Conner, R. (2018) *Holding On; The Troubled Life of Billy Kerr.* [Board game] Belfast: Hub Games Ltd.

Gygax, G. and Arneson, D. (1974) *Dungeons & Dragons.* Lake Geneva, WI: TSR Inc.

Gygax, G. and Perren, J. (1971) *Chainmail.* Lake Geneva, WI: TSR Inc.

Hutchings, T. (2018) *Thousand Year Old Vampire.* Self-Published.

Johnson, J, (1988) *Adeptus Titanicus.* [Board game] Nottingham: Games Workshop.

Liste, F., Rodríguez, G. and Torres, C. (2005) *Infinity N3: Core Book.* Cangas, Galicia: Corvus Belli.

McVey, M., Snoddy, B. and Wilson, M. (2003) *Warmachine.* Bellevue, WA: Privateer Press.

Minkoff, J. (2013) *The Last of Us.* [Video game]. PlayStation 3. San Mateo, CA: Sony Computer Entertainment.

Pagani, W. and Shick, W. (2019) *Marvel Crisis Protocol.* Roseville, MN: Atomic Mass Games.

Roberts, A. (2019) *Star Crossed.* [Boardgame] Chapel Hill, NC: Bully Pulpit Games.

Romero, B. (2009) *Train* [Interactive installation]. Atlanta: MODA.

Warhammer: Age of Sigmar. (2015) Nottingham: Games Workshop.

Wells, H.G. (1913) *Little Wars.* London: Frank Palmer.

Wreden, D. and Pugh, W. (2011) *The Stanley Parable.* [Video Game]. PC. London: Galactic Cafe.

2 A Brief History of Miniatures Games

Miniatures wargames began with gridded movement. First chess, then Johann Christian Ludwig Hellwig's 'Attempt to build upon chess a tactical game which two or more persons might play' (Hellwig, 1780). In it, the German mathematician uses the term *kriegsspiel* (wargame) to describe a game that resembles chess but uses more squares (49 by 33) and new unit types (including artillery). He filled some squares with terrain (mountains, rivers and forests) and provided rules for their effects. Most interestingly, 'he did not dictate a fixed landscape, but instead provided tools that would permit players to design a terrain matching any historical, contemporary, even imaginary space' (Peterson, 2016), taking the first step into non-discrete gaming. In 1797, Georg Venturini combined the abstract gridded playing area with maps of the real world, introducing ground scale (two thousand paces per square in his case) into gaming for the first time.

In 1809, Georg Leopold von Reisswitz dispensed with the grid in favour of a lipped table covered with sand, allowing the contours of more 'realistic' terrain to be affected, and let units be placed freely rather than one to a square as before. Reisswitz also represented his units with wooden blocks of regular size, designed to occupy the exact footprint and scale that a real troop formation would. Without a grid to regulate unit movements, rulers were used to measure movement and shooting, completing the transition of Hellwig's discrete *kriegsspiel* into the first recorded non-discrete miniatures game. Reisswitz published his system in 1812 and 'replaced his sand table with a fine wooden chest to house sculpted terrain segments that players could combine to resemble a desired battlefield' (Peterson, 2016).

In 1824, Reisswitz's son, Georg Heinrich Rudolf Johann von Reisswitz, built upon his father's game in an attempt to make it more realistic. During Napoleon's occupation, Prussian statisticians had drawn up tables of firing probabilities, which inspired the younger Reisswitz to introduce dice to the wargaming table, increasing realism via the imperfect and unpredictable execution of a commander's plan by their forces. The younger Reisswitz also introduced two further innovations: a neutral referee to diminish the omniscience of the players and the reversion to a two-dimensional playing map.

By 1873, the game had spread as far as England, with an Oxford Kriegsspiel Club. An 1898 article described Robert Louis Stevenson at play with toy soldiers in his attic, deploying a similar dexterity-based pop-gun shooting mechanic to that which H.G. Wells would record in his *Little Wars* (1913). Both Stevenson and Wells were overtly concerned with play and game balance over the serious study of war. Also concerned with toy soldiers were Britains, a manufacturer of lead figures, who in 1908 produced the first example of a wargame ruleset distributed with the commercial purpose of selling miniatures, *The Great War Game for Young and Old* (Curry, 2011).

DOI: 10.1201/9781003314820-4

Between the world wars, a handful of wargaming rules were published: *Shambattle* by Dowdall and Glason (1929); Captain Sach's War Game, published in the journey of the British Society of Collectors of Model Soldiers sometime in the 1930s (Curry, 2011); and *Fletcher Pratt's Naval War Game* in 1940 (Pratt, 1940).

In 1957, a California-based caster of metal miniatures, Jack Scruby, published the first volume of the *War Games Digest*. This was to become a small but fertile community of amateur wargame enthusiasts, publishing rulesets, battle reports and articles on military history. It had subscribers on both sides of the Atlantic, including London-based friends Donald Featherstone and Tony Bath, who edited many of the issues.

The early 1960s saw the publication of an increasing number of books on non-discrete miniature gaming, the most influential of which proved to be *War Games* by Featherstone (1962), which included several of Tony Bath's rulesets. The increased availability of a greater range of wargaming rule systems broadened participation in the hobby. Various periods of history and scopes of games were invented and played, from ancient mass battles to Wild West skirmishes.

In 1971, Gary Gygax published *Chainmail* (Gygax and Perren, 1971), a medieval ruleset, in which he included a section on including fantasy elements such as wizards and monsters, the first commercially available rules system to do so. A fellow wargamer in Gygax's gaming club adopted the rules for a dungeon-looting game, and Gygax and Dave Arneson would collaborate on expanding *Chainmail* into *Dungeon & Dragons*, building from non-discrete miniatures gaming into a new kind of imaginative roleplaying game.

Games Workshop began distributing *Dungeon & Dragons* (Gygax and Arneson, 1974) in the United Kingdom in 1977 and formed Citadel Miniatures in 1978 to produce figures for use in it. Just as Britains had 70 years earlier, Citadel Miniatures concluded that a set of wargaming rules would stimulate sales of model soldiers, and Ansell *et al.* (1983) published *Warhammer: The Mass Combat Roleplaying Game*, which was followed by *Warhammer 40,000: Rogue Trader* in 1987.

Since the 1980s, non-discrete miniatures gaming has greatly expanded, with a host of small and medium-sized companies globally producing rules systems, miniatures, or both, for an enormous variety of periods, scales and fantasy worlds. More recently, the ability to publish rules electronically, allowing instant worldwide distribution with little or no barrier to entry, and the rise of 3D printing, which caused an explosion in digital sculpting, have led to more and smaller production becoming possible. We will explore some of those rule systems in this book.

REFERENCES

Ansell, B., Halliwell, R., Johnson, J. and Priestley, R. (1983) *Warhammer: The Mass Combat Fantasy Roleplaying Game*. Nottingham: Citadel UK.

Curry, J. (ed.) (2011) *The Wargaming Pioneers (Early Wargames Vol. 1)*. Morrisville, NC: Lulu.com.

Dowdall, H.G. and Glason, J.H. (1929). *Shambattle: How to Play with Toy Soldiers*. New York, NY: Alfred A. Knopf.

Featherstone, D.F. (1962) *War Games*. London: Stanley Paul & Co. Ltd.

Gygax, G. and Arneson, D. (1974) *Dungeons and Dragons*. 1st edn. Lake Geneva, WI: TSR Inc.

Gygax, G. and Perren, J. (1971) *Chainmail*. Lake Geneva, WI: TSR Inc.

Hellwig, J.C.L. (1780). *Attempt to Build Upon Chess a Tactical Game Which Two or More Persons Might Play*. Leipzig: Crusius.

Peterson, J. (2016) *Zones of Control: Perspectives on Wargaming*. Edited by Harrigan, P and Kirschenbaum, M.G. Cambridge, MA: MIT Press

Pratt, F. (1940) *Fletcher Pratt's Naval War Game*. New York, NY: Harrison-Hilton Book Inc.

Wells, H.G. (1913) *Little Wars*. London: Frank Palmer.

3 The Spatial Relationship

In the first chapter, we proposed that these kinds of tabletop miniatures games are defined by their non-discrete nature. Here we suggest that the central ludic implication of this non-discrete nature is the **spatial relationships** between markers: the establishment and manipulation of spatial relationships between markers provides the primary driver of player interest within them and differentiates them from other tabletop games.

In the majority of tabletop games, there is little interest in the direct spatial relationships between player markers. There may be an abstracted focus on their relative positions. In race-game, *Hare and Tortoise* (Parlett, 1973) players care whether another player's marker is ahead or behind them on the race track, but the game doesn't interest itself in whether a given marker is facing towards or away from another or precisely how far it is placed from another in real space. Only non-discrete miniatures games regularly choose to deal with these sorts of spatial relationships in a direct and non-abstracted way.

Players of a game such as *Warhammer 40,000* (2023) begin a session by carefully positioning their miniatures relative to their opponent's and to the modelled terrain, and then spend much of the ensuing play time directly measuring and adjudicating absolute distances and relative orientations between models in physical space.

These spatial relationships are central to the interest of non-discrete miniatures games and are expressed in three core forms: **line of sight (LoS)**, **force projection** and **relational conflicts**. Successful engagement with these concepts is central to the success of any non-discrete game.

GRIDDED MOVEMENT GAMES

There are a range of miniatures games such as *BattleTech* (Brown, Leeper and Weisman, 1984) and sections of games such as the tactical combat parts of *Dungeons & Dragons* (Gygax and Arneson, 1974) where movement is managed using discrete methods, such as grids. While in such cases, the non-discrete nature of these games is limited to the initial set-up conditions, the feature that persists through and unites these games with those we might consider more definitively non-discrete miniatures games remains their focus on the spatial relationships between player markers, and, if so, we can consider them in many of the same terms as those miniatures games with non-discrete movement.

LINE OF SIGHT

We will examine the technicalities of designing LoS rules in Chapter 22, but for now, LoS is the term given to the theoretical line traced from whatever part of one player marker is designated capable of sight to a part of another player marker to

DOI: 10.1201/9781003314820-5

check if one can 'see' the other, opening options for the two to interact. Managing the ability of one's own markers to see those of an opponent while obscuring or avoiding their returning LoS is often central to the tactics of these games. As we laid out in the previous chapter, freedom in scale terrain, marker shapes and movements is a core feature of these games, and defining how an infinitely varied range of elements interact clearly creates game design difficulties. Concerns with lines drawn through physical space from one point to another (and what those lines encounter) are rare outside of this genre of game and emerge because spatial relationships are paramount to them.

FORCE PROJECTION

When a gameplay marker is moved around the play area, it carries with it a theoretical area it is capable of interacting with, and we refer to this zone as its area of **force projection**. This concept exists within discrete games; in Chess, a rook creates force projection in orthogonal strips and a Bishop in diagonal ones. In non-discrete miniatures games, the direction and application of force projection can be imagined as a series of strips, cones and circles, centred on the various markers. The non-discrete nature of movement in these games allows for these zones to be moved and intersected with others in an infinite number of combinations. How these zones are brought together – to overlap for additional benefits, deny other players free reign and directly achieve a player's goals – is a significant part of how the non-discrete nature of movement in these games becomes so important and interesting. When, for example, three markers variously generate force projection circles of 2″, 3″ and 4″, and how and where those circles overlap with each other and other markers on the table is a matter of interest, the fact that the markers generating them can move infinite variations of an inch when bringing those zones to bear is central in generating player interest.

All non-discrete miniatures games feature a level of **active force projection**, sometimes called threat range, the area over which a unit can choose to interact with others when used by its controlling player, largely defined by LoS and movement rules. The primary form of force projection is temporary and active, coming into play only when a unit is activated and dissipating when activation is completed. A game can extend force projection beyond this active period with **passive force projection**. This comes about in a range of ways, but the two most common are **auras** and **reaction fire**.

An aura is an area of force projection that a marker generates, usually through 360 degrees, either temporarily or permanently. They are either inherent or activated by player actions. For example, in *Warhammer: The Game of Fantasy Battles* (Cavatore *et al.*, 2000), units could benefit from an inherent aura effect called 'Terror', which meant any other unit within six inches of the bearer of the rule would be required to take a test before being moved by their controlling player, which if failed would force them to flee. Terror is an example of a permanent aura purchased during force selection which allows a marker bearing it to generate a constant circle of force projection. In *Malifaux* (Anderson *et al.*, 2013), the Henchman Sebastian has an ability called 'Bloody Harvest', a temporary 3″ aura requiring the expenditure of an activation point and a successful test to force all enemies in range to take a test to avoid damage, making this a temporary, activated aura.

When a marker is inactive, it may have the ability to take an action that interrupts that of another, usually opposing, marker. Most usually, this is to allow a ranged attack to be made (hence the term 'reaction fire') and might require an action to be expended during the marker's activation to enter a specially indicated state of watchfulness (often called 'Overwatch', a military term for positioning artillery to provide covering fire). For example, in *Infinity* (Couceiro *et al.*, 2014), players can declare a reaction order during an opponent's activation when an enemy model moves within its LoS to attack the enemy model. A marker with a reaction fire ability can be thought of as generating a zone spanning over everywhere that its LoS can be drawn to within its range, another instance of force projection. If this projection can result in markers that violate its boundaries being removed from play (shot by the watchful model), it can be easily imagined how bringing these lanes of pressure to bear to direct and pressure the choices of an opponent can generate considerable player interest and interaction.

One of the most common permanent aura force projection systems is forced close combat engagement. In these systems, units have a close combat engagement range (often base-contact). When a unit begins within the engagement range of another and seeks to either take a non-combat action or move outside of the engagement range, the mover may be struck by the engaging unit, simply causing damage, stopping the movement from taking place or both. Since this engagement range is generally projected in a 360-degree area, this system creates an interesting overlap of aura and reaction systems.

CASE STUDY: PASSIVE FORCE PROJECTION – *THE LORD OF THE RINGS: STRATEGY BATTLE GAME*

In *The Lord of the Rings: Strategy Battle Game* (Cavatore and Ward, 2005), every individual trooper has a 1-inch control zone that enemies are not allowed to enter unless they are 'charging' (moving to engage in combat with) the model generating the zone. Once a trooper is engaged, they lose their control zone. This means that control zones can be used to block enemy movement and protect vulnerable characters or objectives, and in turn, the order of movement and engagement are vitally important in the game. The result is an elegant puzzle of constant force projection.

RELATIONAL CONFLICTS

The final form of spatial relationships used in these games, although not ubiquitously, is the related orientation of participants in conflicts. In most games, it matters very little which marker is facing in relation to another. During a game of Chess, if a rook take a pawn it makes no difference whatsoever if the pawn is approached from the front, flank or rear. In a game of *Warhammer*, if a unit manages to come into contact with an opposing unit's rear, it gains a significant advantage. In *Gaslands*

(Hutchinson, 2017), a 'head-on' collision between two vehicles generates more attack dice than one in which the two parties collide in a less dangerous pair of relative orientations. In a game of *Adeptus Titanicus* (2018), shots from an aggressor positioned in the 'rear arc' of a target receive bonuses to their damage rolls, creating a tactical benefit to outmanoeuvring opponents and increasing interest in the miniatures' relative positions and facings.

CASE STUDY: RELATIONAL COMBAT – *BATTLEFLEET GOTHIC*

When unleashing a spaceship's weapon battery in *Battlefleet Gothic* (Chambers, Johnson and Thorpe, 1999), you are required to check the relative facing of your target. You receive more attack dice if the target's facing suggests relative movement that is favourable to you; it is harder to hit a target moving across your sights (i.e. abeam) than one closing or moving away from you. This is achieved by checking which of the target's arcs of sight the attacking ship lies in and modifying the dice rolls by looking at the relative orientations on a gunnery chart.

EMERGENT SPATIAL PUZZLES

Any non-discrete miniature game in play represents a certain kind of three-dimensional spatial-reasoning puzzle. Force projection turns markers into areas of potential and actual pressure, and bringing those pressures to bear in the correct amounts at the correct points is a puzzle needing mental focus and engagement to solve. The puzzle of force projection and unit interaction emerges from the complex interactions between players, making each instance unique and personal to the players creating them.

Whenever two or more people are opposed over the placement of interacting shapes on the tabletop, the puzzle of how to achieve one's own goals while frustrating those of an opponent will inevitably occur, but there are some principles to bear in mind to make them more satisfying when they do.

REDUCE EFFECTIVENESS AS RANGE INCREASES

When a rule allows force projection over a great distance, its average effect on the game should be less than force projection over a short distance. Close combat should be more reliably able to remove units than ranged attacks, and close combat from slow-moving units should be more reliable than that of fast-moving units. This creates an instant puzzle of how many chances it is acceptable for short-ranged units to give their longer reaching opponents and how either side can shift the margins in their favour.

SPATIAL ACCUMULATION CREATES INTERACTION

Whenever zones of force projection are permitted to overlap in a manner that allows their effects to accumulate, a multi-layered puzzle is generated. Players must choose between multiple overlapping zones to increase their effects in return for covering fewer options or a wider but less potent spread, and once they have made their choice, they must find the means to actually achieve it on the tabletop, creating a further spatial puzzle.

Solving the puzzle that emerges from a specific game session results in a moment of pleasurable satisfaction, and over multiple sessions, players can build up a set of tactical and spatial-reasoning heuristics to solve future similar emergent puzzles more skilfully. The acquisition of such skills can be a further source of satisfaction, as we will explore in the next chapter.

SUMMARY

Non-discrete miniatures games have at the heart of their interest **Spatial Relationships** that are **Specific** and **Relative**.

These relationships are defined by:

- Line of sight
- Force projection
- Relational conflicts

The spatial relationship provides mechanisms to create satisfying and emergent spatial-reasoning puzzles.

EXPERIMENTS

Remove anything that could be considered an act of violence from your game. Identify what the units in the game could still be trying to do, and identify why they might still care to be able to see their opposing numbers trying to do the same thing. Gamify that process of doing, seeing and being seen.

Identify each form of force projection in your game as being either beneficial (such as providing buffs or healing) or dangerous (such as attacking). Make each the other kind, keeping the same degrees of power and effect. How does the game change, and why?

REFERENCES

Adeptus Titanicus. (2018) Nottingham: Games Workshop Ltd.

Anderson, M., Caroland, N., Cohen, R., Darland, A., Gibbs, J., Hanold, D., Johns, E., Martin, M. and Weber, D. (2013) *Malifaux: Second Edition.* South Korea: Wyrd Miniatures, LLC.

Brown, F., Leeper, L. R. and Weisman, J. (1984) *BattleTech: A Game of Armored Combat.* [Board game] Chicago, IL: FASA.

Cavatore, A., Pirinen, T., Priestley, R., Stillman, N. and Thornton, J. (2000) *Warhammer: The Game of Fantasy Battles.* 1 edn. Nottingham: Games Workshop Ltd.

Cavatore, A. and Ward, M. (2005) *The Lord of the Rings: Strategy Battle Game*. Nottingham: Games Workshop Ltd.

Chambers, A., Johnson, J. and Thorpe, G. (1999) *Battlefleet Gothic*. Nottingham: Games Workshop Ltd.

Couceiro, A., Azpeitia, F., Rodríguez, G. and Rodríguez, C. (2014) *Infinity: N3 Rulebook*. Pontevedra: Corvus Belli.

Gygax, G. and Arneson, D. (1974) *Dungeons & Dragons*. 1st edn. Lake Geneva, WI: TSR Inc.

Hutchinson, M. (2017) *Gaslands*. Oxford: Osprey Games.

Parlett, D. (1973) *Hare and Tortoise*. [Board game] Placitas, NM: Rio Grande Games.

Warhammer 40,000 (2023) Nottingham: Games Workshop.

4 When Should Something Be a Miniatures Game?

Games all start somewhere, perhaps with an idea for a neat mechanic, a scene from a book or movie or an interest in a genre trope or a historic episode. Like a painter choosing the best medium for their subject, a games designer must choose the right format of game to have the best chance of generating the desired play experience.

When you are approaching a new game idea, how do you know when it should be a miniatures game and when you should consider making it a board game or a card game instead? In this chapter, we will examine what we perceive to be the key strengths and weaknesses of non-discrete miniatures games and attempt to provide guidance as to when a given design is likely to fit the form and when it might be more effectively implemented in another.

CORE AFFORDANCES

The primary focus of non-discrete miniatures games is the **spatial relationships** between the markers. This leads to their first core affordance: their ability to create **complex physical situations** in which the spatial relationships between markers and their overlapping force projection areas can drive a game's interest for players.

The second core affordance of these games is their ability to **accommodate a vast diversity of physical objects** and express their presence within the game. This provides non-discrete miniatures games with their key interface to the hobby loop: the freedom for players to create or acquire their own markers and terrain.

The third core affordance of non-discrete miniatures games is emergent from the first two: games that can accommodate a vast diversity of physical objects and handle their infinite spatial interactions necessarily need rules that are either complex or loose (and often both). Players of these games accept this, and thus players tolerate substantially more complexity in these games' rules systems than they would in a board or card game[1], and simultaneously more flexibility in their application in play (accepting the increased necessity for player agreement during setup and play). This **tolerance of complexity and looseness** by players is a key affordance of this form of game[2].

The ideal design for a non-discrete miniatures game is, therefore, one that combines these affordances: an interest in spatial relationships; an openness to diverse physical objects; and an exploitation of the tolerance for complex and loose rules. If a game idea engages with these, it is likely a good candidate for a miniatures game.

OPPORTUNITIES AND CHALLENGES

The **tolerance for complexity** leads to opportunities for the inclusion of a 'pre-game' preparation stage of the game; a meta-game improvement loop that does not rely exclusively on heuristics learned through play; and the ability to provide players

DOI: 10.1201/9781003314820-6

with a rich canvas for self-expression. Many of these opportunities are shared with trading-card games and, to a certain extent, tabletop and digital role-playing games and are expanded upon below.

The **tolerance for looseness**, combined with the **acceptance of diverse physical objects**, leads to opportunities to provide space in your game for diversity of play, self-expression, model-making and hobby, collaborative creation and shared imaginative play. All these provide opportunities to deliver a strong sense of player ownership and investment in your games, increasing the chance of maintaining player engagement over time. On the flip side, if your desire is to create a game in which the rules remain precise and unambiguous at all times, miniatures games are a poor medium. The imprecision inherent in measuring and moving markers in non-discrete physical space is unavoidable and will always require a certain tolerance of the need for player interpretation during play.

This tolerance for a collaboratively interpreted game space, with the freedom to place any objects into it, also unlocks for players two of the primary aesthetic pleasures of the form: that of **miniatures cinematography**[3] and **miniatures hobby**, providing players with the ability to create their own miniature world, expressing themselves through model-making, miniature painting, narrative fiction and imaginary cinematics. This opportunity carries with it the challenge of communicating your game's vision and tone clearly to a player who may not have a set of pre-prepared components to guide them to your vision.

The **focus on spatial relationships** leads to a natural ability to test your players' skills in spatial perception, prediction and perspective-taking (imagining your perspective as that of a particular model at table level). At the same time, the centrality of real-world geometric relationships to non-discrete miniatures games means that the creation of unique conceptual game spaces (such as those commonly found in board and card games) is hard, and most non-discrete miniatures games are fundamentally testing these same basic skills.

DEPTH THROUGH COMPLEXITY

The tolerance for complexity affords you multiple opportunities to provide depth, either during play or in force construction (or both), that can reward mastery and hold players' interest in your game for longer. While you do not *need* to provide complexity, you *can*, and the advantages of doing so can be substantial for the right sort of player. Two common areas which we will explore in more depth in later chapters are **Special Abilities** (Chapter 27) and **List-building** (Chapter 30).

In the context of a non-discrete miniatures game, **special abilities** represent the opportunity afforded by tolerance of complexity to provide exciting and satisfying ways for players to twist the rules of the game to better express themselves, evoke the fantasy of the game and feel smart and powerful. Miniature games are not unique in their ability or desire to provide depth and differentiation in their component pieces, but if you seek to provide such depth and differentiation, a miniatures game is an appropriate format.

Miniatures games are unusual in that they tend to require players to prepare a **force list** of some kind in advance of the game. It is impossible to play a game of

Warhammer 40,000 (2023) without having prepared an army list in advance (even if that preparation is sourcing a pre-prepared list from somewhere rather than writing it yourself, you still must have one). This characteristic is shared with trading card games: it is similarly impossible to play a game of *Magic: The Gathering* (Garfield, 1993) without having prepared a deck in advance (even if that preparation is sourcing a pre-constructed deck). In the case of miniatures games, this is partly a result of the requirement to prepare physical objects (the miniatures) prior to play as part of the Hobby Game Loop (Chapter 5) and partly a result of the willingness to take advantage of the affordances listed above. A miniatures game does not have to provide a list-building component, but those that choose not to have one miss out on an opportunity for depth and a natural piece of connective tissue between the physical hobby preparation for a game and the mental.

TESTING SPATIAL SKILLS

When choosing the best medium for a game idea, it bears consideration what skills you intend to test and which skills you will abstract.

When a player plays a game of Football, there are specific physical skills that are being tested (those needed to move around the field, control the ball, etc.), as well as other skills related to the judgement of angles and distances (choosing when and from where to strike the ball and at what angle and speed) and the overall strategic understanding of the game (how to configure the players, when to press an attack on goal, when to fall back into defence). When the same player transitions to the tabletop game of *Subbuteo* (Adolph, 1947), they are not able to carry across their specific physical skills; those must be swapped for the specific dexterity skills needed to flick the playing pieces. However, the ability to judge angles and distances, as well as skills in interpreting the overall strategic flow of the game, are more readily transferable to the new game. *Subbuteo* greatly abstracts the physical skills required to play Football, but abstracts these other skills of geometric and strategic judgement to a much lesser degree. A player who has developed their skills in those areas playing Football can potentially enjoy an advantage in *Subbuteo* over one who has not.

A core skill required in non-discrete miniatures games is that of perceiving and predicting spatial relationships and for perspective-taking (imagining your perspective as that of a particular model at table level). A player who can out-see and out-predict their opponent in this regard will be greatly advantaged. As spatial relationships between markers lie at the heart of all of these games, mastery of this skill in the context of one game system provides the player with improved skill in *all* such games.

If your game will test such skills, then a miniatures game is a strong fit. If your game will focus more on testing social skills, dexterity, or any number of other skills that are unrelated to the spatial relationships between markers, your game idea may better suit another format. In particular, each choice you make to abstract some part of the movement, position, orientation or perspective of the miniatures potentially pulls you away from leveraging the form to its fullest and pushes you towards other types of games.

HEURISTICS AND MASTERY LOOPS

> Many games, in order to satisfy players, need to allow players to gain mastery in the game over time. Players typically gain skill by developing heuristics: rules of thumb that help them play the game.
>
> **(Elias, Garfield and Gutschera, 2020, p. 29)**

Games are unusual as forms of entertainment in that, over time, they are able to give players a sense of mastery. Heuristics are the learned meta-rules of how to judge both the current state of a game (e.g. who is ahead) and what actions are most likely to lead to an improvement of that game state for the player. A player's heuristics for a particular game are developed over time through repeated engagement with the game, experimentation, observation and reflection. They are built up in the form of increased skill at the game and an increased likelihood of victory. In the case of non-discrete miniatures, there are three broad buckets of heuristics that a player will develop: spatial heuristics, resolution heuristics and meta-game heuristics.

SPATIAL HEURISTICS

As we noted in Chapter 3, these games tend to share a focus on the skills of perceiving and predicting spatial relationships. This skill, once developed, becomes a set of heuristics that players can re-apply to almost any similar non-discrete miniatures game. As the essential nature of the physical relationships between player markers remains relatively consistent from game to game (not just driven by convention but also by geometry and physical reality), these games are less capable of offering totally new heuristics than other forms. In a card game, for example, entirely new abstract relationships between card positions, orientations and iconography can be established, requiring players to develop a wholly new way of looking at the tabletop to be able to 'read' the game state. This is much less possible in a non-discrete miniatures game. Players experienced in one such game will very likely be able to apply their pre-existing understanding of how such games generally operate when they start a new non-discrete miniatures game. Playing *Warhammer 40,000* will improve one's skill at *Star Wars: X-Wing Miniatures Game* (Little, 2012) in a way that playing *Pandemic* (Leacock, 2008) will not make one better at playing *Mysterium* (Nevskiy and Sidorenko, 2015).

RULES SYSTEM HEURISTICS

While superficially there appears to be a wide variety of resolution and rules systems employed by miniatures games, there are many patterns and commonalities between them, as we explore in Section 2. Beyond the spatial relationships, a player may need to establish new heuristics as they explore and master a specific game's rules systems, such as its initiative, activation, resolution and objective systems. Here, a non-discrete miniatures game can offer an amount of depth and opportunity for system-specific mastery over time, but the overall contribution of this system-specific mastery to their skill at the game will always sit in partnership with their non-system-specific mastery of spatial relationships. During play, the player is developing both their spatial heuristics and their rules system heuristics. This is sometimes described as their 'piloting skill', apart from their meta-game skill.

META-GAME HEURISTICS

Perhaps the most powerful area that a non-discrete miniatures game can offer a unique and satisfying mastery loop is in its meta-game. While not all miniatures games do so, the three core affordances discussed above provide the opportunity to allow players a mastery loop that sits outside of the heuristics they develop in the game. In games without a significant meta-game component, in particular, those that do not feature an out-of-game list-building (or deck construction) activity, players improve their skills at the game by playing the game. In games with a rich meta-game component, additional advancement can be achieved outside of play through the study and theoretical analysis of potential lists or combinations of selectable units and special abilities.

LADDERING AND ZEROING

It is common for non-discrete miniatures games to have a destructive game arc: a player often begins the game with their whole force, and then a process of attrition reduces both players' resources until the game ends with only a fraction of the starting strength remaining.

It is desirable that games achieve acceleration towards their end point. In practice, this is achieved by ensuring that what players can do on their last turn is different from on their first, and there is a sense of the meaningfulness of decisions increasing as the game approaches its end. This sense of acceleration is most often achieved in games in one of two ways: **laddering** or **zeroing**.

Laddering is a process whereby players build up in-game resources and abilities such that they can do more on their last turn than they did on their first. In *Settlers of Catan* (Teuber, 1995), players gather resources to build settlements, to allow them to gather more and more varied resources to build more settlements and cities, and so on. Players who are advancing successfully up the ladder in *Settlers of Catan* will be able to do more on their last turn than on their first.

The other main method of acceleration in a game is by allowing a narrowing of focus during the play session. This approach doesn't have a widely accepted name; we will call it **zeroing**. With zeroing, players can do more on their first turn than on their last. The player starts with a lot of options but no clear picture of where the most meaningful decision will end up being made; they 'zero in' on that spot during the course of the game. They also suffer a reduction in their forces over the game, with the number of available decisions thus trending downwards towards zero across the course of the game (even if it rarely literally reaches zero except in extreme situations).

This process of attrition, rather than construction, does not necessitate that the arc of the game is necessarily any different in terms of the density of meaningful decisions a player faces during the game. In a game built on laddering, the initial decisions may be few but meaningful, such as the placement of your initial settlements in *Settlers of Catan*, which can determine the course of the rest of your game, whereas the decisions available in the final may be numerous, but only a subset lead to victory.

In a game built on zeroing, there may be a wide variable of possible initial decisions, but few that are meaningful in the long term, such as the initial movements of your units out of their deployment positions in a game of *Warhammer 40,000*, which do not overly lock you into any future course of action in the game, whereas the final turn may contain only a few decisions, but each one is pregnant with the possibility of victory or defeat, such as is often the case in the final round of a tense game of *Malifaux* (Anderson *et al.*, 2013), in which the surviving models must often be utilised with pin-point geometric accuracy.

Non-discrete miniatures games are not effective tools for creating laddering and much more naturally fit the zeroing game structure. In large part, this relates to the Hobby-Game Loop (which we discuss more in Chapter 5) that emerges from the acceptance of a diversity of physical objects: if we ask players to spend time preparing miniatures for use in our game, it is natural for them to wish to maximise their usage and presence in the game. Effective laddering structures commonly feature uncertainty about what elements will be selected and introduced by each player during the game (as predictable laddering lessens interest). If a laddering structure permits such uncertainty, it follows that a model or unit that a player has spent time preparing for use in the game may not be used, thus rendering such efforts wasted in the context of this session. This may simply be a question of perception, as they may use it next session, but that perception can veer into a sense of disrespect for a player's investment and bears consideration. As well as the physical preparation stage of the Hobby-Game Loop, the uncertainty of a laddering structure also fights against the mental preparation stage of the loop, such that a player cannot prepare in advance in a way that they might expect to and cannot know what is going to be relevant for a session prior to starting it.

Some miniatures games have experimented with hybrid models. *Malifaux: Second Edition* had a common tournament format in which players are required to prepare a limited pool of models and then asked to select a subset of those models at the start of each game, attempting to strike a balance between respecting a player's hobby investment and offering uncertainty and tactical flexibility at the table. *A Billion Suns* (Hutchinson, 2021) offers players the ability to introduce any unit they wish during play, sometimes creating a problematic situation where the desired tactical choice is obstructed by the necessarily limited pool of physical miniatures available to the player.

Other considerations are the emotional arc of laddering versus zeroing: one is a journey of escalating power, ending with the final denouement of an ultimate expression of strength; the other is a path of attrition, concluding in a handful of heroic final elements fighting to the last gasp. Your game may wish to evoke one over the other.

Finally, laddering may require the introduction of new elements or rules during play, which may be more effectively delivered with bespoke components, such as cards or tokens, that allow players to absorb and track their changing board state. This may push the design of your game away from the do-it-yourself conventions of a non-discrete miniatures game and towards the holistically complete nature of a boxed board or card game.

COMPONENTS

It is worth considering that many of these drivers are part of an accretion of guiding elements rather than a single moment that drives your design one way or another, and one of the ways that this can be most obvious is in relation to the components of your game. If your game is primarily interested in spatial relationships mapped through real, non-discrete space, then it will need a fairly large tabletop with markers placed across it and relatively little else. Players can be expected to gather these items for themselves, and when they do, they will often naturally wish to adorn them appropriately, creating the components of a non-discrete miniatures game. It is certainly reasonable to expect them to gather dice, tape measures and markers. It might be reasonable to expect them to print off quick reference cards and gather a range of different markers. It's far less reasonable to expect them to generate bespoke cards that are unidentifiable from the back, components that cannot be identified by touch or a range of specifically shaped tokens. As the components needed for your game tend further down this path, so too will the benefit of presenting a boxed game rather than a non-discrete miniatures game increase. Once the components suggest a boxed game, the freedom to add a range of previously unconsidered bespoke components can, in turn, free up design space, invite movement towards more discrete elements and allow your game to change, sometimes for the better.

CONCLUSION

It may be the case that you have a strong vision for a game that you believe relies on physical miniatures and scaled terrain but seeks to marry such components with mechanical systems that are ill-suited to a non-discrete miniatures game. Perhaps your resolution system is complex but unrelated to the spatial position of the miniatures, or it is delightful but would endanger their positions (such as a dexterity-based system). Perhaps you imagine a laddering system of unit construction and development, such as in a real-time strategy game. In such cases, the most successful expression of the game may be found by changing the mechanics to better suit the form or relinquish the scale models, or their non-discrete positions, for a more discrete and/or abstract game format. Likewise, if you imagine your game restricting or dictating the scope of markers and terrain it offers to players but choose to design it in the form of a non-discrete miniatures game, you may well be making the game more complex than it needs to be. Perhaps the game would be better served by avoiding the complexities of terrain types (Chapter 23), line of sight (Chapter 22) and other sunk costs associated with systems that accept a wide variety of miniatures and miniature environments and moving towards a more abstracted and/or discrete system.

In the end, your game is an expression of your vision, and if that vision contains miniatures arranged in non-discrete space, our aim with this discussion is simply to provide provocations to stimulate your thinking, and we invite you to approach everything in this chapter as much as a design challenge as a guide rail.

SUMMARY

Non-discrete miniatures games offer three **core affordances**:

- an interest in spatial relationships;
- an acceptance of diverse physical objects;
- a tolerance for complex and loose rules.

The **key opportunities** that arise from these core affordances are:

- The hobby-game loop (see the next chapter)
- Player ownership and self-expression
- Collaborative creation and shared imaginative play
- Depth through complexity
- A meta-game mastery loop
- Testing spatial skills
- Natural fit for zeroing, rather than laddering, game structures

NOTES

1 *Pandemic Legacy: Season 2* is a relatively complex boxed game (with a weight rating of 3.25 out of five on the board gaming community website BoardGameGeek.com), its rulebook is 19 pages long. *The Lord of the Rings Strategy Battle Game* (Cavatore and Ward, 2005) is a comparatively simple non-discrete miniatures game (weight rating of 2.77), its rulebook is 240 pages long.

2 Non-discrete miniatures games share this third affordance with tabletop roleplaying games but offer it in a very different play environment, i.e. one in which the games have a discrete win state.

3 We knowingly use the term 'miniatures cinematography' incorrectly here. We intend to convey the sense that there is an intrinsic pleasure in arranging scale models into a scene which you can then explore in three dimensions, moving your viewpoint around the physical space to create new compositions, and that this scene will evolve unpredictably but systematically over the course of the game, providing a sort of very slow stop-motion film unfolding below you. Even if the models are unpainted, or the model terrain unsatisfying, players can engage in an act of imaginative play, perhaps made easier by the physicality of the 'toys' arrayed before them.

REFERENCES

Adolph, P. (1947) *Subbuteo* [Boardgame].

Anderson, M., Caroland, N., Cohen, R., Darland, A., Gibbs, J., Hanold, D., Johns, E., Martin, M. and Weber, D. (2013) *Malifaux: Second Edition*. South Korea: Wyrd Miniatures, LLC.

Cavatore, A. and Ward, M. (2005) *The Lord of the Rings Strategy Battle Game*. Nottingham: Games Workshop

Elias, G.S., Garfield, R. and Gutschera, K.R. (2020) *Characteristics of Games*. Cambridge, MA: MIT Press

Garfield, R. (1993) *Magic: The Gathering*. [Boardgame] Renton, WA: Wizards of the Coast.

Hutchinson, M. (2021) *A Billion Suns*. Oxford: Osprey Games.

Leacock, M. (2008) *Pandemic*. [Boardgame] Roseville, MN: Z-Man Games.

Little, J. (2012) *Star Wars: X-Wing Miniatures Game*. [Board game] Roseville, MN: Fantasy Flight Games.

Nevskiy, O. and Sidorenko, O. (2015) *Mysterium*. [Boardgame] Poitiers: Libellud.

Teuber, K. (1995) *Settlers of Catan*. [Boardgame] Stuttgart: Kosmos.

Warhammer 40,000 (2023) Nottingham: Games Workshop.

5 The Hobby Games Loop

Quite where the line between pastime, game and hobby lies is at best a question of vagueness that is not within the scope of this work to delve into. However, for our purposes, we might consider a hobby to be a leisure activity which takes up focus, time or money outside of that required to directly engage in the activity. If you stop at the local public course and hire some clubs for a round, you're engaging in the leisure activity of golf. If you research and buy your own clubs, maintain a membership, subscribe to a golf magazine and attend lessons and practice drives in the local park, you're engaged in the hobby of golf.

HOBBY GAMES

To play a non-discrete miniatures game, we are often asked to assemble miniatures and scale terrain, formulate army lists and decide upon a scenario for our session. This requirement for both physical and mental preparation prior to being able to play a game is rare beyond this form. Simply arriving at a table to play without at least some engagement with the mental or physical aspects of a given system is the exception rather than the norm. Such a requirement for preparation is not a weakness; it is an intrinsic component of the pleasure of tabletop miniatures games as a hobby; enjoyment and engagement are not limited to the activity of playing the game itself. Instead, engagement in the game forms a loop, like this (Figure 5.1):

1. **Mental preparation** (preparing a force list, reading rules, planning and purchasing miniatures and terrain).
2. **Physical preparation** (assembling and painting miniatures and terrain).
3. **Playing the game** (playing the game itself).
4. **Analysing the game** (reflecting on the experience, figuring out where to improve force lists and strategies, how to improve your terrain setup or finding new inspiration to paint models, thus returning to step 1).

FIGURE 5.1 The hobby games loop.

DOI: 10.1201/9781003314820-7

Players of these games will recognise that the time spent playing the game can be greatly outweighed by the predominantly solitary time spent in preparing to play. This is part of the attraction of these games. They invite and inspire satisfying and absorbing game-adjacent activities, both intellectual and physical, outside of the necessarily limited time available to play games with others. In essence, the sorts of players who enjoy these games tend to enjoy the hobby aspects that surround them. In fact, players who derive much of their pleasure from the physical preparation step will deliberately create more work for themselves by changing forces or game systems. For such players, arranging to play a game is often the motivation and the excuse to engage with their hobby.

The length of the loop – the more mental and physical preparation required for each game – can have a direct relationship with the perceived value of a game system as a hobby driver to its players. If the loop is too long or too weighted away from the game itself, the players may perceive the game as asking for too much investment for too little pay-off. If the loop is too short, requiring too little preparation, the players may perceive the game as too 'light' on the hobby side, and it may not be offering enough interest away from the table.

An understanding of this loop and the trade-offs within it for different players can help you increase the longevity of engagement with your game and allow it to offer different options to different hobbyists.

HOBBY AS INVESTMENT

The investment of time and money required to play your game is a barrier to entry for new players, but it is also an opportunity. If one of your objectives as a designer is to see your game played repeatedly and perhaps even loved by its players, the hobby loop is a valuable tool. Non-discrete miniatures games ask a lot from their players, more than a boxed board or card game, but asking a lot is what can make them feel so special to their players. We assign more value to things that we have personally invested labour in[1].

If you are successful in motivating a player to source, assemble and paint miniatures and terrain for your game, understand its rules system, write a force list and figure out the first scenario, you will have engendered a significant investment of labour from them. This investment makes it more likely that they will play your game again. Not only are they more prepared for it, making the next session easier, but they are also less likely to walk away from a game that they have invested labour in.

In this way, carefully considering how you create invitations for escalating hobby investment is of value. Consider what you expect from new players and how those expectations can organically grow or evolve as the player engages with your game. You might find ways for new players to start small and branch out, or play modes that inspire their activities to escalate as their interest in your game grows.

LOWERING THE BARRIERS TO ENTRY

Even if we intend to offer a deep and satisfying hobby loop, we likely wish to lower the barriers to entry for new players. There are many techniques to reduce the initial investment in mental and physical preparation and get the player through their first loop as quickly as possible so that they have experienced your game, ideally enjoyed it and feel that they are initially invested and want to participate in the hobby loop a second time.

Reduction of mental preparation may be achieved through:

- **Pre-prepared force lists:** These reduce the need for understanding the force-building rules and overcoming the difficulty of choosing an effective force before you have played the game and understand its rules system deeply.
- **Quick start rules:** You can provide a simplified rule system or tutorial mode that teaches the core mechanics, highlights the most interesting or exciting parts of your game, but avoids the more complex rules. You can recommend players use these quick-start rules for the first game or two and then adopt the full rules once they are familiar with the basics.
- **Obvious first play mode:** By providing a default or starter scenario or by using procedural scenario generation at the table, you eliminate the need to decide on the structure of the first game. See Chapter 28 for more details.
- **Proprietary miniatures:** If you have the capacity, offering miniatures (physically or digitally) that have specific rules within your system reduces the complexity of sourcing the required models.
- **Ready-package force boxes:** If you have the capacity, offering starting boxes that contain a self-contained ready-to-play force can make the selection of miniatures and the preparation of the force list for the first game much simpler.

Reduction of physical preparation may be achieved through:

- **Miniature agnosticism:** By ensuring that your game allows players to use miniatures they already own and selecting settings for which players likely already own miniatures, you increase the chance that a player already has what they need to experience your game for the first time. We discuss this in more detail below.
- **Common scale and settings:** By designing your game in a common scale (such as 28 mm) and in a common setting (such as World War II or medieval fantasy), you greatly increase the chance that players already have the terrain they will need to create a play area for your game.
- **Single-piece models:** If you have the capacity, offering miniatures that are mostly provided as a single piece can reduce the complexity of preparation (at the expense of modularity, which can be important to many hobby gamers).
- **Ready terrain:** Depending on your setting, terrain can be offered as print-as-play papercraft or flat templates, such as offered by *Dropzone Commander* (2021) on their website, or you can describe simple tricks to create an initial set of low-effort terrain, such as using spare toy cars as crash barriers in *Gaslands* (Hutchinson, 2017).
- **Pre-painted models:** Outside of the means of most independent designers, pre-painted miniatures reduce the barrier to a good-looking tabletop experience, but do so at the risk of lessening the players' opportunity for feelings of investment in their miniatures.

MINIATURE AGNOSTICISM

Hobby gamers quickly acquire ranges of the standard miniature tropes, such as skeletons and elves in fantasy genres or power-armoured warriors in science fiction. At which point, rather than being a barrier, these miniatures are a reason to seek out rule sets that can be played with them, similar to purchasing a gaming console being a good reason to seek out the games compatible with it. This is a flexibility rare in tabletop gaming, where the idea of playing multiple different games with a *Monopoly* (Darrow, 1935) set would be bizarre.

Miniatures agnostic games are designed in such a way as to be flexible in their support for the use of miniatures from a range of sources or manufacturers, as opposed to being designed to implicitly or explicitly force the usage of specific (likely proprietary) miniatures.

In contrast, it is possible to design a game where playing with unexpected miniatures is either confusing or mechanically inconvenient. Games such as this might be described as 'miniatures prescriptive'.

The decision to design your game to be miniature-agnostic depends a lot on your scope as a games maker and what you have the capabilities and appetite to distribute. A game that will be sold as a stand-alone rules system would do well to support the broadest range of already-available miniatures, maximising the chance that potential players either already own or can easily acquire miniatures appropriate for the game. This is one of the primary reasons so many rule systems are designed in a 28-mm scale: such miniatures are by far the most widely available.

When designing a miniatures-agnostic game, consider the following:

- **Base sizes:** If you are very strict and specific with base sizes, you make it more likely that models prepared for other games are incompatible with yours. Your rules should avoid directly interacting with specific sizes or shapes of bases (such as having nubs to guide movement templates or shooting templates that fit only on certain base shapes) unless you are providing those bases directly.
- **Refrain from exotic themes:** If your game asks players to source something too specific and unusual, then players may simply fail to do so, and you may need to consider providing proprietary miniatures.
- **Be your first hobbyist:** As soon as you have a rough idea of the background and factions of your game, attempt to source a suitable set of miniatures yourself. This will give you a feel for the difficulty of what you are asking of potential players.
- **Openness to player invention:** You will need to strike the right balance between world-building and openness. If all the available units in a skirmish game are named characters, you leave little space for a player to fit their miniature into the game world if it doesn't fit one of your characters.

COMPONENT AGNOSTIC

Gathering miniatures and terrain is a crucial part of the preparation for play, but the ancillary components – dice, tokens, templates and unit's cards – can be equally important. If miniature agnosticism ensures that a game feels open to the imagination and ingenuity of the hobbyist, careful thought about the components needed to play will ensure the game is not undermined by esoteric or difficult-to-produce components.

Components that need precision in their production, such as objects of an exact regular size or objects that must be indistinguishable when face down, are a big ask for a hobbyist and may be outside of their reach. If your game requires them, you may need to consider how they are to be produced and supplied.

Dice are ubiquitous and regular in shape and size, as are playing cards. We explore these both in Section 2. If markers of a specific size and shape are required, consider using empty bases of a commonly available size.

CASE STUDY: MINIATURES PRESCRIPTIVE – *STAR WARS: X-WING MINIATURES GAME*

Star Wars: X-Wing Miniatures Game (Little, 2012) includes every one of the elements of miniatures prescriptiveness. Its bases are not only of specific and custom sizes but also have specific guides for the placement of movement templates. While its miniatures aren't particularly relevant to gameplay, spaceship miniatures of an appropriate scale are quite difficult to find, even ignoring the attached movies. Toughest for those seeking to play the game without purchasing the attached miniatures, though, is the fact that custom cardboard dials are needed for each ship type to plan their movement, such that the miniatures essentially need to be bought to play the game, whatever the player might prefer to use.

LOW HOBBY GAMES

Some games attempt to minimise the physical preparation. *Star Wars: X-Wing Miniatures Game* provides pre-painted miniatures and requires no scale terrain beyond the asteroid tokens provided in the box; there are a handful of other non-discrete miniatures games that don't seek to offer players the chance to engage with hobby elements. *X-wing* can be played on a space-themed playmat or a simple black sheet with little or no terrain. *HeroClix* (Cook *et al.*, 2002) requires players to use their own, pre-painted miniatures since gameplay is based on their custom bases (featuring a patented element, rare in the world of games). The non-discrete miniatures game *Necromolds* (Bohaty, 2021) asks players to create their miniatures at the table by pressing clay in a simple mould. However, it should be noted that *X-wing* has the Star Wars licence attached while *HeroClix* has the Marvel and DC licence and *Necromolds* is an entirely boxed game. Engaging with hobby elements is, for much of your existing audience, an attraction rather than a distraction. If you remove it to reach a wider audience, you will need to replace it with something that may well be out of your means.

OFFERING HOBBY PROJECTS

For players to stay engaged with your game, they should be inspired to repeat the hobby loop regularly. In order to avoid the loop becoming stale, it can help to offer a variety of hobby projects. A potential added advantage of hobby projects is that they can bring players together to create socially motivated solo projects, ones that can be chosen, planned, discussed and acted on as a group.

- **Set-piece games:** Providing exceptional scenarios that describe noteworthy encounters or events such that they require specific preparation in either forces or terrain. A centrepiece model can be a strong attraction, such as a landing craft in a WW2 beach game. See Chapter 28 for more details.
- **Campaign progression:** Offering the chance to play a series of linked games, or a campaign, can allow players the chance to build stories around particular troopers or characters. Encouraging them to physically change the miniatures for those troops can turn these shared stories into shared hobby events for your players, encouraging them to return to the campaign to show off their handiwork and enshrining in-game events into reality. See Chapter 29 for more details.
- **Factions:** Offering a variety of play styles constrained to specific factions with your force-building system can provide an invitation to start a new hobby project in order to explore the new faction. See Chapter 30 for more details.

GOOD HOBBY DESIGN

When approaching a tabletop miniatures game design, it is critical to understand in what ways your game will engage the hobby-game loop and to design with that loop in mind. This loop stems from the openness of these games; they encourage players to import their own objects, design their own forces and build their own scenarios and units, and this do-it-yourself attitude permeates their attraction and should be present in your design if it wants to really embed itself in its players' imaginations.

Good hobby design is about understanding the process of envisioning and preparing the miniatures that will be needed to play your game and designing to ease that process while adding interesting but achievable challenges to it. The best way to start is by putting yourself through that process, creating the forces and the tabletop that you expect your players to put together. If a particular unit or character proves difficult to create or represent, design it differently. The hobby elements of non-discrete miniatures games spring from freedom, which leads to creativity and self-expression via personalisation and ultimately pride. Understanding and leveraging the hobby loop effectively is a win-win for both you and your players.

SUMMARY

Non-discrete games feature a Hobby Loop:

1. **Mental preparation**
2. **Physical preparation**
3. **Playing the game**
4. **Analysing the game**

Investment of time and money by players is an opportunity for the game designer. There are many ways to **lower the barriers** to entry for a new player.

Miniature agnostic games welcome the use of 'any' miniatures, **miniature prescriptive** games require the use of proprietary miniatures.

There are many ways to **offer hobby projects** to encourage re-engagement with and sharing of hobby activities.

EXPERIMENTS

Go through the hobby loop for your game.

Eliminate at least one possible barrier to entry for your game. Eliminate all of them.

Create a hobby project that will encourage a player who has been playing your game for a reasonable time to attempt something new.

NOTE

1 In a 2011 study, Ariely, Mochon and Norton found that after asking people to assemble their own IKEA furniture, LEGO sets or origami animals, they valued their self-made creations five times higher than they valued similar amateur work they did not personally labour on. Michael I. Norton, Daniel Mochon and Dan Ariely, The 'IKEA Effect': When Labor Leads to Love (SSRN Scholarly Paper, Rochester, NY), Social Science Research Network. (4 March 2011), http://papers.ssrn.com/abstract=1777100.

REFERENCES

Bohaty, C. (2021) *Necromolds*. [Boardgame] Minneapolis: Necromolds LLC.

Cook, M., Grubb, J., Johnson, S., Leitheusser, J., Quick, J. and Weisman, J. (2002) *HeroClix*. [Boardgame] Bellevue, WA: WizKids.

Darrow, C. (1935) *Monopoly*. [Board game] Beverly, MA: Parker Brothers.

Dropzone Commander (2021). https://ttcombat.com/pages/dropzone-commander-resources (Accessed: 19 December 2023).

Hutchinson, M. (2017) *Gaslands*. Oxford: Osprey Games.

Little, J. (2012) *Star Wars: X-Wing The Miniatures Game*. [Board game] Roseville, MI: Fantasy Flight Games.

6 Players of Tabletop Miniatures Games

Games should be fun. Ideally, they should be equally fun for all players. However, different players take pleasure in different things, so how are we to delight all players equally, and how are we to delight players with differing interests as they share the same game? What sorts of fun should we offer?

For our purposes in this chapter and the next, we will define 'fun' as pleasurable engagement with the goals, processes and other players of a game, including any intellectual, narrative, aesthetic and social delight that arises from that engagement. However, not all players find fun in the same places. In this chapter, we will examine some common player personas and what sorts and sources of fun they might be seeking from your game.

PLAYER PERSONAS BY MOTIVATION

The following personas are inspired by Richard Bartle's taxonomy of player types (Bartle, 1996) and by the psychographic profiles Mark Rosewater and his team developed for *Magic: The Gathering* in 2002 (Rosewater, 2002). They are far from exhaustive, but they provide a starting point. Each persona is a framing for a set of player motivations and focuses, not an expression of a real person. All players will be some mixture of each of these personas, expressing their traits and proclivities to varying degrees.

STORY-BUILDERS, PLAYING FOR NARRATIVE

Story-driven players are often thought of as the lore-keepers for systems; they desire that the gameplay on the tabletop should support the narrative attached to it, and by those mechanics, explore the world of the game. Story-builders are the explorers of non-discrete miniatures games; they find satisfaction when an item or character performs the way the background text says they would; they can then combine elements and find answers to 'what if' questions about the world. This could be alternative historical events or entirely fantastical investigations of created lore.

Story-builders wonder what would happen if a certain unit were in a certain situation; how they would fare against another unit, and they play to mutually discover the answer to those wonderings. They engage with the game in the manner that they might a novel or a movie, to discover what will happen to their favourite characters in this dramatic tale. They can sit back a little more and enjoy the unfolding narrative, possibly irrespective of their personal performance within it. Designing for story-builders means that things should do mechanically what they expect them to; grenades should explode; sniper rifles should be slow to fire

 DOI: 10.1201/9781003314820-8

and deadly in skilled hands; ramps should have spectacular and high-risk results. Waving off narrative concerns as secondary to gameplay ones is the capital crime for these sorts of players.

Story-builders can also express themselves during force-building, bringing units to life with names and background stories. They may push against your force-building system if it resists their attempts to create a force that tells their preferred story, but when engaged, they will take pleasure in inventing narrative justifications for those same constraints. They are the players most likely to explore the full list of scenarios in your game to discover the stories they can tell with your system and your setting.

SPECTACLE-MAKERS, PLAYING TO EXPERIENCE

Spectacle-makers are often seen as more casual, social players; they want to see what will happen when they pull on one of the game's levers, and they hope it will be something spectacular. A well-designed game is a series of rules that mesh together so that engaging with one rule will result in a series of cascading effects. Some players simply want to see what happens when some of those rules are engaged with. In fact, most players, based on their first experience with your game, are likely to be playing with this mindset, particularly if they're having the game presented to them by someone else. This is quite relevant since the spectacle-maker is often also quite a magpie, trying out multiple different choices of forces and even game systems.

For spectacle-makers, things need to go boom; for them, the game is a sort of chaotic experiment; operating the levers is generally its own reward, provided they do *something*. They will often be less concerned with winning or losing than whether or not a series of exciting moments emerged from the action, often regardless of who it happens. The cardinal sin for these sorts of players is to pull a lever and have nothing happen; moments of something are vital to their engagement.

In force-building Spectacle makers may tend towards selecting physically impressive centrepieces or force compositions that fire their imagination. Overly restrictive force-building may be a turn-off for them, limiting their ability to make unusual choices in the name of spectacle-generating units. They may prioritise the whole gaming table, seeking a rich and cinematic miniature world, with little regard to the outcome of the game itself.

FINE-POINT COMPETITORS, PLAYING TO PROVE

For fine-point competitors, the primary drive is to win the game. The game is a puzzle, and they want to prove that they can solve it. They like to fine-tune and analyse a game and are more than happy to play using a force created by someone else, as long as it is effective at the tabletop. They enjoy environments in which playing to win is celebrated, such as tournaments, and searching for slight edges at the pinnacle of gaming advantage. They are sometimes referred to as 'min-maxers', from the process of maximising the performance of a force while minimising its weaknesses or unimportant attributes. For these players, choices should provide clear and immediate feedback with some level of reliability, such that when they lose, they feel an understanding of how to re-theorise and improve. There must be enough knobs and dials in the game to allow ongoing tweaking and adjusting to hold their interest. Fine-point competitors will be very present and active in their use of the full scope of the mechanical systems in your game.

PLAYER-ARTISTS, PLAYING TO EXPRESS

Players should have choices in your game, and whenever there is a choice, someone will seek to use it to express themselves. Player-artists seek to express themselves through their selection of units to play your game with they want to find new and unusual combinations of options. Player-artists thrive on confines and conditions, limitations to push against in creating their forces. They want to win, but because a force still being able to win is the most interesting constraint to form a force around, it is far more important to them that they play and win on their own terms, and they would rather lose on their own terms than win someone else's way.

For the player-artists, poorly regarded and even outright sub-optimal units are catnip. Having undesirable choices and a range of options is vital for the player-artist to be able to express their individuality by using whatever it is that no one else looks twice at. They thrive in relation to constraints, boundaries and limitations to push against and shape their expressions around. To a player-artist no greater sin exists than, ironically, perhaps, excessive freedom and balance.

MECHANIC-CONNOISSEURS, PLAYING TO APPRECIATE

Game design is a complex practice that is somewhere between an art and a science, and it has its own tropes along with a rich history of mechanics and systems built upon systems. Any process with this level of background and complexity will inevitably attract its own connoisseurs, those who look to appreciate the process on detailed and esoteric levels, and games are no different. The mechanic-connoisseur wants to appreciate a finely crafted game mechanic, whether one that is original or that pays proper tribute to those it is built on, one that is elegant or labyrinthine in its complexity. They are most often hooked on a single, startling mechanic, something that they can't help but sit up and take notice of.

For the mechanic-connoisseur there is nothing more upsetting than a collection of rules and mechanics they've seen a hundred times before with a new set of clothes on. They would rather see a designer swing big and fail hard than modestly succeed. To appeal to them, you simply need to have a deep and intense understanding of the history and application of game mechanics and use them in a stunning and original fashion.

Of course, player psychology types are nowhere near so clear-cut in reality; most players are a blending of these categories and more. These are game design motivations, but players are just as likely to be drawn to your game by its artwork, its miniatures, its lore or any of a number of more strange and esoteric draws. We're only focused here on the things we can control at the game design stage. In the next chapter, we will explore the sort of levers you have available within a design to generate fun for these different personas.

GAMES AS SOCIAL MEDIATION

Games are socially transformative systems. That is to say, they are able to change otherwise negative social drives of competition and even dislike into positive experiences. Tabletop games in general have a high degree of transformative power due to the separation between players offered by their interacting primarily with the table state rather than directly with each other, and this is no different for non-discrete miniatures games. Often only the most superficial level of direct interaction is demanded, with most tabletalk being player choice rather than a requirement. The value of this transformation versus its cost in terms of lack of direct social interaction is a question that each design needs to answer for itself, but it is worth noting that the apparent lack of direct interaction is not necessarily a social negative.

Multi-sided games are ultimately cooperative social endeavours that feature artificial conflicts with fun as their goal. It is for this reason that they can allow close friends to engage in savage struggles for supremacy while maintaining cordial relationships. Indeed, even if players come together to play the same game, they may not be seeking the same outcomes or playing for the same reasons. For a game to succeed in bringing together players, it is vital that it be understood that the enjoyment of everyone is dependent on having motivations that are aligned between the players and the system, such that the psychological pressure to protect the fun of others can be offloaded to the game (Thi Nguyen, 2020). This alignment must be part of the technology of the game; it cannot be based only on the requirement for players to maintain it. A game must not appeal to players to 'have fun' without a strong contract for how the game thus intends fun to be had. If a game thrusts the responsibility for one's enjoyment onto one's opponent, the result will be only as effective as it would have been if we were not playing; it would be wholly dependent on our relationship outside of the game. In a game requiring direct and brutal opposition, this can taint the enjoyment of the game (or the relationship).

Non-discrete miniatures games require a level of social contract demanding that people place the enjoyment of the game ahead of strict accuracy due to rule complexity and leeway on measurements, but it is vital that this contract not overstep those areas; otherwise, by undermining the transformative power of the game, the request to treat others kindly can, ironically, increase the cruelty between players. One of the key ways for a game to guide its players into alignment is through its victory systems, as we shall explore in Chapter 7.

SUMMARY

Players have a range of motivations in gaming:

- **Story-builders** – Explore and experiment with play narratives.
- **Spectacle-makers** – Seek to experience events through play.
- **Fine-point competitors** – Play to win in balanced and close competition.

- **Player-artists** – Express themselves by how and what they play.
- **Mechanic-connoisseurs** – Appreciate games as well-wrought artistic artefacts.

Games allow players with a range of interests to come together in mutually beneficial social interactions, transform competitive drive and protect player enjoyment.

REFERENCES

Bartle, R. (1996) *Hearts, Clubs, Diamonds, Spades: Players Who Suit Muds.* Available at: https://mud.co.uk/richard/hcds.htm (Accessed 29 April 2024).
Rosewater, M. (2002) *Timmy, Johnny, and Spike.* Available at: https://magic.wizards.com/en/news/making-magic/timmy-johnny-and-spike-2013-12-03 (Accessed 29 April 2024).
Thi Nguyen, C. (2020) *Games: Agency As Art.* Oxford: Oxford University Press.

7 Sources of Fun

Is your game fun? The most basic way to answer this question is to check what players spend the majority of their time doing in your game. Our games are not about what we believe, intend or say they are about; they are about what our players spend their time doing and thinking about while playing them. Whether planning and positioning during movement phases, checking narrative-generating tables or writing the perfect army list, whatever the most commonly executed loop of your game is, it needs to be the most fun part.

In the previous chapter, we proposed a set of personas to help us understand and differentiate between the potential motivations of our players. We defined 'fun' as pleasurable engagement with the goals, processes and other players of a game, including any intellectual, narrative, aesthetic and social delight that arises from that engagement. In this chapter, we propose a framework for examining the different sources of fun within your game and begin to map them onto these personas.

A FRAMEWORK FOR FUN

The sources of enjoyment and pleasure in a game may be said to lie somewhere between **diegetic** and **non-diegetic**, **intrinsic** and **extrinsic**.

Diegetic sources of enjoyment are those that occur within, or emerge directly from, the game world; they exist first in the world of our tabletop avatars. **Non-diegetic** fun is that which we derive from the elements that lie outside of the game world, whether in the mechanics of the game, the enjoyment of the other players' company and so on. If we take pleasure in the cinematic vignette of a model's unlikely six-gunshot through a saloon window into the last-remaining highwayman escaping with the mail coach, we are enjoying a diegetic element within our game. If we delight that the card we drew during the test to achieve such a feat was the ace of spades, we are enjoying a non-diegetic element.

Intrinsic sources of fun are those that emerge from the act of engaging with the game (or the hobby that surrounds it) for its own sake; they are things we do because we like to do them. **Extrinsic** enjoyment emerges from the satisfaction of some external motivation, outside of the pleasure of the act itself. If we enjoy our cinematic gunshot because it is the perfect climax to a tense game and aligns with our internal vision of the white-hatted hero that pulled the trigger, we are taking intrinsic pleasure in the event. If we enjoy the success primarily because the elimination of the final highwayman satisfies the victory conditions, causing us to win the game, we are taking extrinsic pleasure in it.

As should be apparent from these examples, these sources of fun are by no means mutually exclusive; they are separate axes on which any given event may register fun. In fact, the more we engineer our in-game moments to provide fun on multiple axes, the richer such events will seem. In addition, the enjoyment of certain activities

DOI: 10.1201/9781003314820-9

may be intrinsic for some players and extrinsic for others. Some players will paint models because they enjoy doing so, some because they want to have a painted force ready for the next game. For many, it will be a mix of both.

Similarly, it can be tempting to view these sources as a hierarchy, with diegetic intrinsic joy at the pinnacle and non-diegetic extrinsic rewards at the bottom, but we don't believe so: all are sources of wholly valid enjoyment for different players, and – for us as designers – all are tools for the motivation and direction of player intent.

Diegetic Intrinsic

Diegetic intrinsic moments of fun are found when a player does something for the sheer pleasure the in-game reality of doing it provides. This sort of fun often requires a level of suspension of disbelief: to enjoy something happening in the game world in and of itself, we need to believe in that game world to a degree. It is greatly assisted when the game produces a moment in the game world that 'feels right'. A story-builder may choose to cast a fireball spell because that is their imagination of what the fire wizard should do, and when the fireball misses its mark and causes some nearby powder kegs to explode, regardless of whether that explosion harms their models or their opponent's, they can celebrate because it 'feels right'. Then, if the spectacle-maker is sufficiently invested in the world, they can celebrate that same explosion for its sheer impressiveness. Often, that sense of 'feeling right' is linked to the genre expectations of the game, as we explore in Chapter 16. When there is dissonance between the fantasy and the gameplay, diegetic intrinsic pleasure can evaporate.

Aside from ensuring units have access to actions that players expect and exploring ways to chain events together to increase the likelihood of emergent narrative, it is also worth exploring how your handling of failure may be used to create moments of diegetic intrinsic delight. Failure that results in no change to the board state may be the simplest option, but it has the least chance of creating narrative progression. Consider 'fail forward' mechanics, in which failure to achieve an action results in *something* happening rather than nothing. When a model fails during an action in *Rogue Planet* (Spivey, 2015), their opponent receives a free move. When a driver in *Gaslands* (Hutchinson, 2017) fails to control their vehicle, it is forced to move, potentially causing a collision. When a stone thrower fails to hit in *Warhammer: The Game of Fantasy Battles* (Cavatore *et al.*, 2000), the rock scatters, potentially hitting friendly units. Dynamic failure systems can offer opportunities for surprising emergent mechanical results that player-artists and mechanic-connoisseurs delight in playing for and replace moments of nothingness with moments of spontaneous story and spectacle.

Non-diegetic Intrinsic

Non-diegetic intrinsic fun is something done in the real world for its own pleasure, because of the game, but not within the world of the game. At the table, this might be satisfaction from operating the game's mechanics, pleasure at social interaction with other players or pride at one's miniatures arrayed for battle.

The enablement of non-diegetic intrinsic moments of fun is as much about removing barriers as seeking direct stimulation. Mechanical systems that are awkward or complex to manipulate, rules that deviate from convention without justifying that deviation and systems that require players to complete busy work all inhibit intrinsic enjoyment of a game. Generative random numbers can be intrinsically fun: rolling dice and getting the results you want (or those your opponent does not) is a joy that sits outside the game world, the pleasure of which is enhanced by the importance of the roll. Consider making the peripheral parts of your game more predictable and its central activities more random.

Managing player interaction is more complex, but consider including some level of player decision exchange, allowing fluid responses to each other's actions in a pleasurable exchange of gameplay. Hidden information can permit dramatic moments of revelation, the surprise of which can elicit laughter and groans. The inclusion of input randomness (explored more in 14) can provide opportunities for players to feel smart in relation to their ability to play the hand they have been dealt (sometimes literally) even if they don't come out on top, allowing both sides of an interaction to feel good about the results. In Chapter 8, we explore the ways that victory conditions help align players to a shared comprehension of the purpose of the game, and this helps them have a more intrinsically pleasurable interaction over the table.

Non-discrete miniatures games also excel at providing non-diegetic intrinsic enjoyment away from the table thanks to their hobby game loop (explored in Chapter 5). Additionally, the motivation of an organised game day, encouraging oneself to paint a given set of miniatures, can provide peer approval of the achievement, allowing the hobby loop to provide additional extrinsic enjoyment. Structuring your game, its force-building rules, or any campaign systems to engage the hobby loop is a key way to engage story-builders and player-artists.

DIEGETIC EXTRINSIC

Diegetic extrinsic enjoyment is motivated by an outcome or reward, but the reward exists within the game world; the fun is in having done something rather than in doing it. Intrinsic fun isn't always obvious from the rules, but extrinsic rewards are easy to spot; they are the designer giving players something in return for doing something. You can use diegetic rewards to signpost where the fun is in your game: you will have a good time if you do *this*, and so the game rewards you for doing that. Diegetic extrinsic rewards can be used to connect the mechanics of the game to its setting: the people in the game-world want to do *this*, and so the game rewards you directly for doing that. They can also be used to directly incentivise the player to cause their units to act in a narrative-congruous way: it will feel right if this unit does *this*, and so the game explicitly rewards that.

Within a single game session, diegetic extrinsic rewards can take the form of in-world resources granted as a result of taking actions in keeping with their character. These may either indirectly evoke some thematic element (some assassin-type units in *Warhammer 40,000* (2023) generate additional abstract 'Command Points' when they dispatch an enemy character) or directly represent an in-world resource (some models in *Malifaux: Second Edition* (Anderson *et al.*, 2013) are able to create additional 'Soul Stones', an in-world currency, by draining the life-energy of slain foes).

Diegetic extrinsic rewards may also be offered between game sessions as a reward for acting in keeping with the fantasy and the game's objectives and to disincentivise disengaging from the game too early. If you wish to inspire players to play multiple connected games, diegetic extrinsic rewards are a powerful strategy. Units can be rewarded with resources (such as experience points) that can be exchanged for further powers: a reward that only benefits the player if another game is played (for which the player will likely receive further rewards that necessitate playing another game to enjoy to their fullest). If the reward is a modification to an existing unit (necessitating a conversion) or the addition of another unit to their force, this can be used to trigger another turn of the hobby loop, driving both intrinsic hobby fun and further investment in the game.

CASE STUDY: DIEGETIC EXTRINSIC SIGNPOSTS – *GASLANDS*

In *Gaslands* (Hutchinson, 2017), players control drivers racing in a televised death sport. If they manage to reach the higher gears for their vehicle, they are permitted to use the 'long' template, allowing them to move further. Managing the gameplay mechanics sufficiently to reach higher gears and being able to use the long are intrinsically rewarding, which could have been enough; however, the game includes 'sponsors'. If players perform actions listed by their sponsor, they are rewarded with 'audience votes' that can be spent for in-game benefits. One sponsor lists using the 'long' as a condition. The intrinsically rewarding element has been signposted by the extrinsic reward, guiding players towards doing something fun.

NON-DIEGETIC EXTRINSIC

Non-diegetic extrinsic enjoyment is found in a game-related activity that is motivated by a real-world outcome or reward. The three major sources of this sort of fun in non-discrete miniatures games are the hobby, force-building and winning.

There is pleasure in winning. For many players, the possibility of winning is a key motivator in engaging with the game, as we will explore in detail in the next chapter. Fine-point competitors and player-artists are oriented towards this goal, albeit with different focuses. While it is the case that generally only one player can win, multiple players can *almost* win. If scoring is only made at the end of the game, the claim to almost having won can fall flat, but if there is more than one scoring stage in your game, an ultimate loser can have moments of non-diegetic extrinsic enjoyment in having been winning at certain points.

Even without securing victory, the player-artist can find great delight in discovering counterintuitive or novel-feeling solutions to the game's challenges that break the conventions of play but nevertheless 'feel right' within its world. Here arises a blend of diegetic intrinsic enjoyment with non-diegetic extrinsic pleasure in effectively utilising the system for advantage without breaking the verisimilitude of the game-world.

Your game's force-building system will be a key source of non-diegetic extrinsic enjoyment for most players. Some players may intrinsically enjoy the activity of list-building and create lists purely for the pleasure of it, but it is likely that the majority of list-building is done with the objective of being ready to play a session of your game and likely with an eye to having a competitive force. Even story-builders may be found enjoying such preparation, with the goal of having just the right force for the next game and the next chapter in their narrative: different framing, same source of fun.

Players might draw pleasure from other activities external to the game session and far removed from its fantasy, such as studying or discussing rules, lists and strategies in order to increase their chances of successfully achieving their in-game goals (which may or may not be focused around winning). Alternatively, they may wish to discuss or share the game or their hobby activities online with the goal of participating in its wider community or improving their hobby skills.

Thanks to the unique formulation of the hobby-game loop for non-discrete miniatures games, players will often encounter your non-diegetic extrinsic motivators first, before they even play your game, and so they are of critical importance. Beyond your marketing blurb, they are the first signposts to the fun of your game, the first tool you have to set out your stall for the game, and the most direct way to get new players hooked.

ATTAINING MASTERY

Attaining mastery of a game over time arguably registers on all of these axes. It is intrinsically rewarding to get better at a game, both diegetically by having a force that sweeps all before it and non-diegetically by gaining confidence and control over the rules systems and mechanics that make up a game. Having that growth in mastery acknowledged by one's peers extrinsically and non-diegetically feels good and may well go hand in hand with one's units garnering diegetic extrinsic rewards.

Each of these sources of pleasure may be stronger or weaker for certain player types as they obtain mastery over your game: the story-builder may feel more able to control the diegetic narrative to fit their vision; the spectaclemaker may feel more able to reliably set-off the fireworks; the fine-point competitor may feel more able to play at higher and higher levels; and the player-artist may feel more able to uncover original ways to play and win.

CONFLICTING MOTIVATIONS

It is inevitable that there are some parts of your game that are not fun. Players may be able to play in certain ways, choose certain options or interact with other players in ways that erode both their own enjoyment and that of others. This is not an issue unless your game promotes such things to its players. Problems arise when your game provides conflicting motivations and sources of fun that are in disharmony with each other. Let us illustrate this with some specific (non-exhaustive) disharmonies that will likely dismay each of our personas.

For story-builders, power must be narratively consonant. If your system's victory conditions or unit synergies mechanically promote actions that are in disharmony with the setting and the fantasy, the story-builder may choose losing over winning in a way that breaks the logic of the game world. They won't enjoy that loss, but they may conclude it is the lesser of the two evils. To resolve the dissonance, consider making unthematic actions expensive, ineffective or have undesirable consequences.

For both spectacle-makers and mechanic-connoisseurs, the narratively appropriate thing for a unit to do cannot be wholly predictable, passive or boring. They want narrative consonance, but not at the expense of fireworks and mechanical interest. Make sure the things that units would naturally do in the game world are supported by interesting parts of your system, and things that are out-of-character are at best mechanically simple or even boring.

For both spectacle-makers and mechanic-connoisseurs, the path to victory cannot be passive. The one wants you to provide active, energetic and surprising routes to victory; the other wants the maximum opportunity to see the system in action. Restore harmony by finding opportunities to reward units for behaving dynamically, move focal points around the play area or potentially actively punish passivity.

For the mechanic-connoisseur, the mechanically interesting bits must be relevant. If the most novel and intriguing parts of your system lie outside of the path to victory and engaging with them is more of a distraction than a core activity, the lack of harmony between disparate parts of the system will frustrate the mechanic-connoisseur.

In each of these cases, the game pushes players in conflicting directions, asking them to choose actions to satisfy one personal goal that undermines another. Your objective is to identify these opposing forces and restore harmony between them.

SUMMARY

- The sources of fun in a game may be **diegetic** and **non-diegetic**, **intrinsic** and **extrinsic**. These sources of fun are not mutually exclusive.
- **Diegetic intrinsic** fun is something done for the pleasure the in-game reality of doing it provides.
- **Non-diegetic intrinsic** fun is something done in the real world for its own pleasure, because of the game, but not within its world.
- **Diegetic extrinsic** enjoyment is motivated by an outcome or reward, but the reward exists within the game world.
- **Non-diegetic extrinsic** enjoyment is a game-related activity that is motivated by a real-world outcome or reward.
- Attaining mastery of a game can register on all of these axes.
- Problems arise when your sources of fun are in disharmony with each other and your game provides conflicting motivations.

EXPERIMENTS

Find something that players in your game choose to do, even when it is against their own best interests. Make it in their best interests. Make something else and re-create its effects.

Take two disconnected events in your game that, if they occurred in proximity in the real world, would trigger each other and build a mechanic to connect them.

Identify a moment when a given test result causes nothing to happen. Have it make something happen.

Remove at least one mechanic that requires state notation or bookkeeping from your game.

Identify a moment that you think is fun but that is under-utilised in your game; attach a reward resource to doing it.

Create a stage for partially scoring your game before the end of the game.

REFERENCES

Anderson, M., Caroland, N., Cohen, R., Darland, A., Gibbs, J., Hanold, D., Johns, E., Martin, M. and Weber, D. (2013) *Malifaux: Second Edition*. South Korea: Wyrd Miniatures, LLC.

Cavatore, A., Pirinen, T., Priestley, R., Stillman, N. and Thornton, J. (2000) *Warhammer: The Game of Fantasy Battles*. 6 edn. Nottingham: Games Workshop Ltd.

Hutchinson, M. (2017) *Gaslands*. Oxford: Osprey Games.

Spivey, B. (2015) *Rogue Planet*. Palm Bay, FL: Bombshell Games.

Warhammer 40,000. (2023) Nottingham: Games Workshop.

8 The Victory Imperative

There are many forms of play that we would recognise as 'games'. Some, such as Chess, produce a 'winner' while others, such as *Dungeons & Dragons* (Gygax and Arneson, 1974), do not. Nothing inherent in non-discrete miniatures games demands there be a winner, but if your game intends to have victory conditions – rules for determining who has won and when – a number of interesting and useful dynamics emerge which are crucial to understand and leverage in order to engender the most satisfying experience for all types of players. We discuss the specifics of designing victory conditions in Chapter 26; here we will explore the deeper purposes of victory conditions, aside from telling players who won.

PLAYING TO WIN

If a game has victory conditions, it is important that players play the game to win, in order that player behaviour becomes interestingly predictable and victory can be regarded as satisfying to both players. It may seem counterintuitive, but a certain degree of predictability is necessary for a game to be interesting. Imagine that we're playing Tennis; you serve the ball to me, and then reposition yourself for the likely angle of return, watching for my actions and keeping on your toes. However, I'm playing with total disregard for the victory conditions, and so I deliberately hit the ball directly off the court, and I continue to do this throughout the match. You will certainly win, but you will also very likely be bored or frustrated long before the end of the match and find little satisfaction in your victory. A level of unpredictability in a game is valuable, but players need to have some idea of the likely actions their opponent will take during play in order to anticipate and respond.

It is the job of the game designer to ensure there is both sufficient indication of the path to victory and sufficient incentive to follow that path, such that players both know how to play to win and choose to do so. While this may appear initially self-evident, it is absolutely possible to design a game in which the path to victory is obscure, narratively-dissonant, or runs counter to the core elements of fun that the players sought from the game.

However, if the path to victory is clear but a player pursues it in a manner that is all-consuming, where is left the space for intrinsic enjoyment of the mechanics of the game and its imaginative and social pleasures? By playing a non-discrete miniatures game, we choose to engage in a form of play that requires us to place personally curated objects before us and allows us to animate them with a form of imaginary life. A player may disengage from aesthetic and imaginative enjoyment of the game at times when the path to victory is foremost in their mind, but if they find themselves considering the game in purely abstract terms, taking actions exclusively in service to victory, we might say that they are missing the point of playing a *miniatures* game. In addition, as designers, we weave mechanics into interlocking systems that we labour to ensure are fun to manipulate

 DOI: 10.1201/9781003314820-10

and engage with; if a player is focused only on the operation of those mechanics as they relate to victory, we have failed to invite them to enjoy our system for its intrinsic pleasures.

It is important that players play to win, but it is equally important that players do not play *just* to win.

SIGNPOSTS FOR FUN

The way to achieve playing to win and playing for fun at the same time is by building rules that are fun to engage with and victory conditions that are best achieved by engaging with that fun. To put it another way, the victory conditions should be a signpost towards the most fun parts of your game. As a designer, victory conditions are the main way to show your players what you intend for them to be doing. By providing them at the start of a game, you are implicitly saying that you should be doing whatever things advance you towards achieving *this*.

It is also important that both players feel the game is being played in the same spirit. In any game, a player that rejects or ignores the rules destroys it: 'the spoil-sport shatters the play-world itself' (Huizinga, 1949, p. 11). In a game with winners and losers, if we observe a player deliberately playing in a manner that rejects or ignores the victory conditions, we may call them a spoilsport. My chaotic tennis playing is disruptive and destructive; I'm not even trying to win, and I ruin the game. The pernicious truth is that if a player cannot see the path to victory or finds that path is in disharmony with either the narrative or the fun they came to find, they may find themselves tempted or forced to act as a spoilsport, potentially even unknowingly. Clear victory conditions align players with the spirit of the game. If your rules instruct your players to play in one manner, but your victory conditions indicate to them that another manner is more effective, you cannot abdicate responsibility to the player for playing your game 'wrong': you must align the victory conditions with the actions in the game you wish players to take and the manner of taking them that you consider sporting.

If the activities that advance players towards victory are tedious, repetitive, narrative-dissonant or (worse) tend towards the appearance of being a killjoy, while the activities that are fun and narratively congruent run counter to the path to victory, you should expect players to feel frustrated, confused or bored by your game. One relatively safe approach is to make undesired behaviours ineffective as a winning strategy. If you want to dissuade players from taking certain actions or from playing in a certain way, make such things weak. This can be as simple as withholding extrinsic rewards for undesired behaviour. Weakness is relatively safe because if you accidentally apply it to a part of the game that's actually quite fun, that's not necessarily a problem. Many systems have legendarily enjoyable non-optimal choices that players are not only happy to engage with but they also take doing so as a mark of pride. For story-builders, spectacle-makers and even some player-artists, knowing that they're going to lose while enjoying themselves can be an ideal state.

Your victory conditions should lead players to the fun and align players with the spirit of the game. To achieve this:

- Identify the main sources of fun in your game (thanks to the previous chapter).
- Identify what a player who engages with those sources can achieve.

- Through playtesting, identify what constitutes a skilled level of that achievement.
- Make that your victory condition.

ANYONE CAN WIN

It is an oft-heard marketing boast in tabletop gaming that 'anyone can win until the last move', as though this is a desirable goal in game design. If we wish for players to invest time and effort into our game, the ability for 'anyone to win' undermines that, and the ability for 'anyone to win until the last move' calls into question the purpose and relevance of the rest of the game up to that final move.

Instead, a better goal might be that the outcome of the game is unknown for as long as possible. For players of similar skill, that might well be right up to the final move. For players of significantly different levels of mastery, that may well be much earlier in the game session.

ENCOURAGING ENGAGEMENT

When designing victory conditions, it is easy to create points when a player will choose to disengage from your game rather than play it. Being aware of some of the common traps increases your chances of encouraging engagement.

The key question to ask is: why should I engage with my opponent? Is the winning strategy to switch off and sit back from the game? Ask these questions about your design, and challenge your playtesters to find ways to win while disengaging.

Beyond that essential question, some common pitfalls for victory conditions are:

- To have a success threshold (for example, destroy half the enemy units) that does not trigger the end of the game, once one player has passed the threshold, they are incentivised to back off and avoid engagement with the game. Possible solutions are to have the threshold trigger game end or to combine it with a second objective that is easy to achieve if the enemy has disengaged.
- Rewarding one player by default and the other player only if they achieve an outcome. This is common in a siege scenario: the defender wins if the attacker fails to breach the walls. The defender has only limited agency to actively effect the outcome, and their default action is to do nothing. A possible solution is to give both players asymmetrical but active objectives, such as the attacker needing to breach the walls but the defender needing to sally forth and hold an objective beyond their walls.
- Your victory conditions reward a player for defending a location or unit in their deployment zone, particularly if both players have this objective symmetrically. The player is encouraged to sit still; if they move to engage, they split their forces across attacking and defending. Possible solutions include a time limit to force immediate and aggressive play or a secondary objective that allows the bolder player to break the tie.

Victory conditions such as those above can drive disengagement inherently by their inclusion, but there are other conditions that are fine on their own but, when combined with other factors, can become problematic. There are a few abilities that can be regular problems for standard victory conditions:

- **Summoned units:** It is not unusual to allow players to place additional units during play, whether magically risen in fantasy games, airdropped in during science fiction ones or called as reinforcements in historical themes. However, when a victory condition requires that a particular location be held at the end of the game, summoned units that are permitted to score these conditions can short-circuit the engagement otherwise offered by battling to hold a location throughout a game. Units not necessarily present throughout the play may need to have their ability to hold locations curtailed to avoid this.
- **Sudden unexpected movement:** Units that can move distances far beyond the scope of the standard in your game can create a lesser but similar problem, particularly when the location to be defended is large, such as a deployment zone. For most forces, the only practical way of defending large areas is by predicting enemy movement, so movement designed to be unpredictable can destroy the ability to realistically plan for such victory conditions.
- **Leaving the table:** Generally, it is disadvantageous to voluntarily have a unit leave the tabletop; however, in campaign games where damage can have lasting effects, it can be rewarding for players to feel they can make such a potentially counterintuitive choice, and it can be advantageous due to longer-term pressures on their force. As such, allowing units to leave the tabletop at a player's discretion is usually a reasonable option. However, if such a game then includes an (otherwise reasonable-sounding) victory condition, such as to assassinate a leader model, it opens the door to a player simply walking their leader model off the tabletop as their first action. If these options are to be included side by side, consider including something within the rules for the victory condition that accounts for models leaving the table of their own accord.

EVERYBODY WINS

Your game need not have victory conditions to have a satisfying conclusion. While victory conditions are present in many non-discrete miniatures games, strong intrinsic or extrinsic motivations can fulfil a similar role, particularly when playing to find out (as explored in the previous chapter).

Three common scenarios in which victory conditions may be unnecessary are campaign progression, reenactment and story-creation games.

In the first, if the individual session is one of a series, across which the player's force grows and changes, the fear of negative repercussions and the drive for rewards can be sufficient to create the motivation to engage in a measured fashion. A game with sufficiently powerful extrinsic motivators can dispense with victory conditions all together. *Frostgrave: Second Edition* (McCullough, 2020) goes so far as to explicitly state that there are often winners and losers who are not defined by the game in campaign games: each player must adjudicate for themselves if the campaign rewards and repercussions result in a feeling of success for them from a given session.

When the object of a miniatures game session is to reenact a historic conflict, it may be unnecessary to provide victory conditions to motivate action or frame the outcome. For example, miniature gamers often re-stage historic conflicts to see if they could do better or if the world would have turned out differently had Harold Godwinson had slightly less gullible family members. Players in such games play to win because the alternative would be both dissonant with history and defeat the purpose of the activity. Both sides may even be equally invested in seeing either side win, provided they win in an interesting and satisfying manner, as they are playing to both relish the history holistically and find out what could have happened if fortune had fallen differently on the day. In such games, if the extrinsic motivations are agreed upon and shared by the players, the drive to engage is unquestioned, and the hunger for victory is delegated to the inch-high generals.

Related to the motivation of playing to find out what happens seen in historical reenactment gaming, miniatures games designed to create original collaborative narratives can have the same play to find out motivation. While miniatures games lack the examination of the internal motivation of novel-like storytelling, they are excellent at telling epic stories centred on unfolding action. If the narrative of a play session is the sole motivator in a game, it can be difficult to provide players with a middle ground to bring their narratives together; everyone is the hero of their own story. In these cases, a satisfying game is highly dependent on clear communication and collaboration between each player and the designer, explaining that courtesy is entirely reasonable and probably necessary.

A useful design principle to keep in mind is that rules need to be created to stop players from doing things that are no fun but advantageous, but there's no point in writing rules to stop players from doing things that are no fun and disadvantageous. If there is a path that is disruptive to the play experience of others but fun to engage in, offer other players a method to get in on the fun, and it will cease to be disruptive and become transformative.

Without traditional opposed victory conditions, there is room to consider instead a game driven by narrative triggers, even ones that are not directly mutually exclusive, if not outright complimentary. Players will often take a position of basic opposition if there is even a vanishing chance of opposition being present within a game. Discovering a common cause, or at least neutral ground, can be a revelatory experience. Remember, your game is not an opposition engine; it's a fun engine, and mutually achieved goals can result in a greater number of satisfied customers than directly opposed ones. Consider the effects of handing out a series of sometimes complimentary hidden objectives at the start of a game. How long would most players spend blowing each other away before they realised they could have both done better with a little cooperation? Then consider how they will feel when the next time they tell each other that they're all on the same side, it turns out they weren't, and the trap is sprung. For those opposed to overly gentle and cooperative engagement, the potential for kindness can just make the cruelty cut all the deeper.

If the purpose of your game is to provide a tight and clean tournament game of direct competition in its purest form, victory conditions are, of course, indispensable. For other designs, they're just guides to doing what the game was built to make fun, and it is worth considering that they're not really needed. Where they are present, the conditions for victory should illuminate a pathway through your game for players. Make sure it passes through all the best and most fun parts of your game.

SUMMARY

- Games do not need winners and losers.
- Victory conditions should act as signposts to the most fun activities in your game.
- Strong intrinsic or extrinsic motivations can fulfil a similar role to victory conditions in campaign progression, re-enactment and story-creation games.
- To create aligned victory conditions:
  - Identify which activities in your game are the most fun.
  - Quantify what engaging with the most fun activities results in.
  - Test to discover what amount of those results exemplifies mastery of the system.
  - Make achieving such mastery your victory condition.
  - Avoid incentivising disengagement.

EXPERIMENTS

Remove your game's victory conditions altogether.

If your game has either symmetrical or asymmetrical victory conditions, try the other.

Borrow the victory conditions from another game and play with those.

Create a set of victory conditions that directly reward players for taking the actions you think are most interesting in your game.

REFERENCES

Gygax, G. and Arneson, D. (1974) *Dungeons & Dragons*. 1st edn. Lake Geneva, WI: TSR Inc.
Huizinga, J. (2016) *Homo Ludens*. New York: Angelico Press.
McCullough, J. (2020). *Frostgrave: Second Edition*. Oxford: Osprey Games.

9 Fantasy and Narrative

One of the primary pleasures of non-discrete miniatures games is to allow its users to indulge in a fantasy instantiated in tiny physical form before them. This isn't necessarily fantasy as in dragons and elves, although it can be, but rather the fantasy of inhabiting a time, place, character or world in a manner that would be impossible, impractical or unpleasant in reality and then providing the player with the constructed means of exercising their agency within that fantasy (Thi Nguyen, 2020). Because it reflects this agency, this fantasy is not experienced as a single story but through the stories that players themselves tell within it. Our game must provide mechanisms to generate a series of events interesting enough that we can use them to create stories (Schell, 2020, p. 319) and offer 'a narrative world that is capable of supporting many possible stories' (Murray, 2017, p. 203). Strong designs begin with a strong idea of their core fantasy and how the player will be given agency within that fantasy.

Due to the do-it-yourself nature of non-discrete miniatures games, the designer cannot provide this fantasy directly; it must be created in collaboration with the player. As players, we are invited to enter the fantasy, with the overall conceit of the game as our entry point. That overall conceit is supported and expanded upon by setting and backstory, art and imagery, all embedded by the designer. Where the game permits force-building or hobby investment, we use that to establish our personal corner of the game world, expanding the embedded backstory with our own extensions. The backstory must establish the core conflict that we are playing to resolve.

THE OVERALL CONCEIT

The **overall conceit** of a game is the collection of narrative devices that help to explain the game world and provide the player with an explanation of their place and motivation within it. At the highest level, the conceit of a game provides the overall framing for what the player is trying to achieve and how, providing 'a great deal of motivation and explanation for the action' (Elias, Garfield and Gutschere, 2020, p. 213).

It is common to frame your overall conceit as a 'you are' statement: 'you are the general of an army', 'you are pilot of a starfighter' or 'you are a wizard leading a band of adventurers and cutthroats'. In reality, of course, you are a person playing a game, but the overall conceit guides our expectations and provides an entry point into the fantasy. The 'you are' framing invites the player to inhabit a specific individual within the game world, which may or may not be represented by a miniature on the tabletop. As it is common for the player to control multiple units in these games, consider whether you wish the conceit to be pluralised rather than attached to a specific individual, inviting the player to inhabit multiple viewpoints during play: 'you control a squadron of starfighter pilots'; 'you control a band of adventurers and cutthroats'.

In miniatures games in particular, you may need to give some thought to harmonising your desired overall conceit with the peculiarity of the player's omniscient viewpoint, towering over the table with absolute knowledge of their forces' positions

DOI: 10.1201/9781003314820-11

and dispositions along with direct command of their movements and actions. Suspension of disbelief in this regard is commonly achieved through MacGuffins (you are in a command bunker with a heads-up display of the battlefield; you have a crystal ball) or by including rules to interfere with the player's control over their units (see Chapter 24).

However, the overall conceit is given it is critical that you are extremely clear about it and communicate it early and loudly to prospective players. This is not about marketing the game (although clarity of conceit cannot hurt in that regard), but rather the first and most important step in helping the player establish the conceptual framework which they will use to interpret your game and understand its abstractions during play.

MINOR CONCEITS

In support of the overall conceit, **minor conceits** are found at all levels of a game as metaphors to imbue abstract actions with narrative meaning. Indeed, without them, our game rules would be bafflingly opaque and bizarrely worded.

In *Warhammer: The Game of Fantasy Battles* (Cavatore et al., 2000), combat resolution uses a dice roll that is designated 'to hit', followed by a roll 'to wound' and a last roll 'to save'. Each of these is, in reality, abstract dice rolls comparing numerical statistics, but the minor conceits of 'weapon skill', 'strength', 'toughness', 'armour value', 'hit', 'wound' and 'save' all serve to connect these abstractions to our conceptual framework of a warrior swinging a sword in an attempt to strike and harm an armoured foe.

While it is generally best practice to avoid excessive commentary in the explanation of rules (such additional verbiage making it both more difficult to find the pertinent rule and risking accidentally restating the rule with a minor variation), conceits can be the exception to this. If the in-world logic of a given rule is not immediately obvious, it can be valuable to add some commentary before the mechanical description of the rule to help the player integrate the rule into their conceptual framework. This will aid them in comprehending and recalling the rule.

CONFLICT

Conflict is the fuel of every story: '*Someone wants or needs something, but someone or something stands in the way*' (Skolnick, 2014, p. 7, italics in original). Conflict is also the fuel of gameplay: the player needs to achieve something, but the game or the other players stand in the way.

Your game should present conflicts for the players. Your victory conditions (Chapters 8 and 26) and your resolution systems express conflicts mechanically, but such mechanical conflicts are framed and contextualised by the players through conceits and backstory. You should make it clear to the players what the nature of the core conflict in the game world is, how and why their tabletop avatars are involved and what the stakes are for those avatars. This gives players a lens through which to understand the motivations of their avatars, allowing them to choose behaviours that are congruent with those motivations.

It is also important to ensure that the core conflict expressed through your conceits and backstory is reflected by any victory conditions for the game; otherwise, the player will experience a dissonance between the story they are provided with and the actions they are incentivised by the game to take. If your narrative requires that a certain conflict occur, you should use the available tools to incentivise the players to engage with it. As explored in Chapters 6 and 7, it is not a reliable enough strategy to just present it and hope the players choose to engage with it.

NARRATIVE

To use the terms established in *Rules of Play* (Salen and Zimmerman, 2004), narrative elements in games can be **embedded** or **emergent**. Both of these forms of narrative are present to a greater or lesser extent in all non-discrete miniatures games, and most narrative moments within them are formed from a combination of the two.

EMBEDDED NARRATIVES

Embedded narrative elements are placed plainly into the game by the designer. They commonly take the form of backstory, descriptions of the setting of the world, the narrative framing of scenarios and so forth. They also appear in tiny fragments throughout your game in the descriptions of actions, weapons, units and more.

By providing more definitive details to the player, embedded narrative elements leave less to the imagination. For example, you might include some text in a scenario that provides concrete information about the location, the involved characters and their motivations. The Ork player's briefing sheet for the Battle at the Farm scenario in *Warhammer 40,000: Rogue Trader* (Priestley, 1987) begins: 'You are Thrugg Bullneck - an Ork Commander of the Charadon invasion force.' The player is informed that they (Thrugg) and a shifty subordinate (Hruk) have looted some jewels and hid them in a farmhouse nearby. Details of character and setting are provided literally, and the game designer can be confident of the player's understanding and interpretation of the intended narrative.

The primary strengths of embedded narrative elements are that they are simple for players and predictable for designers. They are essential to a degree, lest the player have nothing to pull them into the fantasy, and the specifics can act as triggers for the player's imagination to build on. But too much emphasis on embedded narrative elements can leave the player feeling that they are actors in the designer's story rather than forging their own. The art is to find the right level of specificity to provide to build the story along with your players.

EMERGENT NARRATIVES

Emergent narrative comes from the interactions between the set of tools and systems provided by your game. Emergent narrative elements arise unpredictably during play but can nevertheless very much be designed for.

In the 2014 edition of *Warhammer 40,000* (2014), a table is provided to generate a scenario at random. A roll of a six results in the session using 'The Relic' scenario, which begins: 'Both sides are attempting to recover a valuable relic from the front lines. It might be vital battle plans … or some other irreplaceable artefact that must be recovered at all costs'. The scenario provides a generic objective marker and rules for collecting, carrying and dropping that marker. For a player with an Ork force and a farmhouse in their terrain collection, this set of systems may end up interacting to create a very similar narrative to the Battle at the Farm, perhaps even resulting in an Ork Commander picking up the objective marker, only to be wounded and his shifty subordinate carry it off. The difference is that events emerge unpredictably from dynamically interacting systems, and the players are invited to interpret those loosely framed events to fit a narrative of their own invention. Crucially, the process may be run again with an unpredictable output: the players may begin with the same starting conditions (the same forces and the same terrain), operate the systems a second time and generate an entirely different set of events, using them to create a totally new story.

The power of emergent narrative is that it endows players with a sense of ownership of the game's narrative and an increased sense of investment, value and responsibility. If we imagine four friends playing the *Warhammer 40,000* scenario above, one of the two players sharing the Ork force realises that, through careful placement, he can save his lieutenant (named Hruk in nostalgic honour) from the certainly fatal enemy charge that Thrugg, the overall Ork Commander controlled by his friend, is about to suffer. Death thusly cheated, he is free to claim both the objective marker and the bragging rights for the victory. The betrayal of his comrade is subtle; both Ork players win the game, but a personal story of selfishness and disloyalty has emerged without direct intervention from the designer. Other art forms can make you feel anger at a betrayal of one character by another; only games can make you feel guilt over the same event due to your responsibility for them, and this is most effectively achieved by letting such stories arise emergently from the actions of the players themselves.

TIPS FOR EMBEDDED NARRATIVE

When creating embedded narrative elements, there are a few things to consider, which may be generalised as ensuring that you are setting your players up to be the stars of a story they understand and then handing control of it over to them.

Context, Not Control

Embedded narrative devices work best when they provide context for and framing of the player's decisions and actions, rather than attempting to take control from the players. They should not try to force a conclusion to the story, as the players can feel railroaded or cheated. Provide backstory to the game or to the scenario, which can include force-selection and set-up conditions, explanations of the events and mechanics, and then let go of the wheel. You can even guide players and then ask them to provide their own backstories. Force building rules are excellent for this since they tend to build in guidance within force limitations, and you can calibrate levels of embedding or emergence with them quite specifically. A force could have restricted access to a certain weapon because it has been banned by their government, or due to a rule called 'forbidden arms' with no further context, or simply by a restriction with no context. You are free to set the limitations and invitations of your player's invention.

Influencing the play narrative should ideally be done by setting ongoing narrative features that all players are aware of at the start of play. If a particular character is intended to survive an encounter, it is possible to state this narratively in the introduction of a scenario or by including a special rule to represent this 'plot armour' effect.

This can be done in an interactive fashion; often, the specific narrative of a given scenario requires the characters to take actions that are different from the standard actions that units perform in your game. Presenting these as scenario-specific actions is a simple way to differentiate a particular session and have the players participate directly in the narrative you intend to embed.

Introducing narrative events mid-game is a delicate thing. Consider having such events represent a neutral change in the context of the game world, which the players and their avatars are invited to react to. This makes the event part of the fabric of the players' actions and will be more acceptable to the players than a *deus ex machina* event that directly affects a particular unit without warning. Being told that the fall of night will make combat harder for all participants is easier to accept as a surprise than that one unit's weapons have suddenly suffered a failure.

Leave Space for the Player

When providing embedded narrative elements, leave space for the player. If all the important characters are of the designer's invention and all the interesting conflicts are already centred on those characters, the player is apt to feel that anything they do within the game world is a side note and not part of the grand arc of the setting.

Rather than using embedded narrative to create distance between players and the epic events of your setting, it can be used to involve them directly. If a great hero will be seen before and after the events of a given scenario, players may fear the dissonance created by their killing them off. An embedded narrative comment to the effect that the current scenario is one where the mighty hero was thought lost to darkness, only to re-emerge later, frees them from fears of crashing the story.

Don't crowd out the narrative space. Leave holes in your backstory that the players' avatars can step into. Be generous with the important conflicts and let your players take centre stage in them. Make the game's setting about the players' clever actions, not your clever story. This is not to say that the player's avatars have to be the centre of the game's setting; they may be very marginal, but they have to be at the centre of the narrative that frames the game. The player has to be able to drive the story and be the star of it.

Be Bold

Each set of players will interpret your embedded narrative element differently and will place different importance on them, as they relate to their own game session; they are free to embrace, accept, reject or ignore them. If you want to be confident that your players will experience the story you have in mind, be bold with your embedded narrative elements. For a dramatic last stand, it is not sufficient to have the defender slightly outnumbered and poorly positioned; they should be vastly out-numbered and entirely surrounded.

TIPS FOR EMERGENT NARRATIVE

Emergent narrative occurs when events with intelligent embedded narrative attached leave players to build the connective tissue between them. Building the conditions for emergent narrative relies on having the right systems in place, interconnected in the right ways, and with the right incentives to set them in motion.

Connect Events

Events may be connected or chained together, causing us to read narratives into them. This requires that your systems produce outputs that link to other systems. For example, if the damage system in your game results in a model simply being removed, that pro-vides a narrative event, but it is isolated and inert. If instead you permit the dying model to interact with other models nearby (crying out for help or causing panic) or cause them to leave some trace of themselves (perhaps they may be recovered by teammates or leave resources, like some ammo or a blood stain), there is more scope for emergent narrative as the players attempt to make sense of the causality of the connected events.

Correlate Events

Events do not need to be connected directly for us to turn them into stories: 'we are accustomed to make, almost automatically, a definite and obvious deductive gener-alisation when any separate objects are placed before us side by side' (Eisenstein, 1942, p. 16). In-game events that are not connected may be *interpreted* as connected by players if they share a correlation of location and type.

In *SSO* (Ford, 2018), players are struggling against a malicious A.I. in a stricken spaceship. Events occur which can shut down external systems, driving players outside to repair them, and separate events can shut down the ship's airlock. The two sets of events are entirely independent, but when they occur, players commonly invent a narrative of the A.I. tricking them to leave the ship so they could shut down the airlock to explain the events' proximity in place and time.

Your game's dramatic focus (as defined in the next chapter) provides players with a lens to adjudicate the narrative weight that should be given to each event as they attempt to correlate them; if the game's mechanics emphasise an event, more mean-ing will be ascribed to it.

Uncertainty

Whether we provide events that are directly connected or merely correlated, uncer-tainty between such events 'infuses a game with dramatic tension' (Salen and Zimmerman, 2004, p. 388) and creates variety in the stories that emerge. Not every sequence of events needs to feature uncertainty, but if a sequence of events is always predictable, it can be lifeless; its artifice is obvious. As with connecting events, uncertainty that leads to two forms of action, rather than a decision of action or non-action, can provide more fuel for emergent narrative, albeit at the risk of creating a time-consuming chain reaction which may not suit the pace of the game.

CASE STUDY: EMERGENT CHAOS: *GASLANDS*

In *Gaslands* (Hutchinson, 2017), a weapon can be fired at a vehicle, requiring a dice roll to hit and another to dodge. On hitting, some weapons (such as grenades) cause their target to gain hazard tokens, representing a vehicle losing control. If a vehicle has six or more hazard tokens, it will spin out, and depending on a dice roll, it might flip through the air. Flipping will cause a vehicle to lose hull points, which, if they run out, will cause the vehicle to be destroyed. When a vehicle is destroyed, depending on a dice roll, it might explode. Each of these events is dependent on the previous; no following event is inevitable, and many grenades will be thrown that do not cause a vehicle to flip, explode or cause cinematic devastation to vehicles around it. But when one does, the players can see a clear, emergent narrative based on their actions.

Make Things Act the Way that Players Expect Them to Act

Interpreting the mechanics through the conceptual framework of the game's conceits and backstory, the rules can, at best, melt into the background. With a strong (designed) correlation between what is mechanically effective and what feels right in the game world, decision-making can become predominantly diegetic. It is at this point that the player can lose themselves in the game world. To achieve this, it is important that things act the way players expect them to act.

Merely describing a given weapon as a grenade will not cause it to function as a narrative generator. It must carry with it a set of rules that cause results like grenades, or at least, results players expect from grenades in the context of your game. It should have area effects, be able to be thrown with a trajectory unlike a bullet and perhaps even have the option to be thrown back again. Modelling the way a thing is supposed to act will allow it to more easily click into place within the players' emergent narrative, both when players metaphorically reach for it and when it goes off.

Leave Gaps

Emergent narratives such as these give players a sense of ownership over the stories created, not only because they result directly from their efforts and actions but also because they allow players to fill in some of the narrative gaps between events. Alex Kennedy writes, 'If a player's imagination needs to cross a gap, the player will own the gap' (Kennedy, 2021). However, it should be considered that players proverbially filling in the frames between the panels of a comic book is good, and creating a story from a pile of randomly discovered pictures is bad. There should be clarity and intention even in your gaps.

Open to Interpretation

An event that is expressed mechanically may be presented concretely, specifically, or generically. If the output of the event described in concrete terms and the provided specifics are incongruous with the player's vision of the game-world, the narrative may stall for them. If the element is more generically described, inviting interpretation and invention to incorporate it into the story, the player can use that freedom to weave the event into their imagination of the game world, and a satisfying narrative is more likely to emerge.

Returning to the *Warhammer 40,000* scenario above, the non-specific nature of the 'valuable relic' is emphasised by the designers. The use of the descriptor 'relic' is a little specific, but the scenario text then goes out of its way to neutralise any meaning beyond 'valuable MacGuffin', giving the players latitude to adjust the meaning of the element to fit their own vision of the narrative.

SUMMARY

The **overall conceit** of a game frames its world and the player's place within it, generally framed by 'you are…' statements.

The **minor conceits** of a game frame abstract mechanics and rules within the world of the game; abstract dice rolls are framed as 'rolls to hit' or 'rolls to wound'.

The **conflict** that drives your game needs to be framed clearly and concisely.

Your game's **narrative** can be **embedded** or **emergent**, and will generally arise from a combination of both.

Embedded narrative:

- Is offered by the designer to the player.
- Is set, simple and predictable.
- Should create context while leaving space for player creativity and importance.

Emergent narrative:

- Is created by the players.
- Is changeable, requires player effort and is unpredictable.
- Creates ownership for the players.
- Relies on the connectivity and correlation of events.
- Depends on the verisimilitude of the game world.

EXPERIMENTS

Remove a rule that connects two events explicitly together. Add a rule that connects two otherwise disparate but correlated rules together.

Remove all embedded narratives connected to a class, weapon or set of events in your game, then describe them emergently based on what happens when they are used or occur during play.

Insert an embedded narrative event in the middle of the play. Make it smaller, then larger than you initially decided. Make it affect one unit, then one unit on each side, then all units.

Add a set of randomly assigned post-game narratives loosely explaining the outcome of the game.

REFERENCES

Cavatore, A., Pirinen, T., Priestley, R., Stillman, N. and Thornton, J. (2000) *Warhammer: The Game of Fantasy Battles.* 6 edn. Nottingham: Games Workshop Ltd.

Eisenstein, S. (1942). *The Film Sense.* London: Faber and Faber.

Elias, G.S., Garfield, R. and Gutschere, R. (2020). *Characteristics of Games.* Cambridge, MA: MIT Press.

Ford, G. (2018) *SSO.* Dover: Man O' Kent Games.

Hutchinson, M. (2017) *Gaslands.* Oxford: Osprey Games.

Kennedy, A. (2021) *The Snare of the Tree and Other Perilous Seductions.* London: Amazon.

Murray, J.H. (2017). *Hamlet on the Holodeck: The Future of Narrative in Cyberspace.* *updat*ed edn. Cambridge, MA: MIT Press.

Priestley, R. (1987) *Warhammer 40,000: Rogue Trader.* Nottingham: Games Workshop Ltd.

Salen, K. and Zimmerman, E. (2004) *Rules of Play: Game Design Fundamentals.* Cambridge, MA: The MIT Press.

Schell, J. (2020) *The Art of Game Design: A Book of Lens.* Boca Raton, LF: CRC Press.

Skolnick, E. (2014) *Video Game Storytelling.* Berkeley, CA: Watson-Guptill Publications.

Thi Nguyen, C. (2020) *Games: Agency As Art.* Oxford: Oxford University Press.

Warhammer 40,000. (2014) Nottingham: Games Workshop.

10 Dramatic Focus

Abstract games present players with a game world they view from their own perspective as a player playing a game. Miniatures games almost universally offer players the chance to view the game world from a perspective that is not their own. Some games promise an objective presentation of their game world, and some offer a subjective viewpoint. Whichever you choose can have a significant impact on the player's expectations of your game and understanding of its narrative. Regardless of the narrative goal, game mechanics draw the player's attention and create dramatic focus to help deliver it.

OBJECTIVITY AND SUBJECTIVITY

A game with an **objective** viewpoint will attempt to recreate the steps of causal reality and allow the player to approach that reality with their own opinions and emotions. One with a **subjective** viewpoint is concerned with hitting the moments that tell the story and create the emotions and moments the designer has decided are important. An objective design will generally attempt to include each step in the chain of reactions that connects cause to effect, while a subjective one will skip steps it designates to be of no interest or magnify those it considers worthwhile. Every game or mechanic lies somewhere on the axis between those two poles, and a designer can choose variously to defer either to causal reality or narrative satisfaction.

In games which seek to explore contemporary or historical reality, objectivity tends to be emphasised since it provides a strong sense of verisimilitude within a world. In his foreword to *Harpoon* (Bond, 1987), Tom Clancy describes the game as 'a tool for understanding things that happen in the real world' and, in service of that aim, where resolution systems exist, they aim to recreate the pertinent causal steps in series and with equal weighting.

For games whose primary aim is to evoke the fictional action and genre tropes of movies or books, a subjective approach is more natural, since those works themselves generally adopt their own subjective viewpoint. *7TV: Cinematic Skirmish Rules* (Perrotton, 2023) describes itself as a tool 'to re-create the action set pieces of your favourite movies and TV series, or invent entirely new productions straight out of your imagination' and so takes a more subjective approach, acceding only to the sort of movie logic that recreates the world of the silver screen, over anything connected to the laws of physics.

Neither is more inherently desirable – their applicability will reflect your design goals – nor are they mutually exclusive. Your game also need not apply them uniformly throughout; one area of your game may benefit from a more objective approach, another a more subjective one.

SETTING PLAYER EXPECTATIONS

The Fred Jane Naval War Game (Jane, 1906) is governed by the golden rule that 'Nothing may be done contrary to what could or would be done in actual war'.

DOI: 10.1201/9781003314820-12

While mostly unhelpful as a method of resolving disputes, it is effective as a statement of the intent of the game: we are to recreate reality in a manner coherent with objective facts. This is useful and valuable in aligning player expectations. If players approach a game with different expectations about its purpose and focus, they may not be able to enjoy it to its fullest or, worse, may quarrel as they struggle towards mismatched goals.

Players will bring a wide spectrum of expectations to your game, and you need to help them align both with your vision for the game and each other's. As we discuss more in Chapter 11, the looseness inherent in non-discrete miniatures games requires the provision of some form of catch-all 'golden rule'. This golden rule is an excellent opportunity to establish player expectations around the intent of your game. *Frostgrave: Second Edition* (McCullough, 2020) invites players who encounter unclear rules interactions to ask, 'What would happen in the movie?'. Fred Jane asks that we play to generate realism, and Joseph McCullough asks that we play to build drama.

HONOURING PLAYER EXPECTATIONS

Whether you are striving for a highly realistic modern combat simulator or hope to emulate wildly fantastical cinematic action, maintaining the verisimilitude of your game's fictional world is critical. To maintain a coherent game world, you must honour the expectations that you have set for the players. If you have established expectations of realism or genre tropes in your game, moments of deviation from those elements will be jarring to the players, undermining their enjoyment of its diegetic moments.

This is one of the advantages of using familiar-feeling mechanics. If a player has already seen a set of rules satisfactorily interacting to describe a certain situation in a previous game, they will more readily accept those rules as a method of describing that situation in the current one, making it easier to suspend disbelief. If we wish to engender enjoyment in the diegetic parts of our game, it is necessary for our system to fade into the background at times. Disrupting a player's expectations knocks them out of this enjoyment by forcing their attention back to the non-diegetic machinery of the game.

GENRE AND AGENCY

The most significant challenge to creating genre beats and drama is player agency. When a novel or movie script sets about to place its protagonists in danger to satisfy the tropes of its genre, it does not have to contend with a protagonist who is self-aware, self-interested and active. When we ask our players to move their miniatures into a haunted house armed only with a flashlight, they can simply refuse. Genre emulation is, therefore, an outcome not of mechanical systems in isolation but of the interaction of those mechanics with the motivations discussed in Chapters 6 and 7. To cause genre-evoking outcomes to occur, we must first provide rules to allow genre-appropriate actions to take place and then provide motivations for the players to choose those actions. We explore this more in Chapter 16.

ABSTRACTION AND DETAIL

It is tempting to equate objectivity with detail and subjectivity with simplicity, but they lie on different axes. It is entirely feasible to create subjectivity via detail; if a moment looms large in your protagonist's personal experience, you may wish to recreate its various physical, mental and emotional impacts, and it could generate far more mechanical detail than a recreation of objective reality would require.

When adding mechanics to a game, the challenge is choosing the appropriate level of abstraction for your game. Recreating reality is not a process of adding more and more intricate systems to model every level of existence; it is the art of choosing what level of detail is 'enough' for the purpose of a specific design.

We might describe a detailed mechanic as one that requires many or low-level inputs, and an abstracted mechanic as one that requires few or high-level inputs. The level of output can then vary, but if the detail of output exceeds that of the input, it will create a sense in players that the game is 'playing itself' and that their input has relatively little weight. As an example, visual detection is handled very differently in the highly detailed *Harpoon* (Bond, 1987) when compared to the more abstracted *Victory At Sea* (Sprange, 2020). One requires the specific ship class, size and altitude of the target, as well as the weather conditions and time of day as inputs; the other simply requires the distance between the two units in question. Both produce a simple binary output of whether or not the actor can draw a line of sight to the target.

DRAMATIC FOCUS

Whether your viewpoint is objective or subjective, you must direct the player's attention to the places from which meaningful decisions and memorable narratives are most likely to emerge. We can think of this as a game's dramatic focus. More detailed or involved mechanics require more attention from the player to operate, and so detail can be used as a tool to direct player focus. By extension, simplifying an area of your game, or making it automatic, signals that it is of lower importance. We use the presence and relative complexity of mechanics to direct player attention and create dramatic focus in our games. It is through this dramatic focus that we guide players to actively participate in the idea, feeling or fantasy that we wish to communicate through our design. It is through this dramatic focus that the *meaning* of a game is expressed.

In an objective design, dramatic focus should be drawn to the elements that define the action being replicated and the decisions that are meaningful to those elements. *Harpoon* may be 'the best naval simulation available to the public', but in it, Larry Bond asserts (emphasis ours):

> A game must show the players the *significant* details, and ignore the rest. Some details are just not important to the player at his level of control. A ship or formation commander is not interested in the maintenance record of the aircraft, or the exact frequency settings of his sonars.

Bond's goal is to allow the player to adopt the role of a modern naval commander. In the real world, someone is adjusting the sonar frequency, but the naval commander is entirely disconnected from that activity. As such, it is entirely in line with the goals of creating an objective viewpoint that our players have no direct method for making such an adjustment, and thus Bond provides no rules for doing so. If we wish to tell the story of the actions of the sonar operators and make a different game about the uncertainty of detection in conflicts between surface and submarine vessels, we might well include a mechanic for adjusting the frequency settings of our sonars to direct our players' focus to that part of the narrative.

In a subjective design, we have even more freedom to direct player attention: recall a memorable scene from a movie that exists in the same dramatic space as your game. Think about the action that occurs during that scene that we are most focused on as the audience; those are the activities your mechanics should focus on. If the central interest in the scene is not how accurate the gunslingers are but who loses their nerve first, you can make that the focus of the mechanics. By adding in more resolution systems for nerve, you slow the game down in that part of play, as a director might lengthen a shot or slow down the action. By creating separate systems for the gunslinger's furrowed brow fighting back beads of sweat or their fingers twitching around the triggers of their guns, you zoom the player's attention to those areas. When the pistols are drawn and shots are fired, you can simply abstract that least important part of the resolution to a simple roll; the drama is past; time to get to the next face-off.

Identify the dramatic focus of your game, design mechanics and incentives that draw attention to that and eliminate those that distract from it. Your game is about whatever its mechanics cause us to focus on.

SUMMARY

- Games with an objective viewpoint attempt to model a causal reality and place players in it.
- Games with a subjective viewpoint use the beats of a dramatic recreation to model a personal experience.
- You should align players' expectations with how the game is to be approached and honour those expectations during gameplay.
- Mechanics cause dramatic focus.
  - Detail creates focus, slows and zooms.
  - Abstraction creates speed and wide viewpoints.
- A game is about whatever its mechanics cause players to focus on.

EXPERIMENTS

Choose a dramatically important moment in your game. Add an additional rule to describe what happens during it. Abstract a rule that describes something of no dramatic import.

Create a golden rule that explains what the game is about while resolving disputes. Create one that explains a different version of what the game could be about.

REFERENCES

Bond, L. (1987) *Harpoon*. Bloomington, IL: Game Designers' Workshop, Inc.

Jane, F. (2022) *The Fred Jane Naval War Game (1906) Including the Royal Navy's Wargaming Rules (1921)*. London: History Wargaming Project.

McCullough, J. (2020) *Frostgrave: Second Edition*. Oxford: Osprey Games.

Perrotton, K. (2023) *7TV: Cinematic Skirmish Rules*. Woodhall Spar: Crooked Dice.

Sprange, M. (2020) *Victory at Sea*. Nottingham: Warlord Games.

Section 2

The Raw Materials

There are nine and sixty ways of constructing tribal lays, And every single one of them is right.

Rudyard Kipling

In Section 1, we set out our understanding of the fundamental characteristics of non-discrete miniatures games. We also proposed a number of frameworks for conceptualising how they create both enjoyment and meaning for players.

In Section 2, we enumerate and examine the building blocks from which the majority of non-discrete miniatures games are constructed. There are various answers to and routes around the questions that the design of a non-discrete game throws up, and each is as correct or incorrect as the other, depending on the design in question. We try to offer guidance on why a particular solution may or may not work for a particular design.

DOI: 10.1201/9781003314820-13

11 | Miniatures and Measures

As we have discussed in some depth, non-discrete games are concerned with spatial interactions between (potentially quite oddly-shaped) physical objects on the table-top. Dealing with the vagueness of those objects and putting them into some sort of regular framework is one of the first and most major challenges for designing non-discrete games. In order to allow players to manipulate physical models, movement must be structured in a definite physical way. The most common way of achieving this is to set a scale for the game and rules for physically measuring distances with a tape measure.

MEASURING, VAGUENESS AND PRE-MEASURING

Usually, once a scale has been set (see Chapter 12), markers are given a score relating to their speed across the tabletop. Movement is performed by converting this score into a measurement and physically pushing the marker up to that distance across the tabletop. All pains should be taken to make measurement as simple as possible. Generally, it is sufficient to specify that measurements are made from one point on a model to the same point after movement is completed; however, when pivoting large objects about an off-centre point, it should be clearly specified that it will be necessary to measure from different points at various stages (Figure 11.1).

THE GOLDEN RULE

The prevalence of non-discrete systems in these games, whether measuring between two points while physically moving an object through real space, adjudicating lines of sight across a dense tabletop (Chapter 22), or agreeing the boundaries of home-made terrain pieces (Chapter 23), all in a competitive setting, unavoidably results in vagueness and the possibility for disagreement. As such, non-discrete game rules need to decide how they will deal with player disagreements due to this vagueness. It is common practice and recommended to provide an explicit catch-all resolution method to players for this purpose. A typical example of this type of rule can be found in *Warhammer: The Game of Fantasy Battles* (Cavatore *et al.*, 2009, p. 2):

> If you find that you and your opponent cannot agree on the application of a rule, roll a dice to see whose interpretation will apply for the remainder of the game – on a result of 1-3 player A gets to decide, on a 4-6 player B decides.

This result is fair and (in theory) equitable, at least between two players who are seeking honest engagement with the rules. An alternative approach can be found in *Gaslands* (Hutchinson, 2017, p. 6): 'In *Gaslands*, if a rule is unclear, choose which-ever option results in the most carnage for all concerned'. The *Gaslands* rule is pref-erable since it not only settles disputes but also has a consistent resolution outcome

DOI: 10.1201/9781003314820-14

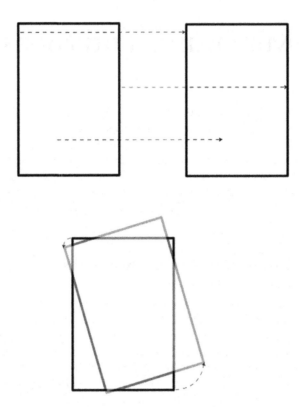

FIGURE 11.1   While measuring straight line movement requires only consistency, different points during a pivot can move different distances.

at every gaming table, while the *Warhammer* version will result in two different rule interpretations being correct in two different instances, at the whim of the dice.

The purpose of such a catch-all resolution should be to cover the cracks where non-discrete theory meets practical miniatures and tabletops, never as an excuse to leave loopholes or create contradictory rulesets.

PRE-MEASURING

Some rule systems disallow pre-measuring, the practice of players measuring out a potential movement or ranged action and agreeing on its achievability before any markers are actually moved or actions declared. Designers rule out pre-measuring to avoid players taking excessive time measuring every possible movement and/or to create performative uncertainty by testing skills of visual reasoning and estimation of distances. The first issue is only problematic when it is indicative of a breakdown in the social contract between players; the rest of the time, pre-measuring is as likely to speed the game up by eliminating options, decreasing analysis time and allowing declaration and agreement of intent to eliminate later debate as it is to drag it out. The second can create interest, but if included, it should be made certain that such requirements are shared equally across forces; for example, those favouring ranged attacks should need to make estimations just as much as those wishing to engage in melee. Regardless of a system's stated intention, pre-measuring is commonly house-ruled by players who prefer one approach or another, so if you wish to explicitly permit or preclude pre-measuring for gameplay reasons, you should consider explaining your rationale to allow players to understand why they should adopt the convention at their table. *Star Wars: X-Wing Miniatures Game* (Little, 2012, p. 6) provides a good example of explicit communication of design intent:

> During the Planning phase, players **cannot** use maneuver templates in order to "test" where ships will end up. Instead, they must plan their maneuvers by estimating their ships' movement in their heads.

MODELS AS MARKERS

Typically, player markers in non-discrete games are miniatures, generally of set physical scales or sizes, and are part of an overarching systemic hobby. These also have specific concerns in relation to game design. The whole purpose of collecting, constructing and preparing miniatures as a hobby is in order to exercise and display creative drives. The result of this is that players will desire to pose and embellish miniatures to make them into larger and more extended shapes than basic production would suggest. Rule sets should be careful to intelligently ensure that such creativity does not advantage or disadvantage the player to avoid the honest modeller falling behind due to their free expression of creativity or the employer of sharp practice from gaining the upper hand due to some outlandish additions to their miniatures.

Artistic player expression in the creation of miniatures will not generally extend to the extension of the core of the represented individual; the trunk and head will tend to remain roughly where originally designed, with extensions taking the form of cloaks, banners and otherwise worn or held objects. Rules tend to allow that miniatures representing living beings attempting to make life more difficult for their opponents will fold back cloaks or lower weapons when taking cover behind stone walls rather than stride about the field in a constant dramatic pose, and so may allow that anything other than the torso and head of the miniature be ignored for targeting purposes (it being harder to fold one's gut away at will, even more so as the years go on). While effective, this can result in additional vagueness and a need for player cooperation, as the line between cloak and torso or head and hair can be difficult to agree upon during a session on a miniature the size of one's thumb. Alternatively, rules can be included to specify percentages of a model, with a certain percentage being required to allow a model to be seen. While this can offer the chance for clarity and allow spindly and ephemeral additions to miniatures with very little risk, it should be remembered that practically, judging the percentage volume of a leg or set of shoulders during play can prove sufficiently unwieldy to create as many arguments as it solves.

ABSTRACTION, BASES AND SILHOUETTES

Most ranges of miniatures come with standardised base sizes, for example, 30, 40 and 50 mm in circular bases or 20, 25, 40 and 50 mm in square ones. One of the more usual solutions to the creative drive in modelling potentially creating game imbalance is to abstract miniatures down to just their bases, essentially making the miniature itself an embellishment with little or no game purpose. It is a simple enough matter to categorise miniatures into set heights such as 1, 2 and 3 and state that whatever shape the miniature on a given base might be, it will not be considered to be taller than its assigned height or wider than its base, creating a tin can-shaped silhouette. Heights can, of course, be assigned asymmetrically to bases to create broad, low shapes or tall, thin ones. This can create a situation, particularly when applied to both player miniatures and terrain, where the tabletop as viewed by a given player is essentially an attractive facade behind which sits the 'true' form of a series of regular cuboids and tin can shapes. This option has the advantage of being impossible to disadvantage oneself by extravagant self-expression, but it can be difficult for players to transfer between 'realities' and it loses some of the very qualities of clarity and direct engagement that make non-discrete games so powerful.

TERRAIN

Aside from miniatures representing the player's forces, the main part of the tabletop will be taken up with scale representations of buildings, furniture, trees, lampposts and any other amount of ephemera to bring to life the location that the forces are encountering each other within. These non-active or player-controlled miniatures are collectively known as terrain. Terrain has a vital role to play in non-discrete games for the purpose of both occluding lines of sight between miniatures and interfering with movement in order to add an interesting order of puzzles to the spatial interactions of the tabletop. We will examine in depth some of the rules for representing these qualities in a later chapter, but for now, it is worth considering that players will tend to fill their tabletop with whatever terrain they have available in the quantities they see fit. Given that these terrain pieces can vary far more wildly than a miniature ever could, are far harder to define in quantity and position and will hugely affect how players experience a game system, it is worth giving serious thought to how a system will define and deal with them. Some suggestions on doing so can be found in Chapter 23.

STANDARDS AND PRE-OWNERSHIP

We are all for breaking standards of design, or at least considering whether they are standards that exist for a reason or not, but it is worth considering that there are standards in scale miniatures and that acquiring a new set of miniatures is an onerous and expensive operation. As such, designing with some of the constraints of what your audience might already own in the way of miniatures is well worth consideration. We will outline exactly what that might mean in the next chapter as far as the size and scope of your games. In terms of motif, this will tend to mean that if you wish to create a system best represented with, for example, large amounts of close-set urban terrain, realistic extremely heavily wooded terrain, canals or water systems and player miniatures that aren't toting some form of weaponry as standard, you will need to be sensitive to the fact that players will want or need to create stand-ins at short notice.

SUMMARY

Measuring can be vague and cause disagreements. This can be combated by:

- **The Golden Rule:** Players can be asked to act in a mutually equitable fashion.
  - A single rule can be offered to default on any disagreement.
- **Pre-measuring:** Measurements can be made before decisions are made.

Miniatures are used as player markers, and creative modelling is part of the attraction of these games. Rules should not constrain such creativity.

Miniatures can be abstracted to **Bases** and **Silhouettes**.

Terrain can be extremely varied and should be carefully defined.

Catering to the player's likely pre-owned miniatures collections can lower your barrier to entry.

EXPERIMENTS

Allow pre-measuring, or restrict it to specific actions.

Base your game on true miniature dimensions, then on abstracted bases and heights.

REFERENCES

Cavatore, A., Pirinen, T., Priestley, R., Stillman, N. and Thornton, J. (2009) *Warhammer: The Game of Fantasy Battles*. Nottingham: Games Workshop Ltd.

Hutchinson, M. (2017) *Gaslands*. Oxford: Osprey Games.

Little, J. (2012) *Star Wars: X-Wing Miniatures Game*. [Board game] Roseville, MN: Fantasy Flight Games.

12 Scale and Scope

The term 'scale' may be used to refer to two very different ideas either the ratio of the relative relationship between the size of a model and its real-life counterpart or the size and scope of the scene being represented, from a duel between individuals to a massed battle between armies. We will refer to the first as **scale** and the second as **scope**.

MODEL AND GROUND SCALE

The relative size of a model in relation to its nominal 'real-world' equivalent is that model's **scale**, commonly expressed as either a ratio (1:72 being a model whose dimensions are 72nd of its real-world counterpart) or as an 'eye height' (28mm being the scale in which a notional adult human has 28mm between its base and its eye level). Even if a game is designed with a specific scale of model in mind, it is common to see rules systems provide suggested adjustments to permit the use of other scales (Figure 12.1).

The **ground scale** of a game is the relationship between distances on the tabletop and the equivalent notional 'real-world' equivalent, exactly as with a map. Knowing the ground scale allows one to calculate realistic movement distances and weapon ranges. Some early rulesets simply state a ground scale and expect the players to research real-world statistics and convert them as needed into game statistics, as may be seen in a number of the systems described in *Naval War Games* (Featherstone, 1965), for example.

FIGURE 12.1 Miniatures of various scales. Photograph by the author.

DOI: 10.1201/9781003314820-15

The adherence to an accurate and consistent ground scale and model scale has the appeal of realism, suggesting a simulation of objective reality, but creates impracticalities on the tabletop, the chief of which is caused by the relationship between the height of a man and the range of a gun. If we have a 28-mm-scale World War Two infantryman, his pistol will shoot perhaps 12" across the table, which is practical in game terms. However, his Vickers K machine gun will shoot roughly 90 feet in-game, which is functionally the same as having an infinite range in game terms. Even in the 1:6000 scale (the smallest commercially available scale for ship models), a World War II battleship gun will shoot 20 feet across the table, requiring play in a sports hall to permit ships to outrange each other. For this reason, many designers have chosen to be flexible with the application of ground scale, particularly as it applies to weapon ranges, in the service of gameplay. We refer to this flexibility as adopting 'game scale'.

GAME SCALE

Games that employ **game scale** prioritise providing an interesting and balanced tactical play experience on a reasonably-sized tabletop over real-world concerns when designating weapon ranges and movement speeds.

As a way of reasoning about game scale in your own designs, let us invent a notional measurement: **Reach (R)**, which will be some fraction of the width of your play area; one-sixth or one-eighth are good options. (If your table is 4-foot across, R might be 6", for example.) We can then design a relative set of distances: standard units can move R, fast ones double R, while most ranged weapons fire between double or triple R. This handily creates a range of tactical relationships where (for example) infantry struggle against ranged troops, who struggle against cavalry, and so archers need the protection of pike blocks in a neat re-creation of real-world tactics. This system is applicable whether the weapons in question are arrows with a fast being a horse, rifles firing at automobiles or lasers shooting at hoverbikes.

In cases of modern or science fiction warfare where different weapons may have vastly different effective ranges, we could set the shortest range to R and make the longest equal to the width of the tabletop, then design the ranges of the remaining weapons on an appropriate curve between the two.

The specific relationship between a game's R multipliers for movement will define whether it is seen as playing in a fast-flowing, dynamic fashion or more of a considered, cerebral one. It will also define the relative balance between ranged and close combat troops and how many turns a game will take before victory conditions based on holding sections of a table become moot.

For example, in *Warhammer: The Game of Fantasy Battles* (Cavatore *et al.*, 2000), a game with a semi-medieval setting, most infantry moves 8" with a table 48" wide, so R is one sixth of the table. Crossbows, handguns and longbows all have a range of 24", triple R, cavalry move double R for 16" and ballista fire the full width of the tabletop. In *Bolt Action* (Cavatore and Priestly, 2012), a game representing combat during World War Two, infantry move 6" with a table 48" wide and 72" long, giving R as one-eighth of the table, short-range pistols fire 6", heavy howitzers fire the full 72" length of the tabletop and rifles fire four times R for 24".

GAME SCOPE

We define the game's **scope** as the number of combatants and the details of their subsequent actions and struggles. The terminology for the description of range in scope is not universal, but generally it breaks into three rough categories defined by whether players control individuals, squads or ranked units. Those that put players in charge of a small group of independently acting individuals may be referred to as 'narrative skirmish'[1] or 'character-driven skirmish'[2] up to 'skirmish' level. Those that involve larger numbers of individuals, some of which may be formed into loose squad formations, usually with coherency rules but without strict formations, can be referred to as anything from 'skirmish'[3] to 'massed battle' depending on quite how many squads are involved, while those that require formations with serried ranks will almost certainly be referred to as 'massed battle'[4] games.

As the scope escalates, it is important not to also escalate the total number of discrete units you ask your players to control. Miller (1956) suggests that the average person can keep their attention and judgement focused on around seven (plus or minus two) things at once, and indeed, most games will tend not to ask players to keep their focus on more than nine units at a time (whether those units are individuals, squads or ranked units). Viewed through this lens, there need not be any difference in the number of units in a small skirmish game between two gangs of street thugs and a massed battle game featuring thousands of soldiers. During a design, we might start with a handful of troopers acting individually. If our scope evolves to a dozen or more troopers during development, we will need to start exploring ways to group them on the table to allow the player to again engage with a number of units less than Miller's magic number. The scale and scope of a game also signal intent to players and set up their expectations. If you want to tell sweeping stories that can affect the fates of nations in battles, then you will want there to be lots of miniatures on the tabletop. The more miniatures you want, the smaller they will have to be and the larger their groups. If you want players to identify closely with individual characters, you'll want a smaller handful of characters.

Between these two extremes, you may focus on groups involved in a mighty struggle but who are moving in a dynamic and dramatic fashion through detailed, realistic terrain. In which case you won't want blocks of units, but you won't want a handful of less than ten people. You'll need loose squads, but they will need to move as a single entity and share statistics to save games stretching into the small hours and breaking the sanity of your players.

In short, decide what your game is to be about; that will tell you how much detail you need an individual to have, how many individuals you want and even how you expect them to move around the tabletop. That will, in turn, tell you what the scale of your game needs to be and what its scope is.

SUMMARY

Non-discrete miniatures games have **Scale**, the relative size of a miniature to its real-world equivalent. This can be converted to measure distances by using **Ground Scale**. Distances in play can be considered using **Game Scale**, relating movement and shooting ranges to table size.

Non-discrete miniatures games have **Scope**, the relative size of the portrayed conflict. This can range from a narrative or **Character-driven Skirmish** to **Skirmish** to **Massed Battle**.

Both scale and scope:

- Control the pace and length of a game.
- Are practical concerns for designers and players.
- Create focus and detail.

EXPERIMENTS

Generate a unit relating your unit's movement distances and ranges to your table size. Reduce and increase it for:

- Everything.
- Shooting.
- Movement.

Gather at least two separate units in your game to be a single larger unit. Divide your units up to be at least two separate units.

NOTES

1 *Planet 28* (Evans, 2020) is subtitled *Narrative Skirmish Gaming in a Baroque future*.
2 The first edition of *Malifaux* (Caroland, 2009) was subtitled *A Character-Driven Skirmish Game*.
3 For example *Burrows and Badgers: A Skirmish Game of Anthropomorphic Animals* (Lovejoy, 2016)
4 For example *Mayhem: Fantasy Mass Battles* (Spivey, 2013).

REFERENCES

Caroland, N. (2009) *Malifaux: A Character-Driven Skirmish Game*. South Korea: Wyrd Miniatures, LLC.

Cavatore, A., Pirinen, T., Priestley, R., Stillman, N. and Thornton, J. (2000) *Warhammer: The Game of Fantasy Battles*. Nottingham: Games Workshop Ltd.

Cavatore, A. and Priestly, R. (2012) *Bolt Action*. Oxford: Osprey Games.

Evans, N. (2020) *Planet 28: Narrative Skirmish Gaming in a Baroque Future*. London: Mammoth Miniatures.

Featherstone, D. (1965) *Naval War Games*. London: Stanley Paul.

Lovejoy, M. (2016) *Burrows and Badgers: A Skirmish Game of Anthropomorphic Animals*. Oxford: Osprey games.

Miller, G.A. (1956). "The magical number seven, plus or minus two: Some limits on our capacity for processing information". *Psychological Review*. 63 (2): 81–97.

Spivey, B. (2013) *Mayhem: Fantasy Mass Battles*. Florida: Bombshell games.

13 Uncertainty

For a game to be interesting, it must not be clear who will win. Tic-Tac-Toe lacks interest for most adults as, after a small number of moves, its outcome is certain. The conflict may be between players, or it may be between the players and the game itself in the case of co-operative games, but the outcome must be uncertain. While not essential, uncertainty in the outcomes of individual events within non-discrete miniatures games is common, allowing mechanical uncertainty to add both dramatic tension and tactical interest to the moment-to-moment play.

Games have many ways of creating such uncertainty. Five key methods are: performative uncertainty; social uncertainty; uncertainty due to complexity; uncertainty of process; and stochastic uncertainty. Not all of these are equally easy to employ in non-discrete miniature games. Which we choose and how we combine them will greatly affect the experience of playing our games. In this chapter, we will summarise each method for creating uncertainty and explore their applicability to these games.

PERFORMATIVE UNCERTAINTY

Performative uncertainty is usual in sports or dexterity games where the result cannot be foreseen since what is being achieved is physically difficult, such as making a basket in basketball. On the tabletop, performative uncertainty is found in **dexterity tests**, in games such as *Jenga* (Scott, 1983) and in **spatial judgements**, such as those commonly found in non-discrete miniatures games.

Dexterity tests can be highly effective at creating player investment. Rolling a dice can create a level of disengagement in players, while testing player dexterity is more likely to cause players to feel direct responsibility for their success or failure. Additionally, they can re-create the events being depicted when trying to hit a target, a player can be asked to throw something at the target, allowing direct identification.

However, dexterity elements can create subgames within the main game, and if used repeatedly, they will slow a game down; even the most assiduous dice roller will pick up and roll more quickly than an attempt to hit a target. They also have a limited ability to provide symmetrical uncertainty, very quickly making the outcome between players largely certain. As such, unless the purpose of the game is to discover who is better at the given dexterity game, they can quickly undermine the game they are part of.

A more usual form of performative uncertainty in non-discrete games is that given by asking players to estimate distances. For example, in *Warhammer: The Game of Fantasy Battles* (Cavatore *et al.*, 2000), players are asked to judge whether an opposing unit is within the distance they are capable of charging before being able to measure; if they misjudge, they will suffer penalties as their unit fails to complete its charge move. Since non-discrete games constantly create highly varied spatial

DOI: 10.1201/9781003314820-16

relationships, these judgements arise quite naturally and so avoid the slowdown of dexterity elements. Also, as they can be used repeatedly throughout a design, failing at a few can be less impactful, meaning they rarely give the sense of deciding a game. It should be considered that in order to include distance judgement and performative uncertainty, a game needs to require no pre-measuring (see Chapter 11).

SOCIAL UNCERTAINTY

Not knowing the intent of another player is a form of uncertainty, specifically social uncertainty. This can take two forms: concealed information (separately from hidden information, which we'll take a look at later) and unknown intent.

Concealed information is any instance where a player selects an option, and concealing it from another player creates uncertainty. This needs no randomness to be involved at all; if I select a number from one to five and ask you to guess it, the process is totally uncertain, although no random events were involved. While concealed information is standard in card games, playing cards is less often used in non-discrete games, considering how ubiquitous they are and the fact that they can be handily used to generate both random numbers and concealed information. Without a hand of cards, concealed information can be awkward to include in a game.

> ### CASE STUDY: CONCEALED INFORMATION –
> ### *FREEBOOTER'S FATE*
>
> In *Freebooter's Fate* (Klocke, 2010), combat is resolved by each player choosing a number of cards based on their unit's combat skills; the cards name body locations. If the attacker has selected at least one location, the defender has not, a hit is scored; if there is more than one location, a critical is scored. The system allows for uncertainty and player interaction via bluffing far more than a simple dice roll.

Concealed information creates chances for bluffing, which can create a feeling of direct contest between players as generals or overseers. When a dice is rolled, it removes player agency, which is perfect for representing the fact that troops are possibly out of direct control once battle is joined. With opposed concealed information, there is much more of a sense of personal agency.

Unknown intent is simply an aspect of games where what the other player is going to do next is unknown. It should be mentioned that in non-discrete games, there is an attitude that since what can be seen at the tabletop is open information, if a player appears unaware of part of this information, it is unsporting to not inform them in the same fashion as when a marker might be unclearly positioned in a discrete game such as Chess. Adopting this approach to the table-based battlefield creates the rather odd situation where, while actual generals often differentiate themselves by reading the terrain and seeing what others do not, we are tasked with making sure that others see exactly what we do. There may be value in reinforcing the nature of subjective player perspectives during play if a game seeks to make use of social uncertainty.

Due to the fact that most non-discrete games then treat all information as open, there are (possibly ironically given the situations being recreated) relatively few chances to conceal intent. We'll look at some of them as they come up, but once a heavily armed close combat unit is thundering towards some lightly armed archers, intent tends to be quite clear. Some hiding of intent is possible in uncertainty due to complexity, though.

UNCERTAINTY DUE TO COMPLEXITY

The sheer range of available choices in a game like Chess or Go means their end states are effectively obscured from all but the most expert of players. These games are theoretically as clear to view as Tic-Tac-Toe, but the human mind is simply unable to hold them in their totality in the same way since the options for viable moves explode too broadly after a few moves. Non-discrete games tend to have far fewer operable markers available than a game of Chess, as we've mentioned, and while they have far more positions available in theory, in practice there are fewer interesting placements in relation to carrying out the goals of any given unit. Still, while a unit's intentions might be highly predictable for the coming turn or two, the range of intentions of a unit and its commander quickly becomes extremely broad after a few turns of future analysis.

Non-discrete games that seek to achieve uncertainty through a pure combination of complexity and social mechanics are vanishingly rare, although they should be more than possible. One possible reason for this rarity is that other mechanics, such as stochastic uncertainty, can provide solace from the much-maligned analysis paralysis (the tendency for a player to remain frozen until they can calculate the exact optimal move). With a few judicious dice rolls, perfect calculation becomes impossible, and players can more easily relax into the fog of war that occurs a few moves into the future. Possibly, this rarity is also due to the perception that social and complexity-based uncertainty are inevitable the moment that two players are asked to place markers with infinite variability of movement freely across a tabletop and then engage with each other, and so relying on them to drive the uncertainty of a game could be seen as under-designing.

UNCERTAINTY OF PROCESS

Cultist Simulator (Kennedy, 2017) puts players in a position of almost total uncertainty about what a given token is for and how to operate with or engage with them; all is left as a matter of pure experimentation. Digital games are extremely good at this sort of process of uncertainty, where a player can be completely unsure of what will happen when they press a given button or pull a certain lever. This sort of uncertainty is difficult for tabletop games to provide due to the player needing to both pull the lever and operate its outcomes, even more so in non-discrete games where rules are generally presented and digested entirely before any game is begun. Some miniatures games – from *War Games for Boy Scouts* (Holladay, 1910) to *Warhammer 40,000: Rogue Trader* (Priestley, 1987) – have required the presence of a neutral additional player in the role of an umpire. The umpire can act fully or partially as the game's mechanism for process uncertainty, with players deciding on courses of action and the umpire fully or partially adjudicating their outcomes, providing for the game to surprise both players. The requirement for umpires in non-discrete miniature games is today uncommon, likely due partly to the potentially unattractively indirect and reactive nature of the umpire's role (although the role of game moderator is common in tabletop roleplaying games).

'Legacy' games such as *Pandemic Legacy: Season 1* (Daviau and Leacock, 2015) provide a form of process uncertainty by sealing additional rules or components into boxes, envelopes or other inventive means of concealment that are opened and explored through play, meaning that players cannot know what the outcome of certain actions will be. As the conventions of non-discrete miniatures games are for players to commonly prepare the components needed for play themselves, employing 'legacy' mechanics in such a game will require investment and/or ingenuity in either physical components or digital technology.

> ### CASE STUDY: DISCOVERY THROUGH PLAY – *GASLANDS: LEGACY*
>
> In *Gaslands; Legacy* (Hutchinson, 2021), the rules contain a series of apparently meaningless code phrases that are earnt by performing certain actions in play. When these code phrases are typed into the game's website[1], additional game material is unlocked. In this way, players cannot initially discover the full scope of the game (without disobeying the game rules, reading ahead and utilising the code phrases before the game authorises them) until they play through it.

STOCHASTIC UNCERTAINTY

Stochastic uncertainty or luck, usually in the form of rolling dice, is by a huge distance the preferred system for producing uncertainty in non-discrete games, for a range of reasons. Dice are not only fast but also efficient; a dice can be picked up and rolled in a fraction of the time any of the previous methods require. They can also be rolled en-masse, allowing as many events to be resolved as a player can hold dice in their hands. Dice are clear to all players; results do not need to be reported or shared; they can be seen from across a tabletop immediately. Dice are fair, and while they might be cruel, there is nothing that players can apply to be better at rolling dice. Dice are well understood; players quickly and easily comprehend that their purpose is to make results unpredictable and understand the limits of their control and the likely range of outcomes.

However, luck can separate a player out from their units. When a dice is rolled, it suggests not that the world is an unpredictable place and sometimes players' best efforts fail, but rather that the world is an unpredictable place and that sometimes the players' minions' (in the form of an imaginarily animated miniature) best efforts fail. This can, of course, be beneficial or negative, depending on a specific design's intentions.

The primary disadvantage of luck is that you can have too much of it. An excess of the other methods mentioned simply changes what game is being designed, but an excess of luck destroys a game, creating a Snakes and Ladders alternative. Luck is so quick and convenient that it can be inserted into every step of a game, so its presence is controlled not by pacing and practicality like the other methods mentioned but by a distinct and clear design decision.

Randomness can be introduced prior to a player's decision-making (input randomness) or used after a player's decision to discover the result of the decision (output randomness). Input randomness provides resources that a player can then think through the application of. It can be used to create intellectual puzzles and a range of knowable options. Output randomness provides uncertainty about the result of a given action, asking a player to weigh the risks and benefits of uncertain paths and affording the opportunity for the delightful (or dismaying) surprise of unlikely events occurring. We explore the mechanics by which dice and cards can be used to create both input and output randomness in Chapters 14 and 15.

Another aspect of stochastic uncertainty is hidden information. If we consider a deck of cards which has been shuffled and stacked, these now form a set of information chosen by stochastic uncertainty and held as hidden information, available but unknown within the system. This can create an interesting sense of power imbalance if viewed by one player but not another. Unknown decks of cards are simply stochastic uncertainty; unequally seen decks of cards become hidden information. If I exclusively know what is on a given card, a sense of unequal competence is created (Engelstein, 2017). If given a choice between guessing the top card of a deck or having another person look at the top card of the deck and then trying to guess it, most players would prefer the former, despite it making no real difference, simply because in the first instance they know as much about the system as anyone alive, while in the second they do not. Offering one player concealed information, even without agency to change or use it, can therefore create a sense of asymmetrical power balance, even if it has no actual effect, which is a useful tool for effecting player behaviour and reactions.

It should be noted that these methods are not mutually exclusive, and many effective designs will include more than one of them. Where other methods are used, luck is generally the workhorse for the majority of resolution mechanics, with a handful of important interactions generated by dexterity or concealed information to avoid the game slowing down too much. With a clear idea of the intentions of a given design and an understanding of the necessity for generating uncertainty, a set of methods and the degrees of their application can be selected.

SUMMARY

Uncertainty in outcomes keeps the conflicts found in games interesting. It can be achieved by:

- **Performative Uncertainty:** Physically difficult to achieve acts, often found in sports.
- **Social Uncertainty:** The choices of other players can be unpredictable.

- **Uncertainty due to Complexity:** The range of choices provided by complex games can make their outcomes uncertain.
- **Uncertainty of Process:** The result of certain actions can be certain but hidden from players by the game.
- **Stochastic Uncertainty:** Random number generation can create uncertain outcomes.

EXPERIMENTS

Take an instance of stochastic uncertainty in your game and replace it with:

- A performatively uncertain event, catching dice or balancing cards.
- A socially uncertain event, having one player conceal a number and their opponent try to guess close to it.

Try to find a way of integrating either or both of uncertainty due to the complexity or uncertainty of the process into a resolution system for your game.

NOTE

1 https://planetsmashergames.com/gaslands/legacy/secret/

REFERENCES

Cavatore, A., Pirinen, T., Priestley, R., Stillman, N. and Thornton, J. (2000) *Warhammer: The Game of Fantasy Battles*. 6 edn. Nottingham: Games Workshop Ltd.

Daviau, R. and Leacock, M. (2015) *Pandemic Legacy: Season 1*. [Boardgame] Roseville: Zman Games.

Engelstein, G. (2017) *Game Tek: The Math and Science of Gaming*. USA: Ludology Press.

Holladay, A. (1910) *War Games for Boy Scouts*.

Hutchinson, M. (2021) 'Gaslands: Legacy', *Blaster*, 3: pp. 79–93.

Kennedy, A. (2017) *Cultist Simulator*. [Video game]. PC. San Francisco: Humble Bundle.

Klocke, W. (2010) *Freebooter's Fate*. Oberhausen: Freebooter Miniatures.

Priestley, R. (1987) *Warhammer 40,000: Rogue Trader*. Nottingham: Games Workshop Ltd.

Scott, L. (1983) *Jenga*. [Boardgame] Bolton: Leslie Scott Associates.

14 Dice Mechanics

Having discussed the reasons to include stochastic uncertainty in your design, let us look at the most popular method of doing so: dice. We will examine their key affordances and discuss some of the more common dice mechanics used in these games. The first question to address when using dice is, which dice?

FAMILIARITY AND AVAILABILITY

The standard D6 has important strengths, the first being availability. It is usual for players of non-discrete games to gather the components for play themselves. If a system wishes to maintain a low barrier to entry, using D6 as the primary or sole form of dice is preferable.

In addition, most adults are familiar with the spread of probability on 2D6 in a way that they are not for any other combination of dice. If you wish for players to make choices based on the probable outcomes of the dice, giving them probabilities they can judge is clearly necessary. A player who does not understand is a player who does not care.

In addition to the widely understood probability ranges provided by a 2D6, the probability of rolling above or under a certain value on a D100 is even more easily grasped by most players. Most players will immediately intuit the probability of scoring over 76 on a D100 because the use of percentage is common in normal life.

GRANULARITY

The main failing of the D6 is that it doesn't have very many faces. This lack of granularity in the generated results restricts available differentiation between the relative skills of units or the strength of abilities. In a system that uses D6s, there are at most five steps within which to graduate skill levels. Dice with more faces affords more granularity to differentiate between units. At the other end of the spectrum, the

DOI: 10.1201/9781003314820-17

granularity of the D100 carries its own considerations: while it offers a much larger range of results if this additional granularity is not used in a meaningful way, you risk your system feeling inelegant and unnecessarily complex.

In addition to the greater granularity available from dice with more faces, it is worth considering the mathematically greater range of divisible affordances available to larger dice. In particular, the D12's broad divisibility means it can perform the functions of a D12, D6, D4, D3 and D2, which can potentially justify the difficulty in acquiring a set.

HISTORY AND AESTHETICS

It is worth being aware that among gaming communities, certain dice carry a degree of history and can evoke reactions among their audience. *Frostgrave* (McCullogh, 2015) uses a D20 for its tests for their ability to evoke another major tabletop franchise that uses D20s, *Dungeons & Dragons* (Gygax and Arneson, 1974), creating atmosphere and player expectation with this simple choice. The fact that D66 were heavily used in Games Workshop products of the 1980s and 1990s means this odd compound dice carries a sense of nostalgia for gamers of a certain generation, and the historical use of the D100 in *Call of Cthulhu* (Petersen, 1981) means it has a strong legacy for horror gamers. While there is plenty of space to carve out a reputation for underused dice such as the D12 or maligned ones such as the D4, following the dice usage of other games can signal intent to new players.

Miniatures games are a holistic experience, and certain dice have both a visual appearance and feel when picking up and rolling them, which can be more or less pleasing. The D4 is unpleasant to pick up a handful of and doesn't really roll when tossed, just sort of plopping onto the tabletop. D8s and D10s are both unbalanced when settled, while D20s are large enough that rolling more than a couple can be difficult. These concerns may seem minor, but just as you might agonise over your world-building and visual expression, you should give equal attention to how your components support or undermine the experience you are looking to build.

CUSTOM DICE

Some games use custom dice, printed with a range of symbols or other elements (Figure 14.1). Often, these are essentially a convenient method of allowing players to intuitively interact with a lookup table. *Gaslands* (Hutchinson, 2017) has a table where a D6 roll of one results in a 'hazard', two a 'spin', three a 'slide' and four to six a 'shift'; alternatively, there are custom dice available with faces showing the relevant results in the correct mix. Dice of this kind can smooth the player experience, but it is worth considering that custom dice are not progressive and so cannot benefit from simple modifiers. For example, in the case of *Gaslands*, there could have been a system where the D6 rolled on the table gained a plus one modifier, allowing the player to avoid hazards altogether and changing slides into shifts, but doing so would make the use of custom dice impossible. Making this sort of choice reduces the design space, which can be acceptable if the alternative would be used so regularly as to be tiresome. It is worth noting that these decisions, which are about an end

FIGURE 14.1   A selection of custom dice. Photograph by the author.

product and experience, sometimes need to be kept in mind even at the early stages of design since they directly alter which mechanics are available.

THE CHARACTER OF TESTS

It is possible to design a game before selecting a dice mechanic. Simply note that a certain test should have a 30%, 50% or 90% chance of success or failure during writing, and then come back and slot in a dice mechanic that provides the desired percentages. However, probability profiles are not the only consideration; each possible mechanic has its own character and feel. Imagine a situation where I want an attacking unit to do five points of damage on average. Two of the ways I could do it are:

1. Players roll 20 D6, each scoring a hit on a roll of a 4+, then they make a subsequent D6 roll for each hit, causing a point of damage on a 4+. Ten hits on average, causing five points of damage.
2. Players roll 1 D10, re-rolling if a 10 is obtained, causing their score as damage. The results are between 1 and 9, with an average of five.

While both have the same average result mathematically, they feel and operate quite differently in games. The first gives a sense of a group of individuals engaging in combat with multiple strikes, parries and misses. Thanks to the use of multiple dice, the probability of producing an average result is higher than that of the other system, but it is also capable of generating no damage at all. Because it produces a single discrete result, the second version feels more like a single strike, and since some damage will always occur, it creates a more brutal and desperate struggle towards inevitable death. Finally, while it will still average out at the same number, there will be a greater variance in individual results, making survival and level of success feel less certain.

Mechanics are the medium by which the art of a game is created. The test results generated by rolling dice are one of the mechanics that players will engage with most repeatedly, sometimes several times in a turn. If those mechanics are selected on a purely functional basis without considering how they will feel for a player, a significant part of the player's time with the game risks feeling flat or disjointed.

SHAPING PROBABILITY

While random events can be useful to add narrative to a game and doubt its result, if you want control over the pacing of your game and to be able to reliably reward good play or construct a narrative, you are very likely to want to shape the probabilities of your dice systems. Unfettered random events within a game make it more difficult to pace the action of a game, reward good play or construct a deliberate narrative. Random number generation needs to be tamed to some degree, and we do this by applying shaping mechanics to the rolling of dice. The following are a set of common probability-shaping mechanics that can be further manipulated by a range of secondary mechanics that we will come on to later.

CUMULATIVE ODDS

All faces of a dice have an equal probability of occurring, so the probability of a given face on a D6 coming up is one in six, or 16.6%. The very simplest system for adjusting the odds of a given event occurring is to require a score of a certain value or greater (or lesser), since this results in the probabilities of a given set of faces being combined. For example, with a D6 requiring a score of four or more results in odds of one in two, this method allows a D6 to generate probabilities of ⅙, ⅓, ½, ⅔ or ⅚.

It is common for the target number of a roll to be based on the statistics of a given unit. If you wish for both high statistics and high rolls to be advantageous in your game, consider having players roll over a set target number, adding the statistic in question, rather than rolling under a statistic.

DICE POOLS

A regularly employed mechanic for evening out fluctuations of chance in non-discrete games is a dice pool. Players are asked to take a number of dice and roll them all, then count up the number of individual dice which achieve a given score or above. For example, they could be asked to take ten D6, roll them all and count up how many of them scored four or more; if six of the dice did so, the result of the roll would be six.

As more dice are rolled, the likelihood is that the spread of results attained will tend towards an even distribution, so if 50 D6 are rolled, the probability that the number that scores four or more is between 20 and 30 will be very high. Such a dice pool can be used to generate either a threshold result or a result by degrees.

A threshold result pool will state first the target number needed for each dice in the pool to be counted as a success and next the number of successes required for the pool as a whole to trigger a given result. If a pool of six D6 had a target number of three or more and required three or more successes to trigger a given event, its result would tend towards that event while being unpredictable. If the same target number were applied to a pool of 60 D6s needing 30 successes, the result would be much more predictable. By using this method, a designer can fine-tune exactly how predictable or unpredictable they wish for a given threshold pool's results to be.

Alternatively, if each success in a given pool results in a discrete event, it instead generates a result by degrees. If a pool of six D6 generated an event for every individual success, it could generate anything from zero to six such events, but will tend towards four. Within such a pool, the overall result of a roll can be more granular, and the probability of a roll achieving nothing is lower than with other systems. Once again, the larger the pool, the more predictable the outcome of the roll becomes.

Typically, a result by degrees will be used to generate a simple numerical result, such as how many wounds are caused by a set of attacks, particularly in relation to the attacks of a squad or ranked unit. A threshold result is more likely when a more narrative event is taking place, particularly when performed by a single character, such as casting a spell.

Dice pools have several advantages. Their probabilities are easily intuited by players – requiring results of a given dice's middle score or more will mean that roughly half the dice in a pool will be successful. They offer practically infinite granularity since players can always add another dice to the pool, and doing so doesn't slow the game down since all the dice are rolled together. On a tactile level, it is satisfying to roll lots of dice all at once, and lots of dice representing lots of power is a visual representation of the situation on the tabletop.

On a practical front, it should be noted that a dice pool is only effective at smoothing probabilities if it contains at least as many dice as the number of faces on the given dice, so at least six D6 or 12 D12, and the pool becomes more predictable as the number of dice achieves multiples of that number. 12 or 18 D6 make for very stable dice pools. This becomes relevant since very few people own anything like 40 D20, and picking up and rolling and then reading 40 D20 is a non-trivial task. As such, if a game decides to use anything other than the ubiquitous D6 for its dice pools, it will raise the bar to entry, potentially significantly.

While many of the later minor mechanics will be applicable to dice pools, it is worth mentioning here two somewhat rarer alternative mechanics that are only appropriate to dice pools: spike dice and single result plus pools.

Spike dice are a single designated die within a pool that has an usual or weighted effect; these are usually singled out by being a unique colour within the pool. For example, in the first edition of *Carnevale* (Esbri, 2011), dice pools included a spike dice called the 'destiny dice' which had different results if it scored its highest value depending on what was being attempted. During movement such as jumping or climbing, it allowed an additional 3" of movement. Spike dice are a curious design choice in that the purpose of a dice pool is to flatten the probability curve of a game, while spike dice cause that curve to spike unpredictably. They can be useful if a game gives players the chance to add a large number of dice to a pool, resulting in undesirably stable results since they create a level of unpredictability that resists total smoothing.

Almost the exact opposite of spike dice, in single result plus pools dice are rolled, and either the highest or lowest score within the pool is taken as the result of the roll, with other scores then having some alternative effect, such as increasing the selected result. For example, in *7TV* (Dawson and Perrotton, 2010), the score of the highest dice in a pool is taken as the result, and it is then increased by one for each other dice in the pool that has scored four or more. Pools of this type cause probability to flatten very quickly as more dice are added, since the result will very swiftly normalise around the highest or lowest available result but allow for significant spikes with fewer dice. This can be highly effective in representing individual characters where more lowly individuals are defined by unpredictability rather than general uselessness.

Dice Combinations

Adding the results of two (or more) dice offers two potential advantages over a single dice. The first is the bell curve of results, with results in the middle of the distribution being more likely than those at each end, offering an easy way to shape the probability of certain outcomes. The second is that adding the results of two (or more) dice together allows you to extract greater granularity from your dice with only one or two additional dice. 2D6 offers an affordance from 2 to 12 with two dice, rather than the 11 dice needed to achieve the same range with a dice pool.

An interesting feature that can be a strength or weakness is that, because the probability of such systems peak significantly around their middle results, modifiers vary in value depending on the target number they are applied to. This is to say, if a 2D6 test is successful on an 8 or more, adding +1 to the result is far more valuable than if the test is successful on a 9 or more. This can be a strength since it creates a headwind for powerful characters, which is to say that once a character succeeds on the middle result or better, any further modifiers have lessening benefit. If modifiers require the same level of in-game expenditure irrespective of who is using them, weak characters become cheaper to gain greater benefit from than powerful characters.

A potential weakness is that it is not convenient to perform more than one dice test at a time. If a system is representing individual characters engaging in single actions, this may not be an issue, but if it represents groups, gangs or units all performing the same action at the same time, it can prove an inefficient mechanic.

As with a dice pool system, results may be binary (success or failure) or by degree (incremental levels of success). Because combined dice provide different shapes to their probability curves, the more extreme degrees of success and failure are more probable with combined dice than in dice pool systems. If that characteristic is useful to a design, it is worth considering combined dice with success by degree.

Nested Rolls

Another common mechanic for taming probability without needing large pools of dice is to nest or link rolls together. The usual example of this is a 'roll to hit' with an attack, followed by a 'roll to wound' and a 'roll to save'. For each roll to be successful, it might require, for example, a four or more on a D6. A dice which successfully hit will then be rolled to wound, and those that are successfully wound will be rolled for a save, and only those that are not saved are finally counted as damage. The stages can be designated as whatever is appropriate for the narrative being presented by your game, and two or three stages are generally sufficient to result in quite predictable outputs. This sort of system can be combined with dice pools to pass a high number of dice through to a relatively stable set of results. Alternatively, they can allow dice types that might be unreasonable to expect players to own in large quantities to be passed through a control system without needing pools of dice.

One advantage of nested rolls is that a unit or model can be made to both feel extremely elite to a player but kept at whatever level of actual power the designer sees fit. For example, if we imagine a system with a roll to hit, wound and save, if the base target number to hit were a four or more, a model with a bonus of three to their hit rolls would feel extremely elite since they are so skilled that they never miss a shot. It would be possible, with a second modifier applied to the roll to wound or save, to make this elite character have the same odds of causing damage as any other trooper, but the fact that they rarely miss their initial 'to hit' roll can make them feel elite to the player, regardless of the actual results.

Look-up Tables

A simple, if inelegant, solution to probability control is to include a table where players use their dice rolls to generate a result. These can provide a broad range of detailed results with very specific probability control. For example, a D66 provides 36 results, each with identical probability, unlike the shifting and set probabilities of a 2D6 roll. A D66 table can then have up to 36 results, and probability can be very exactly controlled by reducing the number of different results and assigning additional numbers to some.

The primary issues with look up tables are, of course, requiring players to look up their results, and that only a single test can be performed at a time. As such, this method should be reserved for tests that require very specific spreads of probability, with detailed or complex results that do not often occur.

SECONDARY MECHANICS

The following mechanics can be combined with the above dice mechanics to further shape and modulate their results.

Rerolls

One of the most basic systems to allow players to mitigate bad luck is the reroll. Players can be provided with the chance to roll dice again in the hopes of achieving a more desirable score. These rerolls can be allowed to roll all or just some of the dice included in a given roll. Alternatively, players can be offered the chance to directly select a dice face of their choice, which can provide players with wider and more interesting tactical choices if specific numbers have specific affordances within your system. Some systems insist that a dice that has been rerolled cannot be rolled again. An elegant and interesting solution in relation to re-rolling pools of dice is to allow players to re-roll as many times as they like but to require that they remove a dice from the pool each time they do so.

It is fairly standard to insist that the new result of a rerolled dice stand and that a player be prevented from reverting to the original result if the new one is worse for them. This avoids requiring the setting aside of the original roll until the new roll is made so the player can choose between them, and it also avoids players using rerolls to attempt to better already successful incremental rolls. However, this also narrows the player's decision space, such that they will only reroll a result that is a definite failure, where any result will be better. The player decision space should be kept as wide as possible for as long as possible, so it is well worth considering offering players the chance to return to previous results post rerolling.

When including rerolls in a rule set, it is worth specifying whether or not rerolls can be used by a player on a dice that they did not themselves originally roll. While dice rolls are essentially public property, that is to say, it should not matter which player rolled them; players have a strong proprietary relationship towards the rolls that they made or that the rules direct them to make. In addition, players will likely react more strongly to losing a success than to their opponent averting a failure, even if the two have the same effect.

MODIFIERS

Modifiers to dice, target numbers or statistics are a simple method of changing the probability of a given roll by altering the dice roll or target number by a set amount. A system that chooses to use modifiers should ideally apply them to one or another part of the system consistently. If one modifier is added to a dice roll, another should not be subtracted from a target number; mixing such options can lead to player confusion. If you implement more than a couple of modifiers in your system, there is a risk that they cannot all be easily recalled during play, and you should consider how players will access that information at the table.

When introducing modifiers, consider if your intention is to allow players to experience automatic successes or failures as a result of combining modifiers. You can tame the impact of modifiers by restricting the maximum modification to rolls (e.g. capping modifiers at +/–3), or reserve certain natural rolls as automatic successes or failures (the criticals and fumbles discussed below). This allows players to seek advantage while allowing you to preserve the integrity of your resolution system.

CRITICALS AND FUMBLES

Any given dice has the highest and lowest possible result; these can have unique properties attached to them when rolled, irrespective of modified totals. This is useful if a designer wishes to give players a high degree of control but still maintain an inviolate level of chance. The total rolled on the dice before any modifiers is often known as the 'natural' result, and in instances where a natural top result is given a special quality, it is often known as a 'critical' and the bottom result as a 'fumble'. The simplest special result is that the fumble is always a failure and the critical is always a success, so if a test using a D6 has a plus 5 modifier, it will still fail on a 1.

This version of the rule is both popular and easy to recall, but it should be considered that automatic failures and successes reduce the granularity of any dice system by effectively removing the benefit in any set of modifiers sufficient to change a six to a failure or a one to a success.

A popular version of a critical rule is known as an exploding dice, in which a critical result allows an additional dice to be rolled that can result in an additional success, and even an additional critical with often no upper limit. A more controlled version of this system is to simply have each critical come with a set number of additional successful test results.

An interesting alternative is to allow the critical or fumble to be alterable into a failure or success, respectively, but bring with it an alternative result. For example, imagine a spy game where a failure would result in a locked door not being opened while a fumble would additionally cause guards to be alerted. By changing the fumble into a success, the door is opened, but the guards remain alerted. Many tabletop role-playing games have experimented with various forms of 'success with a twist' or 'failure with a perk' resolution systems, and it is worth your time exploring systems such as those found in Powered by the Apocalypse games, Fantasy Flight's Narrative Dice System games, or Modiphius Entertainment's 2D20 games. It is good practice to keep these alternative results regular throughout a system; if each test comes with a different fumble and critical additional effect, the result can be difficult to recall for players.

OTHER MECHANICS

MIXING DICE

There are interesting effects that can be achieved by mixing dice of different numbers of faces within the same system. Dice with lower granularities have a far higher probability of rolling a critical or fumble, a ¼ for a D4 vs a 1/20 for a D20. In *Burrows and Badgers: A Skirmish Game of Anthropomorphic Animals* (Lovejoy, 2016), critical results are automatically successful, and different creatures are given different dice to roll. Generally, the higher the result, the more likely a creature in the game is to be successful, so a creature allowed to roll a D10 will tend to beat one forced to use a D4 most of the time, but the D4 has a far higher chance of getting a critical hit, allowing the weak to defeat the strong at fateful moments, giving a strong feel of theme and narrative to the game.

Additionally, while using a system where low rolls are good is generally best avoided due to player dissonance, it does offer interesting options for systems with mixed dice types since rolling under a given number is more likely for a dice with fewer faces. In *A Billion Suns* (Hutchinson, 2021), spaceships have a statistic denoting their size, and different weapons roll dice with different numbers of faces, with a hit being a score under the size of the ship. The game attempts to use narrative congruency to overcome players' natural intuition that bigger numbers are better by building a relationship between the power of the weapon and the size of the target, essentially mapping low numbers to small targets and large dice to powerful weapons.

Dice Reservation

Dice reservation means having players roll a set number of dice at the start of a game turn or round, which can then replace dice rolled throughout the turn, allowing them to alter results as they go along. An interesting option is to allow players to swap reserved dice and rolled ones, meaning that players might choose to swap out successful tests in order to store high dice rolls for more important moments (although this should be avoided in systems where players have the chance to perform wasted actions).

Dice Placement

Dice placement refers to systems whereby players are asked to roll a number of dice at the start of a game turn or upon some other trigger and then place them onto boards or cards in order to activate special abilities. *Saga* (Buchel, 2011) uses sideboards known as 'battle boards' and a set of custom dice which are rolled at the start of each round and then placed onto a player's board to represent abilities which can then be triggered throughout the round (Figure 14.2).

The main advantage of dice placement is that player choices are made in reaction to the dice, rather than players making choices and then having the outcome of those choices determined by chance. Input randomness used in this way can engender a

FIGURE 14.2   Saga Battle Board. Photograph by the author.

more strategic feel to a game, in which plans can be laid out with more certainty as to their outcome, which may or may not be preferable.

An interesting option with dice placement is to add a level of semi-permanence, particularly in relation to combinations and sequences. For example, if a set number of dice, say five, are rolled for placement purposes each round and can be placed onto a board but only released if triggered, then an ability that requires a sequence of one, two or three on dice for a powerful effect creates an interesting choice. Few rolls will hit the sequence immediately, so do players lock a one and a three, hoping to find the two on a later roll and reduce their placed dice, or do they opt for more immediate rewards?

OPPOSED TESTS

There are two general forms of opposed tests: opposed statistic tests and dice-offs. Opposed statistic tests ask players to compare two sets of statistics to generate a target number for a roll. *Warhammer: The Game of Fantasy Battles (sixth edition)* (Cavatore *et al.*, 2000) has an opposed test to wound, with the target being the defender's toughness minus the attacker's strength plus four, or greater. This allows a broader range of statistics in a system using low-granularity dice like D6, that is to say, if a test asks players to achieve a total above 8 by adding a character's strength to a D6 roll, then the maximum meaningful strength score is 7, but in an opposed statistic system like that in *Warhammer*, any strength score is meaningful so long as there is a relatively close toughness score available.

A dice-off asks players to roll a dice with the highest score winning. While an unmodified dice-off can be the most effective way of randomly deciding between an unknown number of players, with two players, it is simply a coin toss, except that it can result in a draw and so should be avoided in favour of a single roll with the available scores spread evenly between the players. Modified dice-offs can be useful for non-random selection, but with multiple modifiers on both sides, a dice-off can quickly become difficult to comprehend or predict for players. A dice-off mechanic can be combined with a dice-pool mechanic in multiple ways, for example, a pool from which the highest roll is selected and compared to that of an opponent, as in *The Lord of the Rings: Strategy Battle Game* (Cavatore and Ward, 2005), or by comparing the numbers of successes.

OTHER USES

Dice can be used within a design for purposes other than random number generation.

BOOKKEEPING

If any miniature in the game has a status that can be simplified to a number and the rules are not explicit about how this should be noted, players will invariably place whatever dice they have to hand behind the miniature to note it. It is worth bearing in mind that, therefore, if a game is based on D6s but requires tracking status numbers over six, players will need to use multiple dice, requiring miniatures to trail a conga line of dice around after them. A note in favour of the humble D6 is that after the much-maligned D4, their shape is the most stable of all the standard dice, assisting in their reliability as methods for notation.

DESCRIBING

If a set of three or more dice is rolled onto a tabletop, a shape can be created by tracing lines from one dice to the next. It is possible to give the shape the so-described rule properties. For example, the shape could represent a shield, either magically or through future science generated, offering those within its boundaries a protective quality. If the dice used are required to generate specific powers, players can then be offered an interesting decision space where picking up dice to use their powers will re-shape or remove the tabletop effect.

BAG PULL

The Bag Pull mechanic consists of placing a number of objects into a bag and then asking players to reach in and pull one out randomly; dice work well for this. *Bolt Action* (Cavatore and Priestly, 2012) uses a set of custom-ordered dice for this purpose. Each player acquires one dice colour-coded to their force for each unit they bring. At the start of each activation, a dice is pulled from the bag and handed to the player whose colour it matches, allowing them to activate a unit. Any set of appropriately coloured dice can be used for a similar purpose.

It should be considered that bag pull mechanics introduce an element of 'bag building'. As long as a player's choices can manipulate the contents of the bag, then doing so will become a potentially powerful concern for players. If the intention of the bag pull system is to result in roughly evenly randomised events between players, you may need to consider some limits on the abilities of players to control the contents of the bag.

FACINGS

We are usually concerned only with the face of a dice that is pointing directly upwards. However, they have other faces, and the other faces could be aligned with the edges of units or orientated towards or away from them. D6 has four neatly arranged faces that align with the front, flanks and rear of any given unit. A unit could have a D6 placed next to it, aligned as a player wishes, with its faces used to provide additional actions or modifiers to actions performed in the direction of their facing. The orientation of the dice could map to the configuration of energy shields or the direction of a commander's fury. There are unexplored opportunities here.

DEXTERITY

Dexterity mechanics are generally not well represented in non-discrete gaming, which is both a pity and slightly odd since they share many of the concerns of the non-discrete game, such as physical relationships between playing pieces and using non-discrete movements and measurements. Because dexterity games share many of the concerns of non-discrete games, they actually fit neatly into them; specifically, balancing and landing point mechanics should be seriously considered. We have omitted throwing mechanics, but that option does exist in a game that makes it quite clear that miniatures will be struck with little plastic missiles.

Balancing

Dexterity-based mechanics around stacking and balancing dice could be considered for both resolution systems and status tracking. In the former case, imagine a mechanic in which a unit is permitted to roll as many dice as the controlling player wishes, provided they are able to then stack those dice up without them toppling. In the latter, imagine a game that tracks a unit's fear by stacking dice on its base or movement tray, and the unit breaks and runs if the dice tower falls. Players would have to consider their movement and the physicality of the models all the more. These forms of dexterity mechanics can naturally include a push-your-luck element that may be appropriate for your game.

One of the major issues of any game, and particularly with non-discrete games due to their potential for complexity, is downtime for players between turns. A simple way to avoid downtime is to allow simultaneous action; however, it can be difficult to organise since player actions can occur at mismatched speeds. Asking players to move balanced objects is an effective way of slowing players down without creating downtime. If miniatures are able to use as many dice as are stacked next to them and then placed at their final destination without falling down, players need to make a choice between multiple single-dice abilities, obviously being very easy to move without dropping, or fewer multiple-dice abilities as speed decreases with power increasing in such a system. If a design wishes to level the playing field between gamers of differing mental powers, such as one that hopes to allow adults and children to play in opposition, dexterity mechanics are an excellent method to explore.

Landing Position

Generally, where a dice lands is of little interest in relation to the result of the dice itself, but it is possible to require dice to be rolled onto a printed sheet marked with a grid of different values. *Space Fleet* (Johnson and Jones, 1991) came with a grid printed on the inside of its box lid into which dice, or any object, could be dropped to generate a result. Landing positions in such a system can create secondary results, modifiers or secondary effects for dice. Alternatively, these systems can be dexterity-based, with players being encouraged to aim their dice rolls at certain parts of the sheet or grid. There is also the option to allow players to drop or throw in turn onto the same sheet or grid before resolution, creating a tactical dexterity mini-game where players must both decide whether to hold back important dice results until no shots can be made to displace them and whether to sacrifice their own landing position to dislodge an opponent.

By explicitly requesting that players roll dice in the play area, more physical affordances are opened up. Games of *Moonstone* (Greenway, 2017) begin with the dropping of a handful of D4 into the play area; these become resources that players wish to claim. One could envisage the landing position of a dice being used to create an unpredictable movement system. Imagine allowing players to roll a dice in the play area, move a unit up into contact with the dice and then additionally move by the number rolled on the dice. Then add the caveat that all movement for that unit is forfeit should the dice strike any enemy unit. Now we have combined dexterity, non-discrete physicality and chance into a single playful mechanic.

Dice are elegant, simple and familiar. They are also physical objects of predictable shapes and weights. They seem to be the ever-present companions of our miniatures, and so we encourage you to turn them over and see them in a new light.

SUMMARY

Dice are useful for generating random numbers. When considering which to use:

- D6 are familiar and widely available, but lack granularity. The opposite of both is true for dice with more faces.
- Dice have their own history within gaming and aesthetics generally.

While random numbers are useful, some control of them is often desired. This can be obtained by:

- Cumulative odds – assigning success to more than one face of a dice.
- Dice pools – more dice rolled create more predictable results.
- Dice combinations – 2D6 has a useful result distribution that 1D6 lacks.
- Nested rolls – more rolls create more predictable results.

These can be combined with:

- Rerolls.
- Modifiers.
- Criticals and fumbles.

The design space can be further expanded by considering:

- Mixing dice types – creating different probabilities of rolling maximums.
- Dice reservation – holding back dice until they are required.
- Dice placement – rolling and then assigning dice.
- Opposed tests – basing target numbers on the statistics of opposing units.

Aside from random number generation, dice can be used for:

- Bookkeeping.
- Describing an area of the tabletop.
- Bag pull mechanics.
- Dexterity mechanics, including:
  - Balancing and stacking.
  - Landing positions.

EXPERIMENTS

Recreate the same probability of a resolution sequence in your game using a dice type that the game does not normally use.

Find a way of recreating the probability of a resolution sequence in your game with whichever it does not use:

- Cumulative odds.
- Dice pools.
- Dice combinations.
- Nested rolls.

Assign criticals and fumbles in your game, if they are not already, and have them:

- Generate additional successes.
- Create exploding dice.
- Create secondary effects that cannot be modified, but allow hitting or missing to be modifiable.

Have players roll five of the most common dice in your game at the start of a round and use them throughout the round to replace any five dice of their choice for either player.

Replace one resolution step in your game with a dexterity mechanic using dice.

REFERENCES

Buchel, A. (2011) *Saga*. Evesham: Gripping Beast.

Cavatore, A. and Ward, M. (2005) *The Lord of the Rings: Strategy Battle Game*. Nottingham: Games Workshop Ltd.

Cavatore, A., Pirinen, T., Priestley, R., Stillman, N. and Thornton, J. (2000) *Warhammer: The Game of Fantasy Battles*. 6 edn. Nottingham: Games Workshop Ltd.

Cavatore, A and Priestly, R. (2012) *Bolt Action* Oxford: Osprey Games.

Dawson, G. and Perrotton, K. (2010) *7TV*. Lincolnshire: Crooked Dice Game Design Studio.

Esbri, D. (2011) *Carnevale*. Barcelona: Vesper-on Games.

Greenway, T. (2017) *Moonstone*. Wales: Goblin King Games.

Gygax, G. and Arneson, D. (1974) *Dungeons & Dragons*. 1st edn. Lake Geneva, Wisconsin: TSR Inc.

Hutchinson, M. (2017) *Gaslands*. Oxford: Osprey Games.

Hutchinson, M. (2021) *A Billion Suns*. Oxford: Osprey Games.

Johnson, J. and Jones, A. (1991) *Space Fleet*. [Boardgame] Nottingham: Games Workshop Ltd.

Lovejoy, M. (2016) *Burrows and Badgers: A Skirmish Game of Anthropomorphic Animals*. Oxford: Osprey Games.

McCullogh, J. (2015) *Frostgrave*. Oxford: Osprey Games.

Petersen, S. (1981) *Call of Cthulhu*. Michigan: Chaosium.

15 Card Mechanics

Dice are ubiquitous as random number generators in non-discrete miniatures games. Though less commonly used, cards can achieve as much, or possibly more, in the same role. This chapter will explore the affordances cards provide, their potential uses in non-discrete miniatures designs and some of the considerations for choosing to use them or not in your own designs. Standard playing cards are cheap and widely available (vital qualities in a form that requires players to gather their own tools of play) and open up a broad design space that is well worth consideration. Game-specific custom cards afford a partially overlapping set of affordances, which we will also discuss.

WEAKNESSES

Cards have interesting affordances and advantages, but they have two significant weaknesses that will rule them out of some designs. The first and biggest issue is that they are good at producing a single discrete result but not a pool of results. While it is simple to pick up and roll a handful of ten D6, flipping out ten cards to achieve a result is quite onerous. If your design requires players to sometimes simulate a lot of things happening at once while also sometimes only one thing, such as in a mass battle game where a whole unit might need to attack or a single trooper, it can be a significant disadvantage. The other, more minor, issue is that while most people are familiar with standard playing cards, they are commonly less familiar with their probability distributions. That is to say, the average gamer can confidently state that the most likely result from rolling two D6 is seven, and they have a good instinct on what the odds are of a six or eight. They are also less likely to be able to name the most likely result when flipping and adding up two playing cards from a deck, particularly if aces are high or court cards count as tens. Unless they are professional gamblers, once half the deck has moved to the discard pile, the possibility of accurately judging the probabilities of playing card combinations drops to more or less zero. Cards provide the designer with an ability to shape the probability distribution of random number generation, akin to the shaping that summing multiple dice affords, but with potentially more opacity over the likely results; this can be a benefit or a disadvantage, depending on your design.

COMPETENCE AND PRIVILEGE

With dice, we generally have two forms of information: open (the value of the dice once rolled) and unknown (the value that the dice is about to roll) and a single level of competence in the system in relation to that information (everybody knows as much as each other). Cards introduce a third sort of information: privileged information (I know what's in my hand and may be allowed to look at cards in the deck) and

DOI: 10.1201/9781003314820-18

different levels of competence in the system (we know different amounts and types of information). Not only that, but the privileged information can be easily moved around, noted and maintained. This opens up a huge range of design space, as we will examine in this chapter, but it is worth taking a moment to consider that differences in competence within a system can put players off, even resulting in irrational choices. If cards are used to provide privileged information, roughly the same level and availability of privileged information should be provided to both players, or it will result in a sense of imbalance beyond what is actually present.

CASE STUDY: PARTIAL INFORMATION: *MOONSTONE MELEE COMBAT*

Moonstone (Greenway, 2017) is a miniature skirmish game which uses a custom deck of combat cards to resolve melee combat. At the start of combat, players draw a number of cards from a shared deck containing three copies each of six attack types. As the deck is shared, both players have partial information about what attack cards are available to their opponent and may use this information, combined with their knowledge of the engaged models' abilities, to make an estimation of what their opponent will choose to play (and thus what their opponent will suspect them of playing, what the counter to that counter would be and so on), creating a rich moment of decision-making and player interaction.

RANDOM NUMBER GENERATION

The first advantage of cards is the broad affordance they provide when used as random number generators. When flipping a card from a standard 52-card deck, it generates the equivalent of a coin flip (since it can be one of two colours), a D4 (since it can be one of four suits) and a number. The number itself can have a wide affordance; it can be between one and thirteen, one and ten with court cards can be given additional separate qualities, or not, or one and 52 if all the suits are ranked in order. Jokers can be included or not, and if included, they can provide numbers at the top and bottom of the order or be used as wild cards (with a different distribution from the other face value cards). Aces may be valued as one or fourteen or both. Certain combinations, sets or runs of cards may be valued arbitrarily (if a reference guide is provided) or trigger additional effects. Cards can trigger additional effects depending on whether or not they match previously played cards. Unique cards (say, the ace of spades) may be inscribed with specific meanings in specific contexts or for specific units or factions. The sheer affordance of numbers and events a card can provide is staggering.

In addition, a card offers many of these affordances *simultaneously*. When a dice is rolled, it provides a single number. A card offers the ability to resolve and trigger multiple effects with different probabilities from a single random generation. Flipping a king could result in an eleven at the same time as triggering a king ability and a heart ability. Cards offer the chance to trigger multiple effects with a single action.

CASE STUDY: CARD MASTERY – *MALIFAUX*

Malifaux: Second Edition (Anderson et *al.,* 2013) is a great example of the player agency and design affordances that cards can provide when used for random number generation. When taking a test in *Malifaux*, players flip a card from their deck; if they are at an advantage, they flip more than one and select one; if they are at a disadvantage, they flip more than one and take the worst. At the start of each round, they draw a hand of 'control' cards, which they may choose to use to replace a flipped card, but only if they were not at a disadvantage. When a test is taken, the combined score of a character's skill and the card flipped will be used to generate a result, and the suit of the card will designate which additional abilities the character can use during the success or failure, so a low card with a more useful suit may be preferable to a high one. Furthermore, cards are grouped by rank such that they also designate the level of damage that attacks they generate cause. It is a deep and satisfying resolution system that makes rich use of a simple card flip.

PHYSICAL QUALITIES

Cards have a range of affordances that relate to their physical nature. They can be placed into decks and hands, face up or down or placed into the play area, which opens up interesting design spaces not given by dice.

DECKS AND DISCARDS

It is common practice to form cards into a deck, draw or play cards from that deck and then, once played, place the cards in a discard pile. The deck and the discard pile have a *memory,* something that no dice can have. This means, first of all, that while dice are fair, decks are just. Everyone gets the same number of kings as deuces, and if things went well for you at first, you know a bad time is in the post. Dice are chaotic, and decks are lawful.

Card decks have a memory, as do players, and players can track cards and remember what they have seen. It should be said that if you are going to use cards in your game, you should specify precisely whether players are allowed to check the cards in the discard pile or not, and when. Unless there is good reason to restrict checking, this should be considered similarly to allowing players to pre-measure, which is to say that it might slow down the game if allowed without restriction, but if not permitted, it will give an advantage to players with skills other than tactical acumen and manipulation of the game, which may create a meta-game not connected to and even at odds with the main game and the atmosphere you wish it to generate.

Decks and discard piles can be searched, and specific cards can be taken, discarded or retrieved. A unit could have the ability to search a deck for the first card of their suit or to search an opponent's deck for a court card and discard it. A high card could be retrieved from the discards and shuffled back into a deck or a low card for an opponent.

Decks can be stacked to shape the pacing or structure of a game or to programme orders for a unit. The game could ask players to shuffle cards of a particular range and stack them at the top of a deck and those of another range at the bottom, ensuring bigger numbers as the game advances. It could ask for the aces to be shuffled into quarters of the deck and trigger events when they are flipped. It could ask players to stack their decks at the start of the game to programme early movements.

CASE STUDY: DECK STACKING VICTORY POINTS – *A BILLION SUNS*

In the space fleet game *A Billion Suns* (Hutchinson, 2021), victory points for objectives are set by stacked decks of cards, but different objectives call for different stacking. They may require that the cards be:

- Shuffled, to represent random rewards, such as mining space asteroids.
- Stacked in ascending order, to represent resources where the most valuable will be claimed first, such as scientists from a failing facility.
- Stacked in descending order, to represent resources where the least valuable must be taken first, such as arresting criminals where henchmen must be cleared before the crime lord is arrested.
- Shuffled with a single trigger card where the trigger card scores the entire objective, to represent needing to search for a single valuable reward, such as searching for vital information.

In this way, the same mechanics for claiming and scoring cards can be used to provide mechanics with very different in-game effects.

If a discard pile is shuffled whenever a deck runs out to form a new deck, then the cards are an infinite resource. If, however, they are not, they can act as a limited resource for players who could have to default to weaker abilities or a pre-set result when they run out. They could even be a timer. In an alternating activation game, for example, a deck being exhausted could be used to trigger the end of a round.

A further interesting option is to not allow discard piles to be shuffled when they are stacked to be used as a fresh deck, so they remain in the same order as when they were discarded. In this case, how players use cards in one round will dictate how they arrive in the next. By managing the order they play cards in and setting up runs of good or bad fortune, they can plan ahead and affect their future luck.

The existence of discard piles offers a simple facility to 'rewind' the game; if errors are made in the rules with dice, rolls are certain to be forgotten before they can be corrected, and with cards changes can be made by reference to the cards flipped. Furthermore, rather than simply correcting errors, the ability to rewind time could be part of the mechanics of a game, allowing a player to trigger an ability to rewind time and take a different action with the same cards, or by allowing some units to take parallel actions with the same results as their fellows.

Decks can be shared or player-exclusive. If shared, when one player has a card in their hand, their opponent cannot, making cards a discrete, exclusive resource in a way that dice results can never be. If player-exclusive, then players can stack and control their own deck and know that luck will always be even between players throughout the game.

If decks are player-exclusive, they can be built asymmetrically. Which is to say, if before play each player is allowed to remove ten cards from their deck, each can have a different set of cards. If suits have a set of purposes and powers, then it could be that simply pulling out the lowest value cards is not the wisest choice.

HANDS

It is a familiar concept for players to draw and hold hands of cards. With the caveat that it should be considered how unwieldy a hand of cards can become, particularly in relation to accessibility issues with those who struggle to hold and manipulate large numbers of cards, this is a process that most people are comfortable with. Once players have a hand of cards that they can put into play when they choose, they can select the order of their own luck, either entirely, playing all cards through a player's hand, or at moments of intervention, such as in *Malifaux*. In a hand, cards become a resource, both to play and to reserve, since the exclusive nature of cards means that if a bad card is kept in hand, a player cannot flip it by chance.

Once cards are in hand, they can be played as pairs, runs or sets, opening up a range of additional planning and probability.

CASE STUDY: RUNS AND SETS – *HEARTS OF PLASTIC*

The short-form game *Hearts of Plastic* (Schlief, 2023) simulates skirmish combats between sets of plastic army men and triggers a range of effects from players putting runs, sets and combinations into play. For example, playing a card that makes a run with three previously discarded cards allows a player to place three cards onto the battlefield, representing areas of suppressive fire, or playing a card that matches the value of a previously discarded card allows a card to be placed onto the battlefield, representing the effect of a grenade. By using some of these principles familiar from the traditional game of *Cribbage* (Suckling, 1630), the system requires players to plan and engage at different levels of play.

POSITION AND ORIENTATION

Playing cards have a range of useful physical features that can be used in play. Face-down playing cards open up options for bluffing and hidden information. Face-down cards are an excellent option for secret deployment systems since units can be assigned a card which can proxy for them during the deployment phase. They allow for hidden, prepared abilities since a card can be placed next to a unit and moved with it. Cards can be played next to a unit and remain next to them to note effects, powers and abilities for instant and intuitive book-keeping. Rather than generating a result with a dice and then noting it with a token, the card which generated the result can become the token. Stacks of cards can be moved around the tabletop as easily as one, meaning that, for example, movement can be programmed with stacked cards which move with the unit, being revealed as each activation comes. Many of these affordances for tracking hidden information are shared with tokens, but playing cards have the benefit of being readily available.

While it should be noted that there are variations between deck types (bridge decks being slightly narrower than poker decks, for example), the cards of a deck are of a regular size. This means that cards can be used for measurement, with their short and long edges offering different ranges. *Kobolds and Cobblestones* (Burman, 2018) and *Pirates of the Spanish Main* (Ernest, Mulvihill and Selinker, 2004) each use cards for this purpose. A card can become a template for an area effect, such as a deployed minefield or area of suppressing fire and a template that notes (potentially secretly) its own level of power and additional effects.

Cards can be used for dexterity tests to create performative uncertainty (see Chapter 13). Cards can be flipped, dropped, grabbed, sorted, spun or used to build fragile structures.

Manipulatable

To change a dice in such a way that it will be reliably and permanently transformed can require some quite specific tools. To permanently change a playing card requires nothing more than a marker pen. If your game allows players to have asymmetrical decks, it may allow players to alter the values or suits of cards before play, or if players are encouraged to play a series of connecting games due to the actions taken during play. Cards can have additional effects written on them. Each player can create a deck of cards that is unique to their forces during their story and that changes how they play and as they play.

CULTURAL

Cards have cultural associations, particularly with gambling. If you are designing a game set in the Wild West or any of its weird and alternative permutations, cards give off a good deal of atmosphere. A game requiring a suave spy to sneak around casinos in Monaco or depicting the battles of organised crime in Las Vegas would similarly do well to consider cards to evoke the genre.

Standard playing cards are not the only option. Tarot cards have all the qualities stated so far with an additional set of major arcana cards with a set of additional numbers attached. If a game is about witches or cultists, tarot cards could help immerse players in the fantasy. Japan has a few interesting standardised decks of cards, such as Hanafuda, Kabufuda and Karuta, although these are much less accessible to players in the west.

Aside from decks with different card distributions and values, standard playing card decks come in a wide and fantastic variety of patterns and styles, allowing players to extend their hobby into curating just the right set of playing cards (as many players will do with dice), which can further enhance the atmosphere of playing with them.

COMBINED POWERS

There is, of course, no reason whatsoever that dice and cards cannot be combined, and many of their more interesting features gain additional nuances when combined. A card can be face-down with a dice placed on it, which will be added to its face value when revealed, creating partially hidden, partially open information and additional levels to any bluffing that a game might include.

If dexterity and physicality are of interest, dice can be rolled down or flipped off of cards. If, after a roll, all dice that are touching each other must be removed, then a player increases all dice that can be covered by a single card by the value of that card. Players may wish to group dice for a high card and risk losing some, or take a spread with little raising for a low card. The combinations of mechanics and ideas available are a barely explored area of design and have many possibilities. There is plenty of space to do something genuinely new here.

CUSTOM CARDS

Aside from pre-printed standard card decks, there are additional options and concerns opened up by custom-printed cards or card-like items. Decks of professionally produced custom cards bring their own issues of supply as a product line, it is worth considering how players might acquire them. If sold as a separate product, consider how and if the game can be played without the cards, should they be unavailable to a given player. If sold with specific miniatures or expansions and used as unit upgrades, consider if you are creating a 'pay-to-win' situation where players with more cards and so more options have a better chance of victory. If you are providing cards as a freely downloadable print-and-play resource, consider the burden of production you are introducing for your players. Those caveats aside, if your players can acquire custom card sets for your game, there are many advantages available.

Cards make excellent quick reference tools; players can decide for themselves which parts of the game they need reminding of and take only the reference cards that they need, keeping them in view at all times and picking them up without needing to flick through a book. From easily forgotten rules to overall turn order, rules reference cards can speed up play and learning. Unit statistics, special rules for items, abilities or powers can all be easily forgotten during play, and having them on cards can speed up play significantly.

Random narrative elements such as events, locations, wandering creatures or terrain effects can be provided as card decks, saving players from generating numbers and then needing to hunt down tables in books. Flipping a card and having the information immediately available is quicker and more elegant. If using emergent scenarios (see Chapter 28), then decks of scenario elements can be used to generate the scenario and then act as quick reference cards during play.

Units can have special abilities triggered by drawing or flipping custom cards with their details listed on them. Furthermore, putting those abilities on cards can allow players to put together their own decks, with restrictions and requirements adding another layer of strategy to your game. Custom cards used as templates can have corners or edges with additional effects for targets they touch.

Cards are barely explored in non-discrete miniatures games, despite the ease of acquiring them, people's familiarity with them and the massive range of design space they open up. Consider what they can do for your game; you'll not look back.

SUMMARY

When considering using cards, their potential **weaknesses** must be understood:

- They are poor at creating pools of results.
- Their odds can be tough for players to calculate.
- They create possibly unbalanced levels of **competence** and **privilege** in relation to information.

However, they have a significant range of strengths.

- Cards can:
  - Generate a huge range of numbers.
  - Generate a range of results from a single card.
  - Allow for runs and sets.
  - Can have meaning attached to orientation and position.
  - Easily be transformed physically.
  - Be custom printed.
  - Bring cultural associations.
- Decks and discard piles:
  - Can be stacked.
  - Have a memory.
  - Can be searched and manipulated.
  - Shuffled into one another, or limited to a single pass.
  - Shared, split or asymmetrical.
- Hands of cards create player exclusive resources.

EXPERIMENTS

Replace dice in your game by asking players to flip a card from a deck to generate random numbers. Then:

- Replace re-rolls with:
  - Flipping a new card from the deck.
  - Using a previously flipped card from the discards.
  - Using a card from a hand drawn at the start of the turn.
- Base test or skill modifiers on suits.

Find three more mechanics or processes you can replace with cards.

REFERENCES

Anderson, M., Caroland, N., Cohen, R., Darland, A., Gibbs, J., Hanold, D., Johns, E., Martin, M. and Weber, D. (2013) *Malifaux: Second Edition*. South Korea: Wyrd Miniatures, LLC.

Burman, R. (2018) *Kobolds and Cobblestones: Fantasy Gang Rumbles*. Oxford: Osprey Games.

Ernest, J., Mulvihill, M. and Selinker, M. (2004) *Pirates of the Spanish Main*. [Collectible game] New Jersey: WizKids.

Greenway, T. (2017) *Moonstone*. Ganarew: Goblin King Games.

Hutchinson, M. (2021) *A Billion Suns*. Oxford: Osprey Games.

Schlief, N. (2023) 'Hearts of Plastic', Hearts of Plastic, 2023; Hearts of Plastic by Frankenstein (itch.io) (Accessed: 8 January 2023).

16 Genre, Theme and Setting

In tabletop games, 'theme' is a term generally adopted for a range of concepts in a manner that is both confusing and arguably just wrong. What is collected under the term 'theme' are ideas that might be better addressed as genre, tropes, conceit and setting. Tabletop games tend to be collected in general categories of 'thematic', such as *Monopoly* (Magie, 1935), and 'abstract', such as Go. While it is possible to create an abstract, non-discrete miniatures game, they are generally highly thematic and understanding the collection of concepts that make a game thematic and their purposes is therefore important to an effective design. This chapter builds on the ideas of Chapter 9 and focuses predominantly on the creation of games with fictional conceits.

SETTING

The setting of a game is the collection of narrative pieces created to frame and explain the world in which it exists, creating the setting for play. Sometimes referred to as the background, 'fluff' or 'lore', this is generally presented in sections of text clearly separated out from the main rules text and may drive specific rules concerns. The primary purposes of the setting are to draw players into investing in the game as a whole and to provide them with signposts as to how their in-game avatars will participate in that world. It may be presented faux-factually, as a birds-eye-view description of the world, or narratively, showing the world from the eye-level of its inhabitants.

The advice for embedded narratives found in Chapter 9 applies to the creation and presentation of your setting, in particular leaving space for the player and inviting them to provide their own portions of the setting and backstory. The purpose of providing setting detail in a miniatures game is to enhance the game experience by connecting the player to the world they will inhabit during the game, the forces they will command and the conflicts that will drive their sessions. Strong setting writing in game rulebooks shows the reader how to become a participant in the story. Counterintuitively, it should avoid satisfying narrative arcs, instead presenting ongoing conflicts that the player's avatar can become an actor in resolving. The setting must leave space for the player to become the author of the unfolding story.

GENRE

For our purposes, a genre is a set of media that shares common characteristics in theme, tone and subject matter, and that genre is built by the presence of expected tropes. A game could be in a particular genre of *game* (with 'tabletop miniatures games' being the genre of game we are examining in this book), but it could also

 DOI: 10.1201/9781003314820-19

evoke the genres of other media, such as science fiction, in which case it would become a science fiction miniatures game. If you wish to let your players tell a certain kind of story within a certain genre, you will need to consider which of the tropes of that genre are needed for players to feel that the game successfully evokes the genre and create rules to suggest those tropes. We summarise some of the tropes and design challenges for common genres later in this chapter.

THEME

Theme has two distinct meanings. If I decorate a restaurant with jolly rogers and serve Blackbeard burgers, my restaurant has a pirate theme. Conversely, the theme of *Three Colours: Blue* (1993) is emotional liberty. While the first meaning is potentially useful to us, it is already adequately covered by setting and genre. The second meaning is different but important: what is the idea or purpose behind a game's creation? Where games are usefully definable as an art form, they are best thought of as a method of inscribing moments of agency, as painting is about seeing and music is about hearing. When considering themes, it can be useful to look at the form of agency that a particular game intends to record. The theme of a game, then, might be the sense of choosing how best to sell the lives of one's men in a hopeless last stand or assigning limited resources where every mistake leads to death. A game's themes can therefore be understood as separate from its genre and setting.

It is easy to pay little heed to a theme in non-discrete miniatures games; they are a series of choices relating to placement and positioning, often within a framework of direct conflict, which is often taken as sufficient theme, but to do so is a potentially serious mistake. A clear and powerful guiding theme is one of the ways that games avoid being lost within the mass of similar titles and can work to support, subvert or altogether avoid the necessity for genre in a design.

Consider why you are designing a particular game, what emotions or reactions you wish to garner from your players, what events you wish to recreate, or which mechanical concepts you intend to investigate. These are the themes of your game, and referencing them throughout your design process can guide you to a more coherent communication of your vision to players.

SOME TYPICAL GENRES AND THEIR TROPES

For reasons that we aren't fully able to explain, miniatures games are currently almost exclusively rooted in action-oriented genres of fiction and non-fiction: military history, fantasy, science fiction and horror (or at least monster movies). It is less common to find miniature games based on romance, mystery or crime (even though heists are a perfect fit, as we'll get to).

Miniatures currently labour under a conceptual limitation in their utilisation, with games focusing on physical activities (running, shooting, climbing and punching) far more than the social activities that characters in movies and books often spend their time doing (asking, arguing, lying and seducing). While non-discrete miniatures games absolutely tell stories (see Chapter 9), the sorts of stories each can tell are limited by the verbs provided to the players. Mental and social activities are just as natively supported by the core affordances of these games (their ability to model complex physical situations and effect projection) as physical ones, but the game design community has yet to take significant risks in that creative direction (and thus an audience of players has yet to be developed for such games). We are hopeful to see more of that, just as roleplaying games evolved from *Tunnels and Trolls* (St. Andre, 1975) to *Star Crossed* (Roberts, 2019), and video games offer an *Animal Crossing* [Video game] (2001) as often as a *DOOM* [Video game] (Hall, Petersen and Romero, 1993).

However, accepting that action-orientated genres are both popular with players and well-suited to the affordances of non-discrete miniatures games, let us survey some of the tropes that define them and how they might be evoked effectively in your designs.

The genre definitions below are not absolute. Their borders are blurry, and we encourage you to blur them further. This is simply a note of some of the commonalities that non-discrete miniatures games set in these genres share, along with directions to the chapters that expound upon some of the possible solutions to meeting (or subverting) players' expectations of these genres.

MILITARY HISTORY

The progenitor genre of non-discrete games is military history, the recreation of actual battles and conflicts as recorded within history. This genre in miniatures gaming is rooted in attempts at historically accurate simulation of statistics, scales and strategy; realism is its primary defining trope. Historical battlefields and forces are, however, not originally crafted for enjoyable gaming on a dining room table. Weapon ranges, unit movement and the impact of terrain cannot all be modelled accurately at the same time as providing a balanced and engaging game experience. How a design deals with the compromises required will define its success as a historical game.

FANTASY

One of the most popular genres for non-discrete miniatures games is fantasy, and high fantasy is particularly prevalent, likely due to the enduring centrality of *Dungeons & Dragons* (Gygax and Arneson, 1974), *Magic: The Gathering* (Garfield, 1993) and the Warhammer worlds[1] within tabletop gaming as a whole. An extremely common trope is that of faux-medievalism, with most fantasy being set in a world somewhere technologically and socially akin to the dark ages, though usually taking liberally from across that broad period to allow otherwise anachronistic warfare technology to face off on the battlefield in the interests of tactical range.

High fantasy settings create an entirely fantastical world with its own races and physical rules, its primary tropes being fantasy races and magic. The standard fantasy races have their own sets of tropes within non-discrete gaming so well established as to be more or less requirements of their representation: goblins must be numerous, weak and cowardly; orcs must be muscle-bound and belligerent; elves skilled and refined; dwarves must be stoical and tough; and attempts to subvert these expectations should be well worth the effort. Chapter 30 surveys some of the considerations when designing list-building factions to represent such races. While magic tends to be restricted to a subset of powerful individuals and has deadly consequences for its misuse, it remains central to the genre, so most forces should have access to it, albeit in a limited capacity and when it goes wrong, its wielders should be conclusively damned for their hubris. We examine many of the ways of achieving such effects in Chapter 27. High fantasy heroes are often superhumanly powerful, wading single-handed into small armies of opponents with gusto, while mythical monsters and fantastic beasts abound.

Low fantasy has two related patterns. The first[2] is made by taking some of the tropes of high fantasy but placing them within a world otherwise recognisably similar to our own. The world of *His Dark Materials* (Pullman, 2000) is akin to our own Oxford, but with spirit familiars and inter-dimensional travel. The second is to place the action within a fictional world apart from our own, but to limit the prevalence of high fantasy and mythic elements. *Gormenghast* (Peake, 1950) is infused with much of the same grim and perilous atmosphere that pervades other fantasy settings but contains no magic or mythic creatures; it has plenty of dungeons but no dragons. Low fantasy games tend to focus more on the prosaic actions of 'regular' people, albeit with the convenience of detachment from reality. Tabletop action is likely to be closer to that in military history games of a comparable period or set in insalubrious locales. Players may expect to embody low-status characters, anti-heroes and criminals.

SCIENCE FICTION

Science fiction is a widely represented genre among miniatures games, with its most valuable property being the Warhammer 40,000 universe, a space opera setting. In all cases, the most significant trope of science fiction in non-discrete miniatures games is ubiquitous ranged combat. Despite the prevalence of science fiction games, dealing with shooting in strategically interesting ways on the tabletop is a non-trivial task, as we explore in Chapter 22, and doing so will likely define your success in delivering a satisfying non-discrete game in any science fiction genre.

Space opera blends the tropes of science fiction with many of those from high fantasy, and miniatures gamers will anticipate space magic, space monsters and powerful space heroes. You will need to find ways to mesh together powerful ranged attacks with tropes that were incubated in melee-focused environments; otherwise, players may be disappointed to discover that hokey religions and ancient weapons are no match for a good blaster.

Hard science fiction has its representation as well, with near-future and cyberpunk-themed games such as *Infinity* (Liste, Rodríguez and Torres, 2005) and military-minded miniatures games that eschew aliens and space magic, such as *BattleTech* (1984). Players of hard science-fiction miniatures games may be looking for a blend of the tropes of science fiction with those of military history.

POST-APOCALYPTIC

Miniature games in post-apocalyptic settings are numerous. Their tropes include small groups of survivors banding together; most are skirmish-level games of no more than a half-dozen models a side. Many feature a focus on scarcity and survival; models will often be found collecting resources and avoiding making noise, which would attract environmental threats.

HORROR

Interestingly, unlike its genre representation in almost every other medium, horror in non-discrete games very rarely makes anything more than a cursory attempt to generate the emotions of fear or disgust in its audience. Rather, the primary trope of horror in these games is the use of the cosmetic trappings of the genre, such as monsters and mad scientists. The inclusion of deeper horror themes is mostly limited to the simulation of the effects of fear within the agents of a player, usually resulting in a range of control removal effects as agents refuse to act as a player wishes or flee the tabletop (see Chapter 24) and stealth mechanics to represent being stalked by monsters.

CROSS-OVER GENRES

One finds a great many miniatures games that lie at the intersections of science fiction, horror and fantasy. Both steampunk (science-fantasy with Victorian-era inspired technology and aesthetics) and weird west (the American west during the frontier period, but populated by supernatural or technologically anachronistic individuals) are found on our tabletops far in excess of their showing in any other media. These settings generally require that the standard tropes of their parent genres be subverted in some way, often by colliding them with the tropes of other genres, either from their historical realities or representations within the wider media. Players may expect to find real-world groups, historical figures or archetypes represented in uncharacteristic ways, blended with fantasy races, magic or anachronistic technology.

NON-VIOLENT GAMES

The defining feature of most non-discrete miniatures games, regardless of genre, is the presence of violent conflict. This is probably due a little to a history stemming from simulations of military conflicts and a little to the fact that combat is a quick and clear way of explaining why two or more individuals should care exactly where and in what attitude each other stands. However, violence is far from the only reason to care where a person might be standing. In daily life, physical violence of any kind is mercifully rare, yet spotting friends in crowded or complex locations is a regular concern. There are a handful of alternative genres to consider with tropes that could replace direct violence.

Heists form an entire sub-genre of cinema. Spies, con-men and thieves stealing a valuable item from under the noses of its guards could quite easily be re-imagined as a non-discrete miniatures game. Stealth, a popular trope in video games, is based entirely around line-of-sight properties. The primary issue to deal with in relation to stealth in a multi-sided game is that the players controlling the patrolling guards have an omniscient view of the table and can thus simply see where the thieves are. Guards can, however, be controlled by simple AI systems or abstracted to leave players as competing groups of thieves, or hidden movement mechanics can be used to create an asymmetrical game system.

Distracted Observation, for want of a better term, provides a basis for many possible miniatures game conceits. Forcing one figure to maintain a watch on another while both are moving and possibly engaged in other distracting activities could simulate all manner of narratives, different from outright stealth. Traders moving through a marketplace may wish to both trade at a particular stall while keeping an eye on what their rivals are selling and how it might affect prices. A detective might wish to keep two or more suspects in view as they both move towards potential targets for crime or need to move to a clue site while keeping watch on a suspect. A lover might wish to pass a note to their beloved without their overbearing parents witnessing the exchange. All such events make line of sight and position interesting without introducing a need for violence.

CASE STUDY: ALTERNATIVE GENRES – *REDWOOD*

Redwood (Raimbault, 2023) is a boxed, non-discrete game in which players are nature photographers. Movement is template-based, and players need to line up shots on animals such that they align with suitably attractive backdrops. It has non-discrete movement and line-of-sight rules and is in every way a non-discrete game. However, rather than being a tabletop miniatures game, it has been presented as a boxed game, possibly because there is a perception that the audience for tabletop games not based around direct and clear violence is limited.

Sports, whether real or invented, make ideal conceits for non-discrete miniatures games, as they possess a number of relevant characteristics. They tend to provide their own conceit (we are here to play this sport and wish to win the match). They tend to feature a constrained play area. They provide clear objectives. Arbitrary rules and restrictions on activities are more readily acceptable (as they are common in real-world sports). They often provide a dynamic focal point for action, in the form of a ball or similar, that forces an ever-changing tactical situation and naturally demands the movement of participants. Notable examples for study are *Blood Bowl* (2016), *Guild Ball* (Hart and Loxam, 2015) and *Dread Ball* (Thornton, 2012).

Races are a great subject for non-discrete miniatures games, as they are centrally concerned with the relative positions of competitors in space. *Gaslands* (Hutchinson, 2017) is a non-discrete car racing and combat game, but there is no inherent reason for the combat part of that equation. The primary trope of racing games is momentum: speed and control are the two main focuses of a racer, but they are in direct opposition, neatly creating an interesting puzzle for players to solve. Key considerations will likely be: how to deal with a literal runaway leader problem; how to balance player agency with simulating loss of control; and how to handle the inherent violence of collisions.

THE TROPES OF NON-DISCRETE GAMES

It is worth acknowledging that non-discrete miniatures games have their own tropes and that any design which challenges them may suffer from players who expect those tropes to be fulfilled. Aside from direct violence, other, more arbitrary tropes exist. Sessions of non-discrete games are expected to last for five to seven rounds, despite the fact that a round is an arbitrary definition: some players may find drastically different numbers of rounds off-putting (*A Billion Suns* (Hutchinson, 2021) has three; *Star Wars: X-Wing Miniatures Game* (Little, 2012) can have a dozen). Non-discrete miniatures games are expected to be thematic (rather than abstract), use dice to generate random numbers and allow players to select from a range of factions to produce a force with powers asymmetrical to those of their opponent. We encourage deviations from these tropes, but they will require players who are already accustomed to their norms to consciously depart from their habits and expectations, and so such deviations should be intentional and carefully considered.

SUMMARY

- Games have a **setting** and commonly evoke a **genre**.
- Games use **conceits** to orient the player and to aid understanding and recall of game mechanics.
- A game's **theme** is the unifying idea or purpose behind its creation.
- Genres have expected **tropes**.
- Non-discrete miniatures games have expected **tropes**.
- Non-discrete miniatures games may have **non-violent subject-matter**.

EXPERIMENTS

- Use your game's mechanics to simulate another genre.
- Play the game with miniatures from another genre.
- Play your game with plain wooden blocks or empty bases.
- Remove the violence from your game.

Think of your favourite movie that isn't about direct violent conflict; evoke it using your game.

NOTES

1 Both the original 'Old World', as continued to be explored by product lines such as *Warhammer Fantasy Roleplay* (McDowall and Law, 2018), *Warhammer: The Old World* (2024) and *Blood Bowl* (2016), and the 'Mortal Realms' explored by games such as *Warhammer: The Age of Sigmar* (2021), *Warhammer Age of Sigmar: Soulbound* (2020) and *Warhammer Underworlds: Shadespire* (2017).
2 Also known as intrusion fantasy.

REFERENCES

Animal Crossing [Video game]. (2001). Kyoto, Japan: Nintendo Co., Ltd.

Blood Bowl. (2016). Nottingham: Games Workshop Ltd.

Brown, F., Leeper, L.R. and Weisman, J. (1984) *BattleTech: A Game of Armored Combat.* [Board game] Chicago, IL: FASA.

Byrne, E., Dale-Clutterbuck, D., Guymer, D., Lithgow, E., Luikart, TS., McDowall, D., Ostrander, K., Reynolds, J. and Werner, C. (2020) *Warhammer: Age of Sigmar: Soulbound.* County Meath: Cubicle 7.

Garfield, R. (1993) *Magic: The Gathering.* [Board game] Renton, WA: Wizards of the Coast.

Gygax, G. and Arneson, D. (1974) *Dungeons & Dragons.* 1st edn. Lake Geneva, WI: TSR Inc.

Hall, T., Petersen, S. and Romero, J. (1993) *DOOM.* [Video game] Richardson, TX: id Software, Inc.

Hart, M. and Loxam, R. (2015) *Guild Ball.* Salford: Steamforged Games Ltd.

Hutchinson, M. (2017) *Gaslands.* Oxford: Osprey Games.

Hutchinson, M. (2021) *A Billion Suns.* Oxford: Osprey Games.

Law, A. and McDowall, D. (2018) *Warhammer Fantasy Roleplay.* County Meath: Cubicle 7.

Liste, F., Rodríguez, G. and Torres, C. (2005) *Infinity N3: Core Book.* Cangas, Galicia: Corvus Belli.

Little, J. (2012) *Star Wars: X-Wing Miniatures Game.* [Board game] Roseville, MN: Fantasy Flight Games.

Magie, E. (1935) *Monopoly.* Beverly, MA: Parker Brothers.

Peake, M. (1950) *Gormenghast.* London: Eyre & Spottiswoode.

Raimbault, C. (2023) *Redwood.* [Board game] Longchamps, Belgium: Sit Down!

Roberts, A. (2019) *Star Crossed.* [Boardgame] Chapel Hill, NC: Bully Pulpit Games

Sanders, D. (2017) *Warhammer Underworlds: Shadespire.* [Board game] Nottingham: Games Workshop Ltd.

St. Andre, K. (1975) *Tunnels & Trolls.* Scottsdale, AZ: Flying Buffalo.

Thornton, J. (2012). *Dread Ball.* Nottingham: Mantic Games.

Three Colours: Blue (1993) Directed by Krzysztof Kieslowski [Film] Paris: Canal+.

Warhammer: The Age of Sigmar. (2021). Nottingham: Games Workshop Ltd.

Warhammer: The Old World. (2024). Nottingham: Games Workshop Ltd.

17 Resources

Non-discrete miniatures games are, at their most basic, games of resource management. Each player starts with a finite set of units and must deploy and apply them effectively. In this chapter, we will look at some of the common resources found in non-discrete miniatures games and discuss some of the strategies and considerations for including them.

A **resource** in a non-discrete miniatures game is a discrete mechanical factor that can change during the course of a session and which can be traded for some further game effect. (Most systems also include list-building restrictions such as points and unit allowances, which *are* resources, but do not act in a dynamic fashion during play and are therefore considered in Chapter 30 instead.)

WOUNDS AND ACTIVATION POINTS

The near-ubiquitous resources found in non-discrete miniatures games are **wounds** and **activations**.

Whether recorded with numerical tokens or the removal of figures, each unit will likely have a maximum number of 'wounds' (or damage) that it can receive before it is removed. This accumulation of wounds is a critical resource in most non-discrete miniatures games. Across their force, the player has a limited supply of wounds, which must be spent wisely (by putting some units in harm's way and others not at the right times) to achieve their objectives. If, through better positioning, tactics or luck, a player causes more wounds than they receive, they will achieve an important resource advantage.

Within the limit of a game session, each unit has a finite number of activations available and perhaps also a number of activation points within each activation. These limited activations must be utilised strategically to ensure they achieve their goals before the session ends. If they unwisely or unknowingly spend precious activations on actions irrelevant to victory, they may find themselves unable to claim their objectives. If a player successfully baits their opponent into spending activations unwisely, they will achieve a critical resource advantage.

CHARACTERISTICS OF RESOURCES

Wounds and activation points illustrate the main four characteristics of resources. If a unit can spend its limited activation points on many possible actions, then those activation points are a **fungible resource**. Wounds tend to be used for the single purpose of avoiding the model's removal from play, making them a **non-fungible resource**. Wounds are a **negative resource** activations are not. Activation points are a **recoverable resource**, wounds tend not to be.

 DOI: 10.1201/9781003314820-20

FUNGIBLE RESOURCES

Fungible resources are those that are mutually interchangeable; each may be exchanged for a range of possible outcomes, effects or activities (possibly on behalf of a range of units). Fungible resources can add interest to a design because they offer a moment of decision-making.

In the context of a system with activation points, a unit's activation points may be fungible, as any given activation point is as good as any other for triggering available actions, although it is also possible to constrain the fungibility of activation points by designating some as being only available for certain actions.

CASE STUDY: SEMI-FUNGIBLE ACTIVATION POINTS – *MALIFAUX*

In *Malifaux* (Anderson *et al.*, 2013), units are given two activation points as standard, which can be exchanged for actions such as attacking or shooting, costing a single activation point each, or charging, which costs two points. However, each unit can also make a single action which costs zero activation points each turn, and an action costing zero activation points cannot be triggered by spending activation points. In this way, a neat halt is put on the fungibility of activation points; they may be spent freely, but not for zero actions, and no matter how many additional activation points a unit might gain, zero actions remain safely boxed away from over-usage.

In the context of a player's whole force, a given unit's activations are likely *non-fungible*, as they may only be spent on actions for the unit that generated them. The same is commonly true of wounds, although *Rogue Planet* (Spivey, 2015) provides players with a single pool of wounds (called 'energy') across their force, inviting the player to decide where and when they wish to expend their fungible wound resource. Some games, such as *Infinity* (Couceiro *et al.*, 2014), provide the players with a pool of fungible activations for their force, which may be spent on any of the player's units. Some games, such as *7TV* (Dawson and Perrotton, 2010), go further, providing a resource that may be divided across both activations and other options, such as boosting dice rolls or triggering special abilities.

CASE STUDY: EMERGENT PUZZLES – *7TV*

Despite being a strongly narrative game, *7TV* builds excellent emergent puzzles due to its use of a fungible resource: 'plot points'. These points are required to activate units, trigger special abilities and boost the effectiveness of rolls. By employing this single resource in multiple spots, players are constantly forced to consider whether more activations but less certainty of effectiveness is preferable to fewer more powerful activations, and that tension creates a constantly engaging puzzle throughout play.

Other common examples include the command abilities of leaders, stored dice or cards and resources to trigger special abilities such as spells, psychic powers, or whatever stands in for them in your system (see Chapter 27). Whatever form they take, players should have a clearly digestible set of options at any given time for any given fungible resource. As a rule of thumb, limit them to three or four options if multiple different sets of options are presented over a given round (*Malifaux* units tend to have two to four specific action options beyond the standard set of actions to spend their activation points on, easing slightly the mental load of having to skip between and co-ordinate these options between seven or eight units) or six to ten if only a few sets are to be confronted each round. *Saga* (Buchel, 2011) battle boards have around ten options; *Warhammer: The Game of Fantasy Battles* (Cavatore *et al.*, 2000) spell lores have six or seven options, and players may have to engage with two or three sets of them each round.

Players should find the choice between what to expend resources on to be a tricky decision a couple of times each round; more than this, and a game can bog down as players are caught in 'analysis paralysis', less and the resource isn't doing its job. Ideally, beginners and experts should experience the same level of internal struggle in resource balancing, as at first the subtlety of some exchanges is lost on learning players, and when they later come into view, earlier struggles become easy choices.

Non-fungible Resources

Non-fungible resources are those that may be exchanged for a single and specific outcome, effect or activity. One resource may not be exchanged for another.

Actions with limited uses, such as weapons with limited ammunition, are an example of non-fungible resources. The ammunition can only be used to fire that specific weapon. The interest comes from *when* to spend the resource for that action, rather than *whether* to spend the resource on that action versus another action. There may be thematic reasons to introduce such a restriction, but it is always worth considering whether a non-fungible resource can be redesigned into a fungible one to increase the density of decisions and compromises available to the player.

If a non-fungible resource is limited within a game session rather than within a round or an activation, it can fall foul of players' natural inclination for loss aversion (more below), not being utilised as players hoard the resource 'just in case'. This can make taking the related actions feel more painful to players, which might add to the desired game feel (if you wish to evoke the sensation of scarcity), but can also have negative impacts on the game experience if used too liberally, as players may feel that the game is resisting their natural desire to have things happen.

One design goal to bear in mind is that resources, particularly non-fungible ones, should be a drag on decision-making and absolutely should run out at some point. If there is a non-fungible resource attached to an action (such as ammunition for shooting) and a player performs that action every time they get the chance (firing whenever they see an enemy), but the resource regularly fails to run out during a session, then you've only created an additional piece of book-keeping for your players. If the resource never stops a player from triggering its action, it should be removed.

NEGATIVE RESOURCES

Where resources are something a player desires to have, they may be said to be **positive**. Where they are something a player would rather not have, they are **negative**. Negative resources work best when they are either the downside of an active beneficial choice (increasing the tension in the choice) or gained as a result of actions by an opponent (as a reward for their choices). Negative resources can then create further choices based on their removal.

Wounds are the most common negative resource. They are most often visited upon a unit by an opponent, with the ultimate result of removing the unit, but may be used as a more fungible and self-inflicted resource. In *Frostgrave* (McCullogh, 2015), wizards may inflict wounds on themselves to boost their spell-casting actions.

In *Gaslands* (Hutchinson, 2017), resolving the game's skid dice brings 'hazard tokens', a negative resource. In order to participate in the core game loop by increasing their gear number (getting more activation opportunities), the player must accept the gaining of hazards and suffer a penalty if they gain too many. The game provides a number of ways to remove them, including by spending other fungible positive resources.

Similarly, units in *Star Wars: X-Wing The Miniatures Game* (Little, 2012) may accept a 'stress token' in exchange for performing certain manoeuvres. While the unit has a stress token, it may not perform any further stressful ('red') manoeuvres and the token may be removed by performing a 'blue' manoeuvre. The stress token is a self-inflicted negative resource that offers tactical power in one activation at the cost of a dip in flexibility in later activations, creating interest.

Saga requires units to take 'fatigue' when they activate multiple times, engage in combat or have a friendly unit eliminated. It can be removed by opponents in return for reducing a unit's abilities or by players resting the units. This makes fatigue a highly interesting negative resource in that it is flexible in its method of application, removal and effects, and its usage and management permeate throughout *Saga*.

Many games have status effects such as poison, burning or being pinned, which amount to forms of negative resources with certain effects and removal conditions. For example, *Malifaux* (2013) has a condition called 'burning' which, if applied to a unit at the start of their activation, causes them to take damage, but which another unit can remove by spending activation points.

The inclusion of negative resources beyond the central resource of wounds and model removal should be carefully considered. Ideally, the negative resources should spring from a player's own actions and/or be removable by a player's actions, so that there is a level of control over them. They should alter a player's decision space by adding or changing options, not simply reduce that decision space. We require players to suffer from having their toys removed from their game incrementally over a play session against their will; we should be careful about forcing them to have them exhausted, poisoned, burned and driven insane against their will as well.

RECOVERABLE RESOURCES

Resources can be recoverable, either automatically or by an action. Activation points tend to recover automatically at the start of a round, as do command points in

Warhammer 40,000 (2023) or a player's control hand in *Malifaux*, while something like wounds or ammunition might require an activation or action to be restored.

Automatically refreshing resources give you an emergent method for controlling the tempo of your game. If resources run out and are refreshed at set points, it is the use of resources that will define the rounds of your game. In many ways, a round is just the point at which activation point resources recover. You can create a rhythm in your game by dictating when resources recover and how.

Resources that require player actions to recover are more difficult to design. Firstly, it can be a tempo drop in the game, with an action spent on bookkeeping rather than a direct change in the physical table state. Players may struggle to justify spending a high-value fungible resource like an activation to recover another less-flexible resource. If, for example, a weapon runs out of ammunition on the next to last turn of the game, then reloading it may be tactically difficult to justify. This may lead to emergent changes in decision-making, or it may cause frustration. Lastly, player behaviours can vary broadly; if players spend too long refreshing or not refreshing resources, it can upset the balance of resources in a game.

LOSS AVERSION

People overvalue resources they already have and prefer a sure gain over a possible loss (Ruggeri *et al.*, 2020). As such, if you hand a player a set of resources at the start of a game, particularly non-recoverable ones, you will often see them still holding those resources at the end of the game. This can hold true even if those resources have absolutely no purpose in end-game scoring and no meaning other than to be spent. Resources that are handed to a player as a one-off event at the start of a game which they have a choice not to spend will often go unspent.

If possible, it is a better idea to give players a smaller amount of a given resource at the start of every round than a larger amount at the start of a session. Additionally, taking excess resources away at the end of a round will encourage freer spending than allowing stockpiling. If you intend for players to spend a resource freely and repeatedly, mitigating their natural loss aversion is critical.

THE SHIFTING VALUE OF RESOURCES

The value of any given resource shifts over the course of a game. If designed for, this can provide an emergent catch-up mechanic. If a resource provides more value to a lagging player than to a leading one, the economy of the game tilts in favour of the underdog. It might be tempting to simply give the lagging player additional resources, but this runs the risk of feeling like unearned 'pity points' to the recipient and like an unfairness in the game to their opponent, perhaps experienced as being punished by the game for winning. A more subtle and effective design is to create options for spending resources that naturally shift in value depending on the relative game state.

In *Gaslands*, players can generate a fungible resource known as 'audience votes' which allows for a vehicle to change gears outside of its activation as one of the options for its use. For a vehicle that is doing well, such an option is largely valueless, but for one that is struggling, it can be the difference between activating once or five times in a round. The result is that votes are more valuable to a struggling player than to a leading one. They provide an emergent catch-up mechanic which helps level the field while allowing the laggard to feel smart for seeing the option and the leader to feel the game is fair (as the other player is just using universally available rules and no special treatment has been given).

SUMMARY

Your game contains **resources**, most usually **wounds** and **activation points**. Resources are:

- Fungible – Not limited to single effects or units and potentially exchangeable for other resources.
- Non-Fungible – Locked to a single effect and unit and not exchangeable.
- Positive – Something a player wishes to have, generally generated and spent on achieving goals.
- Negative – Something a player wishes not to have, generally imposed by an opponent or taken as a cost for achieving goals.
- Recoverable – Automatically or by a specific action.
- Non-Recoverable – Generating at the start of play and not returning, this can lead to loss aversion.

The value of resources is not necessarily fixed and can shift with game state and player actions.

EXPERIMENTS

Whenever a player in your game spends an unacknowledged resource (such as an activation point), have them collect and spend physical tokens to do so.

If players gain a non-fungible resource during your game, make it fungible. If they gain a fungible one, make it non-fungible.

Add a negative resource to your game's most powerful actions. Have it be spent by an opponent to do something powerful.

REFERENCES

Anderson, M., Caroland, N., Cohen, R., Darland, A., Gibbs, J., Hanold, D., Johns, E., Martin, M. and Weber, D. (2013) *Malifaux: Second Edition*. South Korea: Wyrd Miniatures, LLC.
Buchel, A. (2011) *Saga*. Evesham: Gripping Beast.
Cavatore, A., Pirinen, T., Priestley, R., Stillman, N. and Thornton, J. (2000) *Warhammer: The Game of Fantasy Battles*. Nottingham: Games Workshop Ltd.
Couceiro, A., Azpeitia, F., Rodríguez, G. and Rodríguez, C. (2014). *Infinity*. Pontevedra: Corvus Belli.

Dawson, G. and Perrotton, K. (2010) *7TV*. Lincolnshire: Crooked Dice Game Design Studio.

Hutchinson, M. (2017) *Gaslands*. Oxford: Osprey Games.

Little, J. (2012) *Star Wars: X-Wing The Miniatures Game*. [Board game] Roseville, Minnesota: Fantasy Flight Games.

McCullogh, J. (2015) *Frostgrave*. Oxford: Osprey Games.

Ruggeri, K., Alí, S., Berge, M.L., Bertoldo, G., Bjørndal, L.D., Cortijos-Bernabeu, A., Davison, C., Demić, E., Esteban-Cerna, C., Fredemann, M., Gibson, S.P., Jarke, H., Karakasheva, R., Khorrami, P.R., Kveder, J., Andersen, T.L., Lofthus, I.S., McGill, L., Nieto, A.E., Pérez, J., Quail, S.K., Rutherford, C., Tavera, F.L., Tomat, N., Van Reyn, C., Većkalov, B., Wang, K., Yosifova, A., Papa, F., Rubaltelli, E., dan der Linden, S. and Folke, T. (2020) 'Replicating patterns of prospect theory for decision under risk', *Nature Human Behaviour*, 4: pp. 622–633. https://doi.org/10.1038/s41562-020-0886-x

Spivey, B. (2015) *Rogue Planet*. Palm Bay: Bombshell Games.

Section 3

Miniatures Rules Systems

One gets to the heart of the matter by a series of experiences in the same pattern, but in different colours.

Robert Graves

In this section, we lay out the practical rules mechanics and systems commonly required when designing a non-discrete miniatures game. The concerns of these games are all linked by the nature of the form, but the way these concerns are answered varies subtly in a multitude of different ways. We attempt to signpost the way to answers that might work for your design.

DOI: 10.1201/9781003314820-21

18 Setup and Deployment

One of the many joys of non-discrete games is the freedom to incorporate almost anything into the shared fantasy before us. Piles of books can become rocky outcrops, impassable on all sides without climbing gear. Grubby coins can become critical military objectives or priceless treasures, for the capture of which dozens of miniature warriors may give their lives. The physical components of the game, be they miniatures, scenery or tokens, can really be of any source in any scale, as long as we – as players at this table – agree with their meaning.

As players sitting down to a non-discrete game, we must create a shared local agreement as to what these objects in front of us represent. Only then can we set up our play area and put our models in their starting positions. As a designer of a non-discrete game, we must provide players with the tools to crisply and simply define their play space, allowing setup to be kept short and sweet while still ensuring that all this freedom doesn't undermine the players' desire for a game that is fair and fun.

THE TABLETOP

Non-discrete games are generally played on a tabletop rather than a board, and as such, any limitations on the size of their play areas need to be specifically delineated and the results of crossing their boundaries declared before anything can really happen. There is clearly a practical consideration to this choice since the maximum tabletop size that people can reasonably be considered to have access to is usually accepted to be 6′ by 4′ and so the majority of rule sets restricts the play area to 6′ by 4′ for massed battle systems, usually cutting down to 4′ by 4′ or 3′ by 3′ for smaller narrative skirmish level games of squads or individuals. The typical system of requiring a square, or at least rectangular, playing space immediately suggests several of the basic aspects of play, specifically the facing off of players against each other and the direction of their advancement and attention. These sizes and shapes of tables are easy to lay out and clearly understood by players; most gaming clubs or regular players will have sets of boards and other playing surfaces of exactly these dimensions ready and waiting.

However, the convenient suggestions that come from the shape of such a playing surface can also be restrictive, even when playing a system that doesn't require direct conflict between players by physically facing them in direct opposition to each other immediate conclusions about territory and intent are made. The sense that this is 'my' side of the table is almost universal and immediate. In addition, while experienced gamers will have acquired access to a solid, stable and flat 6′ by 4′ surface, most non-gamers will struggle to obtain such an area of play. As such, it is well worth considering unmooring a system from such requirements. The space combat game *A Billion Suns* (Hutchinson, 2021) requires players to designate two or three surfaces of any size they choose as playing areas that their models can jump

DOI: 10.1201/9781003314820-22

between, representing the ability of interstellar ships to cross between star systems in the blink of an eye. Systems such as *Fairy Meat* (Leaton, 2000) and *ZynVaded!* (Vogel, 2010) represent games of 1:1 scale with standard household surfaces and objects as the terrain that small beings the size of gaming miniatures battle over. More flexible play zones can open up a game to a wider audience and suggest different ways of playing for gamers. In order to free up such choices, deployment zones and movement rules need to be more flexible to contain even more range in choices among players, but the rewards can be significant. Choosing to define your game's setup parameters in relationship to the centrepoint or centreline of the play area rather than its edges is one simple way of making your system welcoming to tables of many shapes and sizes. Games with more prosaic settings can still benefit from this approach. Donald Featherstone's *Naval War Games* (1965) records the idea of *Tabletop Islands* by Joseph Morschauser, where various flat surfaces can be used to represent small islands, such as those of the Pacific during the Second World War, with ships mounted on broom poles used to ferry troops or shell positions. This even allows for the splendid inclusion of foot-stool reefs.

Once the playing area has been defined, however tightly or loosely, rules need to be created to designate the effects of a model leaving the playing area. This can be easily overlooked as seemingly obvious, but it can be surprisingly rich with problems. Common issues include:

- If destroying a unit grants victory points and your game can be played by more than two people, who scores if I walk my unit off the table?
- If a rule triggers when a unit is destroyed in a certain part of the playing area, does a unit leaving the playing area at an edge in the designated section count? Does it make a difference if only part of the unit leaves the playing area?
- If a model can be chased as it leaves the playing area, what happens to its pursuer? Can models leave the playing area and then return? If so, when and from where?
- If your game forces models to move from certain effects, does it make a difference if a model leaves the playing zone voluntarily or not?

Very few playing areas will represent areas that are cleanly delineated in real life. If the playing area represents an open field and models that step over an imaginary line on that field are instantly destroyed, what is the logic behind that occurrence?

TYPES OF TERRAIN

Once a playing area has been designated, it will generally need to be populated with appropriate scale models of trees, hills or buildings and lamp posts, or something in between, commonly referred to as **Terrain**. We explore terrain in depth in Chapter 23, but some rules of thumb apply when setting up a play area.

If a game has minimal shooting and large block units, then sight-blocking terrain will tend to have little effect, and so its rules are best kept to a minimum, particularly since such units will often have sight line-limiting effects of their own. Conversely, if a game consists of individuals or loose units with panoramic sight lines and powerful ranged capabilities, solid rules for sight-blocking terrain are necessary to generate an interesting game. Almost the exact opposite can be said for movement channelling terrain since it will have minimal effect on freely pivoting lone models but can sharply define the tactical possibilities for larger or more lumbering units if they are unable to change direction freely.

If a game consists primarily of units or squads, you will need to consider your rules for interactive terrain carefully and potentially refrain from providing interactive terrain rules at all. Rules designating how many members of a squad can fight through a window, for example, or how foot-troopers move into and out of buildings have rarely proven satisfying, particularly when playing with modelled terrain pieces that do not physically allow players to place models inside them. If a game uses true line-of-sight rules (where a player is required to bend down to the model's level to check if it can see something), it should be considered that seeing from a model's perspective when the model is inside a building is often practically impossible. If your design requires interaction with buildings, or destruction of terrain, as part of its cinema, consider the limitations and abstractions that you can use to ensure clarity and simplicity during play.

Many rulesets suggest that players should agree with their opponents on the definitions of terrain pieces without actually going into much detail on what they should agree on. All terrain collections require some degree of abstraction and vagueness since terrain models rarely end flat and flush to the table, meaning that standing trooper models as tightly to them as players would wish is generally impractical, and few modelled forests consist of anything like the density of undergrowth needed to actually block sight, so agreeing where and when true lines of sight or actual terrain shapes can be ignored can be vital. Even with experienced players, each game system puts different weights of importance on different terrain pieces and allows for different levels of freedom in movement and engagement, so an outline of which terrain definitions matter to get exactly right and which can be left on the vague side for your system can assist in the maintenance of the social contract and, by extension, the enjoyment of players.

AMOUNT OF TERRAIN

The amount of terrain required to provide a satisfying game in a given system can vary massively and is not always obvious to new players of that system. Getting it wrong can devastate any possibility of an enjoyable or satisfyingly balanced game, particularly with a system that allows for armies of primarily close combat or shooting specialties to face off against each other. You should consider if you are providing enough information to reduce the risk that inappropriate terrain density results in a negative first-game experience. Avoid relying purely on player experience or on a player sticking around for a second game after suffering through an unsatisfying first experience. Attempts have been made to suggest percentages of tabletops that should be covered with terrain or even to provide boxed sets of terrain with rulesets, but this is an area where a picture speaks a thousand words, and you should consider supplying annotated maps or photographs to illustrate a handful of sample tabletops,

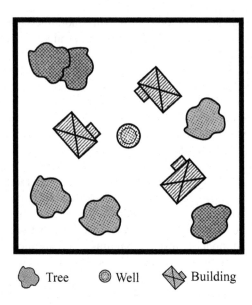

FIGURE 18.1   Map illustrating an example terrain layout.

potentially explaining the designation of the pictured terrain and the reason for its placement and amounts. If, for example, your game plays better with terrain that can create sniper positions, ambushes and lanes of fire, explaining to the player how to set the terrain up to achieve such situations will increase their chances of a positive first-play experience (Figure 18.1).

DEPLOYMENT ZONES

Now that the playing area is defined and filled with suitable amounts of suitable terrain, it's time to get some player-controlled models on the tabletop, but where and how are they to be placed?

A **deployment zone** is the area on the tabletop that a player is permitted to arrange their models in at the start of the game before play proper begins. In many games, these take the form of a strip of a certain depth, the length of the table edge that a player is standing next to. The depth of these strips can be driven by either how much space is needed to array a standard force in an interesting range of strategic configurations or by how far apart the opposing forces should start to ensure a compelling game. If a given game uses ranked-up units, then a deployment zone needs to be sufficient to allow those units to fit in. If players are encouraged to deploy strategic defence in depth, then the deployment zones need to be deep enough to allow players to place units in depth without forcing them to be so serried that the definition between one unit and another is lost. For example, games of *Warhammer: The Game of Fantasy Battles* (Cavatore *et al.*, 2000) were commonly played with a 12″ deep deployment zone, in order that hill-mounted cannon might have units stationed between them and the enemy at the start of a battle.

Alternatively, you might calculate the minimum distances between the starting positions of units in your game required to establish interesting strategic play and provide deployment zones based on that. If we return to our consideration of game scale in Chapter 12, if standard units move R, fast ones 2R and ranged units fire 2R-3R, we clearly want armies to be more than R distance from each other at the start of a game to ensure that the faster units have a purpose and an advantage in our game. In this hypothetical game, we might prefer that armies begin a minimum of 3R apart with the option of a deep enough deployment zone to begin 4R apart to allow for a variety of strategic approaches. Defining standard deployment zones can be done as easily as deciding how far apart the forces should start, positioning this no man's land centrally across the centre line of the table, and allowing any remaining tabletop to form the deployment zones.

OTHER DEPLOYMENT ZONES

Two opposing strips of deployment zones have many advantages. They are commonly encountered, easily understood, simple to set up, physically convenient (players don't have to reach across the tabletop during setup) and instantly create a clear narrative for players: this is my territory, that is yours. However, such clearly opposed opening lines of conflict can have the effect of directing players towards simple destruction as their primary tactic. If the narrative of your game is something other than direct and relentless conflict, standard deployment zones can conspire with player habits to undermine your design intent. Furthermore, even if direct and relentless conflict is the primary focus of your game, you may find that experimenting with setups other than both forces beginning as flat lines stretching across the table in direct opposition leads to more interesting and dynamic conflicts. Managing pincer movements, enfilading fire, or rolling up a flank become rarer when just breaking a line can end a game session. As such, it can be valuable to investigate a range of different deployment zones. There are an almost infinite variety of ways of shaping deployment zones, and we'll only cover a few here. It is sufficient to say that experimentation can be worthwhile and that so long as all your players' models get onto the table and you understand the implications of the potential range of available opening distances and configurations of units in any available setup, all are potentially valid.

DIFFERENT SHAPES

Most deployment zones are a strip of some depth along the longest available table edge; any significant variation on this shape can offer significant variation in play. L-shaped zones, including a second table edge, can open flanking deployments and enfilading fire options; a zone with a spur into the table can allow for vanguard actions or more effective defence in depth deployment.

SPLIT DEPLOYMENT ZONES

A deployment zone can be split into a number of contiguous parts, with players forced to deploy certain units in each sub-zone to provide interesting constraints.

Another option is to split a player's deployment zone across several non-contiguous areas of the tabletop. For example, if players are required to deploy in strips that alternate with their opponents, interesting and dynamic pockets of conflict can develop.

CASE STUDY: EXTREME SPLIT DEPLOYMENT – *MALIFAUX*

In the narrative skirmish game *Malifaux*'s second edition (Anderson *et al.*, 2013), an option for 'Blind Deployment' is offered: a deck of cards is constructed with one card for each model to be deployed and each player having a colour randomly designated to them (so a player designated black with seven models would contribute seven black cards). The deck is shuffled, and then players take turns deploying cards without looking at their faces. The cards are then flipped, and players take turns deploying one of their models anywhere on each of their cards. Essentially, their deployment zones have been split into as many pieces as they have models and spread across the table. An extreme solution, but one that we have found to create exciting and memorable stories.

ASYMMETRICAL DEPLOYMENT ZONES

One of the fastest methods of creating a tabletop narrative is through the use of asymmetrical deployment zones. The iconic example is for one force to deploy in a central position while their opponent deploys surrounding them, such as found in the scenario 'Forenrond's Last Stand' in *Warhammer Fantasy Battle* (third edition) (Priestley, Halliwell and Ansell, 1987). Another common approach is to constrict the deployment of one force while granting their opponent much greater latitude, as found in the scenario 'Battle At The Farm' in *Warhammer 40,000 Rogue Trader* (Priestley, 1987). Depending on the system, the effects of such asymmetrical deployment zones can range from minor narrative flavour to significantly affecting the balance of the game. As a general rule, if a game gives bonuses to flank or rear engagement or has a lot of powerful shooting, a player with a more widely spread deployment zone will have an advantage over a more narrowly confined one. This can be evened out by offering the confined player defensive structures, a points advantage or asymmetrical victory conditions.

SHARED DEPLOYMENT ZONES

A more unusual method is to create some form of shared deployment zone. *Gaslands* (Hutchinson, 2017) simulates violent car races; as such, it has a shared deployment zone in the form of a starting grid where players alternate the placement of vehicles in rows, ensuring immediate player interaction from the first activation. Shared deployment zones generally suit a system whose primary victory conditions are not the destruction of enemy units, such as reaching or controlling a certain part of the tabletop; otherwise, the game will tend towards an immediate and potentially stagnant brawl. If your game values non-destructive victory conditions, shared deployment zones are worth considering for their ability to create immediate player interaction and dynamic play.

Unanchored Deployment Zones

Pre-defined deployment zones allow for clear designer-created tabletop narratives, but they can restrict player freedom, reduce game variability and restrict player-created narratives. As an alternative, players can be given the means to define their own deployment zones by placing a marker and deploying units anywhere within a given distance of the marker, or by dynamically defining a deployment zone with markers or models and deploying units within that 'safe-zone'. The primary difficulty in unanchored deployment systems is giving players a sufficient sense of the game's strategic shape at the start of the game session so that they can be confident in making such a significant choice before a single model arrives on the table.

CASE STUDY: UNANCHORED DEPLOYMENT – *A BILLION SUNS*

A Billion Suns (Hutchinson, 2021) does not provide predefined deployment zones. Instead, it asks players to place a token anywhere on the table and use the area within a certain distance of that token as their deployment zone. This novelty is explained to players in that, since *A Billion Suns* is a deep-space sci-fi fleet battle game, the tokens represent interstellar jump gates. It has the added bonus that once deployment zones are detached from specific parts of a table, play need not be restricted to a single table, allowing multiple tables representing multiple battlezones to be used during play.

SUMMARY

- Define the size of the **Playing area**, which will affect game length and rhythm.
  - Define what happens when units encounter its edge.
- Consider **Terrain** amount and types, which can be:
  - **Sight blocking**, shaping firing lanes and charge arcs.
  - **Movement channelling**, guiding the speed of the game.
  - **Interactive**, creating central and peripheral objectives.
- Define **Deployment zones** creating:
  - Game length, by setting the distance between forces.
  - Narrative, by setting the relationship between forces, with zones being:
    - Unusually shaped, rather than table-long strips.
    - Split, rather than one per player.
    - Asymmetrical, rather than identical.
    - Shared, rather than one per player.
    - Unanchored, rather than defined by the scenario.

EXPERIMENTS

If your game's playing area is 9′ square or less, double it; if it is more, halve it. If your game plays on a square, make it a rectangle with the same volume; if it is already a rectangle, make it square.

Create a shape that is not used for your game to define its deployment zones; use it instead of its existing zones.

Give each player one additional deployment zone, separated from the standard one by at least one full move.

Give one player a deployment zone double the area of their opponent. Have one player deploy in the middle of the play area and the other on any edge of it.

Give each player a token to set on the table before play, centre their deployment zone on the token, make this zone circular, then share. Make these deployment zones unable to overlap, then make them able to overlap. Make them static, then allow each player to move them after deploying half of their forces, then force each player to move them.

REFERENCES

Anderson, M., Caroland, N., Cohen, R., Darland, A., Gibbs, J., Hanold, D., Johns, E., Martin, M. and Weber, D. (2013) *Malifaux: Second Edition*. South Korea: Wyrd Miniatures, LLC.

Cavatore, A., Pirinen, T., Priestley, R., Stillman, N. and Thornton, J. (2000) *Warhammer: The game of fantasy battles*. 6th edn. Nottingham: Games Workshop Ltd.

Featherstone, D. (1965) *Naval War Games*. London: Stanley Paul.

Hutchinson, M. (2017) *Gaslands*. Oxford: Osprey Games.

Hutchinson, M. (2021) *A Billion Suns*. Oxford: Osprey Games.

Leaton, S. (2000) *Fairy Meat*. Waukegan: Kenzer and Company.

Priestley, R. (1987) *Warhammer 40,000 Rogue Trader*. Nottingham: Games Workshop Ltd.

Priestley, R., Halliwell, R. and Ansell, B. (1987) *Warhammer Fantasy Battles*. 3rd edn. Nottingham: Games Workshop Ltd.

Vogel, J. (2010) *ZynVaded!* Fargo: We have issues! Publishing.

19 Activation and Initiative

Once units are deployed onto a well-laid-out battlefield, we need to know who gets to activate what when. We need rules for deciding which player goes first in a given game round and in what manner they activate their units.

ROUNDS, TURNS AND ACTIVATIONS

When playing a game with six game turns, each of which can have two player turns, during which players take turns to move their models, during which movement they might change direction using turns. It becomes clear that the word 'turn' is problematic in our context. Let us agree on some standard terminology: we play a game system during a game session. A single **game session** consists of a number of game turns, which we refer to as **rounds**. Within a single round, there are a number of **player turns**, or turns. During those player turns, the player usually activates one or more of their units, each being an **activation**. During one player's turn, the other player is inactive, experiencing **downtime**. Using this terminology, we can have a session of a (hypothetical) system in which we play six rounds of two turns each, during which one player completes all their units' activations before their opponent has a turn to activate theirs and the round concludes.

ROUND STRUCTURE, PHASES AND DOWNTIME

In our experience, most non-discrete game systems break the game session into between three and ten rounds, after which a victor is decided. It is common to break the rounds and/or player turns into **phases**. Phases are a way of providing a structure, either within a player's turn or spanning across them. Breaking gameplay into phases allows players to focus on one part of the system (for example, the movement rules or combat rules) at a time, allowing them to confidently ignore large chunks of your system's complexity during a given phase. In a system in which a unit has full freedom to complete any supported action during their activation, the player will have to hold a much larger proportion of your system in their head as they reason about and then enact their unit's activation. This may be desirable for your game, or it may not.

The structure of your rounds should consider four key elements: handover, downtime, resolution order and flow and complexity budget.

The more discrete gameplay chunks you break your gameplay into, the more times players will have to handover control of the game. Each time a player hands over control of the game, there is an opportunity for the pace of the game to drop and for the game time to be extended.

While smaller chunks of gameplay increase player hand-over moments, they also decrease the duration of each chunk of downtime. Downtime is the negative space that surrounds gameplay. Large chunks of downtime carry the risk that a player will

DOI: 10.1201/9781003314820-23

become disengaged from the game, potentially becoming distracted, losing context and exiting their flow state. This can lead to slower handovers as the distracted player re-engages with the board state and thus increases the other player's downtime.

When designing gameplay phases and round structure, it is important to consider the flow of the game state and how and where you want players to be able to change the game state or act on those changes. This can be as much a narrative concern as a mechanical one: do you want the cinematic image of bowmen shooting at the enemy warriors as they charge in, or do you want the thundering charge to be the first narrative beat in your game round? The order in which the sub-systems in your game are resolved in the game round can be very impactful on the feel of the game and which unit abilities and sub-systems are important. If your round structure allows a strong unit to move and attack before any enemy unit, the 'highly-mobile glass cannon' type unit may well be more effective in your game than in a game in which all movement is completed before fighting.

PLAYER INITIATIVE

Player initiative refers to which player chooses to act first in any given round. Since activating a unit can often eliminate threats or achieve objectives, activating first can be a significant advantage and how the first player to activate is chosen can be significant. This can be designated in one of several fashions but tends to split out into **random**, **earnt**, **bought** or a mix thereof, and can be **static** or **shifting**.

RANDOM INITIATIVE

Random initiative is selecting the player to go first in some random fashion, usually a dice roll, coin toss or card flip. Commonly, when player order is random, it is also **static**, which is to say that the order decided during set-up is maintained throughout the game. If you are designing a game with **shifting** initiative, such that the player order can change from round to round, you might consider making the initiative semi-random. For example, in *The Lord of the Rings Strategy Battle Game* (Cavatore and Ward, 2005), a dice roll is made each turn, but the player who did not have initiative on the previous turn wins ties.

EARNT INITIATIVE

Earnt initiative is any system where a player's actions during the game can earn them initiative on a given turn. For example, in *Dracula's America* (Haythornwaite, 2017), players select and play cards from their hand to decide initiative order, sacrificing the ability to play higher scoring cards later in a round in return for an earlier activation than their opponent. Earnt initiative is commonly shifting, although, if triggered by an in-game state, it can become static for a short time. For example, in the 'Death Race' scenario of *Gaslands* (Hutchinson, 2017), player initiative is passed only when the player with the initiative crosses through a race gate, resulting in an initiative that shifts irregularly based on player actions. You should consider whether earnt initiative is available to all players equally in your game, should they decide to aim for it, perhaps by spending some sort of fungible in-game resource, so players need to choose initiative over other valuable options. In *7TV* (Dawson and Perrotton, 2010), players are permitted the chance to activate twice in succession, but only once per 'Chapter' of the game. Spending this chance at the right time can be the difference between victory and defeat.

BOUGHT INITIATIVE

Bought initiative is where a player uses their force building options for an initiative advantage. In *Star Wars: X-Wing The Miniatures Game* (Little, 2012), the skill of different pilots, purchased before the game begins, decides the order in which players will act within certain phases of the game. This can allow for additional balancing options among forces, although it should be noted that since any initiative value or bonus is predominantly a relative value between factions or forces, it can be difficult to price fairly. Bought initiative can be combined with random shifting initiative, as in *Epic Armageddon* (Johnson, 2003), in which your faction provides a strategy rating, which is a number that you add to your initiative dice roll each round.

HYBRID INITIATIVE SYSTEMS

It is possible to have a system that ties together all of these options into a complex, shifting initiative system. For example, in *Malifaux* (Anderson *et al.,* 2013) players flip a card to decide initiative randomly but can then spend a card from their hand to replace the flipped card, creating an earnt initiative event. Additionally, they can purchase units that give a bonus to the initiative flip or that can allow for two consecutive player activations, including a bought element.

Many games deal with initiative in a perfunctory manner, defaulting to a basic random static or random shifting system. While this may be appropriate for some games, you should examine this default when designing your game. The determination of the first player can potentially have a big impact on the game session, perhaps swinging the game significantly to one player, and having that impact result from a coin toss can leave a certain kind of player cold. It is our opinion that it is no coincidence that a successful break-out game like *Malifaux* has such a rich initiative system.

ACTIVATIONS

Once a player is chosen to take their turn, the first thing to know is how many of their units they can activate before passing the turn. There are three usual methods of allowing players to activate their units: **Full Force Activation, Partial Force Activation** and **Single Unit Activation**.

Full Force Activation is commonly referred to as 'I go, you go' or 'IGOUGO', and Single Unit Activation tends to be known as 'Alternating Activations'. However, since all activation systems feature an alternation of activations in which first I go and then you go, the common parlance terms are synonyms. For this reason, we choose to use new, unambiguous terms that make the scope of the exchange of activations clearer.

FULL FORCE ACTIVATION

In a Full Force Activation system, players take turns activating all of the units they have available and then pass play to their opponent to do the same. This system is commonly found in mass battle games, such as *Warhammer Fantasy Battle* (Cavatore *et al.*, 2000), where each player will activate all their units in a turn. The primary advantage of Full Force Activation systems is that they allow for strategic play. Plans can be formulated and put into action on a grander scale with less interference from an opponent. For example, unit movements may be coordinated and executed across an entire force, allowing units to support each other and combine their force in a way that is more difficult or risky in Single Unit Activation systems.

If you want to enable your players to enact complex and holistic strategy plays, you may wish to consider an activation system in which players activate a good proportion of their army in an uninterrupted manner. This can be Full Force Activation, or Partial Force Activation, wherein a player activates a set number of units or a division of their army (perhaps determined during the force-building step). *Warhammer 40,000 Apocalypse* (2019) sees players organise their units into a handful of detachments during force construction, and the players take turns to activate a single detachment each in the game's activation phase.

A perceived disadvantage of Full Force Activation systems is that they have a lot of downtime – periods in which a player is inactive within the game. In actuality, though, while these systems have large blocks of downtime, they have relatively few moments of player hand-over, meaning that time lost to players re-calibrating on having play returned to them is relatively low, so there is often actually less overall player downtime in these systems than in Partial Force Activation systems.

To combat the sense of downtime, games with a Full Force Activation system will often ask players to engage with mechanics such as making rolls to save their models from elimination. When considering the inclusion of such a mechanic, you should examine if it is important to your game that it provides moments of decision-making for the inactive player or if it is acceptable that they are simply completing a mechanical resolution task.

CASE STUDY: INTERRUPTIBLE FULL FORCE ACTIVATION – *BLOOD BOWL*

Blood Bowl (Johnson, 1994) is a popular game representing a fantasy version of American Football which uses a Full Force Activation system in which each player activates their entire team in a turn. However, if an individual team member fails an action, the turn is interrupted, and play passes to their opponent. This results in players needing to carefully judge and order their activations to achieve the maximum potential for a turn.

The biggest issue with Full Force Activation games is that the ability to activate an entire force allows a more strategically competent player to leave an opponent unable to respond after a single powerful turn, commonly referred to as an 'alpha-strike'. In such cases, the first player is able to pass a game state to their opponent that is so overwhelmingly against them as to be essentially unrecoverable. Indeed, if the first player can remove just a single unit from their opponent's side of the tabletop with the use of their entire army on their first activation, then the opponent's initial activation is with a lesser force, creating the first step of a possible spiral towards defeat.

CASE STUDY: DEFANGING ALPHA-STRIKES – *WARHAMMER 40,000 APOCALYPSE*

The *Warhammer 40,000 Apocalypse* rulebook laments: 'every wargamer has experienced that moment of dismay as they watched their lovingly built and painted centrepiece model removed as a casualty before it has a chance to fire a shot'. This mass battle system deals with the issue of alpha-strikes by moving the resolution of damage into model-removal to the final phase of the game round after all unit activations are complete. This allows all the units that began the round to contribute to the change of game state, even if they sustain mortal damage during the round.

SINGLE UNIT ACTIVATION

In a Single Unit Activation system, players take turns activating a subset of their units before passing play to their opponent, usually repeating this process until all units have activated before beginning a new round. Often, players are permitted to activate just a single unit each time, although many systems will offer methods of activating two or more units before passing play. Single Unit Activation systems can give a greater sense of player activity and reduce the perception of downtime; however, due to the increased number of player hand-over moments, Single Unit Activation systems can actually increase downtime and extend gametime.

A key consideration with Single Unit Activation systems is that they lead to a relatively minor exchange of incremental game state change after each player turn, creating commensurately simplistic tactical questions rather than more strategic ones. When a player can only activate a single unit at a time and they are aware that their opponent can immediately make a similar activation, their thinking can often, of necessity, become purely tactical. They identify the biggest threat or greatest priority objective and the unit they have capable of dealing with it directly, activate and deal with it, rinse and repeat until the game is over. You can mitigate this by providing mechanics to stop players from being able to freely activate the unit of their choice, forcing them to prioritise differently and make interestingly tactically sub-optimal choices. There are many ways to approach this, and we outline some of the more common approaches below: pull systems, push your luck systems, programmed activations and unreliable order systems.

Pull Systems

Another way of orchestrating unit activations is to assign a set of physical items, such as dice or tokens, to them and then those items can be randomly pulled to select a unit to activate next. *Test of Honour* (Davey, 2017) uses a **pull system**, a bag containing a set of tokens representing either a character, a unit, miss a turn or end the round. Players take turns pulling tokens and activating units until the round ends. Players do not know if they will be able to activate a character or a unit next, or if they will get to activate all their units at all. *Bolt Action* (Cavatore and Priestly, 2012) has each player place as many coloured dice as they have units into a container; the colour pulled indicates which player gets to activate next. Unlike *Test of Honour*, where both players share a set of chits and players always alternate turns, *Bolt Action* can allow a player to activate multiple units in a row if their dice are pulled, increasing the uncertainty of the tactical situation, although it guarantees a player will be allowed to activate all their units at some point during the turn. Similar to pulling an item from a bag, cards featuring units can be shuffled into a deck, either shared or individually for each player, and then drawn to show the unit to be activated.

Push Your Luck

In *Song of Blades and Heroes* (Sfiligoi, 2007), players may roll between one and three dice to see how many activations they will have, aiming to score more than the quality of the units they are activating, but if they roll two or more failures, they miss their turn. One dice is a safe choice; two or more is a player pushing their luck and can lead to unexpectedly missed activations. This sort of system can be interesting since it taps into player psychology, but it can lead a game away from purely tactical play since if a player loses an activation due to bad luck, they can feel more driven to attempt further activations to replace their missed chance. Psychology can be interesting, but it can be hard to control.

Programmed Activations

In *Dropfleet Commander* (Chambers, 2016), players begin the turn by arranging a stack of cards, each representing one of their units. This creates a fixed order in which the units will activate, created in the knowledge of the starting game state, but not the order in which their opponent will activate their units. Players reveal the top cards from their two activation decks, and the unit with the higher strategy rating gets to act first. Once both revealed units have activated, the players reveal the next two cards. This provides a Single Unit Activation system containing elements of bought, random and shifting initiative systems, presented using tactile game components.

Conversely, while in *Star Wars: X-Wing Miniatures Game* (Little, 2012), the unit activation order is mostly known, thanks to a bought initiative system (with a random tie-breaker mechanic), players are asked to use cardboard dials to select all their units' movement actions before the first unit is activated. So, the content of activations is selected simultaneously and with incomplete information, creating a satisfying guessing game for both players as well as the opportunity for unexpected moves to create enjoyable chaos.

Unreliable Orders

Various game systems use mechanics to simulate the uncertainty of orders being given across a chaotic battlefield. These have the advantage of both obscuring immediate tactical choices and creating a simulationist effect.

The usual method of simulating battlefield command is to designate a certain number of character models as commanders with a 'command range', a distance in inches over which they can exert their influence. Units within the command range of a character will then activate at the same time as that commander; those outside of all of their side's command ranges will activate last and will often require passing a test to do so. Furthermore, the number of units a given commander can activate may be limited, as may the number and complexity of orders they can give. This sort of command range system means players must select movement ordering and placement based on the longer term strategic concerns of maintaining a network of command as well as applying pressure to their opponent.

In addition, orders can have degrees of complexity; the skill of a commander and the training level of those ordered can be used to find the likelihood of the order being carried out correctly. In addition, a penalty can be attached for failed orders, ranging from ending a player's activations for a turn or adding negative modifiers for following order attempts to forcing units to make disadvantageous activations. In each case, players need to choose between vital or advantageous but unlikely orders or less useful ones that are likely to succeed.

Activation Advantage

The significant design challenge with Single Unit Activation systems is activation advantage. If we imagine a game with asymmetrical forces where one player is controlling a group of elite knights while the other controls poorly trained goblins, then we would assume that the goblin player has significantly more models than their opponent. If we also assume that if directly and simply opposed in combat, the two forces would be fairly balanced, then it tends to follow that the goblins actually have a huge advantage due to activation advantage.

If a given player has more models than their opponent, then they can activate less important or expendable models first, allowing them to see everything their opponent is planning or doing before activating their most important models, gaining an advantage. In addition, if the victory conditions are based around completing objectives, they generally require simply the presence of a unit or basic actions to be achieved, meaning that whoever activates most or last has an advantage in scoring them. This is exacerbated as a problem since, as mentioned above, one of the issues of Single Unit Activation is that players need to act tactically rather than strategically. If one player has a clump of unopposed activations, they can begin to act more strategically, as they essentially play half of their turn under Single Unit Activations and half under a Full Force Activation system, and so gain both the chance for more long-term options and advantages and even enjoy the game on a deeper level, making activation advantage both powerful and enjoyable for players that attempt to leverage it and so causing an excessive amount of the game to be about seeking it out.

The most basic fix for activation advantage is to allow the player with fewer activations to pass the chance to activate should they wish, then they can reserve the number of activations they believe necessary to counteract their opponent's until the end of the round. A more complex but satisfying solution is to use push-your-luck or order systems as outlined above. Elite commanders being able to activate their units more reliably or issue more complex commands can balance out the more numerous but unreliable or basic activations of less sophisticated forces. A final solution is to give each force an equal number of activations, which they can spread as they wish around their units. The less elite force still has the bodies to absorb more damage and outlast their opponents, but cannot directly out-activate them.

TIMING SIMULATIONS

As an aside, there is a potential debate over which of the two overarching systems best simulates the nature of simultaneous actions in a turn-based system. That is to say, in a given instant during a conflict, all participants will be acting at the same time, while on the tabletop, this is generally impossible. There are arguments either way. Full Force Activation systems have entire armies standing and watching while multiple opponents speed towards them across the battlefield. They benefit from units at least advancing shoulder to shoulder with allies in a relatively simulationist fashion. They can create a situation where armies appear to move in waves of alternating assault and defence, which does have a cinematic logic if nothing else. On the other hand, while Single Unit Activation systems mean that it is never very long before a unit reacts to the opponent's actions, it can also mean that an individual unit apparently moving at the same time as an ally can see said ally move, assault and be repeatedly counterassaulted before they physically move at all.

Charge systems, particularly in hybrid systems, can go a long way towards exacerbating or alleviating this issue, as we will outline in Chapter 21. Suffice to say for now that it is worth considering whether a unit that has been moving at full pace across the battlefield should suddenly be considered totally stationary and 'receiving the charge' simply because another unit had initiative on the turn that they came within movement distance of each other.

HYBRID SYSTEMS

Many of the weaknesses of Full Force Activation and Single Unit Activation systems are exacerbated by player turns and unit activations being played out in their entirety. As such, an effective alternative is to split rounds into phases within which players take turns with activations only able to perform actions suitable to the current phase. For example, a round could contain a movement phase during which each player moves all of their units and a combat phase during which each player fights with their units, such that all units move before any units fight. This effectively removes the possibility of a superior unit picking out a weaker unit in an unbalanced encounter and means no units need to begin their journey to a given location side by side with another and reach it long after the other unit has not only arrived but been hacked to death. Phased systems with Single Unit Activations can result in significant downtime since they split up pre-existing activations, increasing the number of handover points. However, they allow for relatively painless Full Force Activation by eliminating first-strike problems while significantly limiting downtime blocks and still allowing for a good deal of strategic thinking. *Hobgoblin: Brutal Fantasy Battles* (Hutchinson, 2024) structures its game rounds into phases – movement, magic, missile, melee and morale – and then asks players to alternate the activation of their entire force in each phase. Balancing the number of player 'hand-over' moments with maintaining the engagement of regular back-and-forth play and not leaving players inactive for extended periods. An added and elegant bonus is that moving first during a movement phase is a disadvantage, while attacking first in the combat phase is an advantage, significantly lessening the problems of initiative assignment. *Last Days* (Barker, 2018) features Single Unit Activations within a phase-based hybrid system, such that each player takes turns activating a single model for movement and non-combat actions, then takes turns shooting and finally alternates close combat. However, when initiative is decided by a roll off, one player is designated the 'Aggressor' and one the 'Defender'; the aggressor activates first in the non-combat and close combat phases, while the defender activates first in the shooting phase. This means that overly aggressive movement can result in exposure to excessive shooting and discourage outright, unanswered aggression.

CASE STUDY: PARTIAL FORCE ACTIVATION – *FROSTGRAVE*

In *Frostgrave* (McCullogh, 2015), players take part in wizard-led warbands raiding a frozen city for esoteric treasures. It uses a hybrid system where players take turns activating their wizard and up to three troopers within three inches of the wizard, then repeating the process with the wizard's apprentice and finally activating all remaining troopers. The result is relatively little handover time, but by effectively splitting a Full Force Activation system through three blocks throughout a turn, the ability to strike without response is significantly reduced. Additionally, positioning troopers within the wizard or apprentice's activation bubble offers players an interesting additional puzzle.

FUNGIBLE ACTIVATION POINTS

Activation Point systems are common in skirmish games, generally providing each unit with a number of 'activation points' (or AP) to spend during a unit's activation, with various actions such as movement or shooting costing a certain number of AP. However, *Infinity* (Liste, Rodríguez and Torres, 2005) uses a force-wide Fungible Activation Point system by providing each force with a number of AP that can be shared unevenly across a force as the player wishes. By providing players with a single pool of fungible resources to designate activations, each tactical activation becomes inherently linked to an overall strategy. Spending points on one model, or early in a round, can leave other models without the chance to react to developments.

SIMULTANEOUS ACTIVATION

Simultaneous activation systems are rare in non-discrete tabletop games. Simultaneous selection of orders, activation sequence or actions is the closest most have come to simultaneous play, such as the secretly designated movement choices in *Star Wars: X-Wing Miniatures Game*, which provide a sense of simultaneous action since all major decisions were made with a vision of a single game state.

The most immediate challenge with simultaneous activation systems in a non-discrete setting is the physical requirement to move models fairly and accurately and to make subsequent adjudications of range or line of sight in a mutually acceptable manner. As discussed elsewhere, we have – as players of these sorts of games – established reasonable social etiquette around such areas, and the potentially frenetic nature of simultaneous activation would potentially require clear guidelines for new etiquette.

Initiatives can be designated by speed or dexterity systems. Players could be asked to programme actions, either by open or hidden systems, with the player who finishes first taking the first activation, allowing for initiative to come as a reward for forward-planning or simplicity of strategy. One can imagine using this with either of the previously discussed programmed activation mechanics above. In particular, manipulation of tactile physical components could become a dexterity or speed-calculation mechanic, such as creating a stack of dice the fastest or completing a sequence of cards.

EXCHANGE OF GAME STATE

Player turns can be seen in terms of an exchange of game state: as a player, I take actions to modify the game state, and then I hand control over to you, hopefully having created a game state that presents a tactical or strategic puzzle for you to overcome. A game in which the player is permitted to change a significant amount of the game state before passing play to their opponent can feel more strategic and premeditated, but may feel more passive and unengaging for the inactive player. A game in which the player is permitted to only change a small amount of game state before passing play makes it harder for a player to set up complex strategic puzzles for their opponent and will likely feel more tactical and reactive but also more immediate and urgent. The choice of activation system will greatly influence the feel of your game and the balance of strategic and tactical concerns it presents to your players.

SUMMARY

- A **Game session** is a series of **Rounds** which may break down into **Phases** and consist of player **Turns** where units have **Activations**, between which players suffer **Downtime**.
- The **Initiative** of which player goes first can be:
  - **Random** usually this is **Static**, staying with one player as opposed to **Shifting**.
  - **Earnt** by player actions during play.
  - **Bought** during army list construction.
- During activations, players might activate all units as a **Full Force Activation** system or only some of their units in a **Single Unit Activation** system. These can be combined in a **Hybrid** system.
- In partial activation systems, units can be chosen by:
  - **Pull systems**, picking random tokens to indicate activations.
  - **Push your luck**, where players test for additional activations.
  - **Programmed activations**, pre-selecting activations, asking players to plan and predict.
  - **Unreliable order**, basing activations on proximity to commander units.

EXPERIMENTS

If your game uses a static initiative system, repeat the selection process at the start of each turn to make it shifting; if it is shifting, maintain it from turn one to become static. If initiative is not chosen randomly, make it randomly chosen; if it is randomly chosen, give it to the player with the least spent points on the table, then to the last player to cause a wound.

If your game uses a Full Force Activation system, try it with a Single Unit Activation system, and vice versa.

Using a Single Unit Activation system, divide units into general types and assign each type a range of cards. Assign a colour to each player and shuffle up an appropriate number of cards and flip to select a unit. Try again with each player stacking their own deck at the start of the game or whenever it becomes exhausted.

Using a Single Unit Activation system, whenever a player activates a unit, they may choose to activate up to three. They then roll three dice; if they get at least as many 3+ as the number of units they selected, they can activate them; if not, they lose their turn.

REFERENCES

Anderson, M., Caroland, N., Cohen, R., Darland, A., Gibbs, J., Hanold, D., Johns, E., Martin, M. and Weber, D. (2013) *Malifaux: Second Edition*. South Korea: Wyrd Miniatures, LLC.

Barker, A. (2018) *Last Days: Zombie Apocalypse*. Oxford: Osprey Games.

Cavatore, A., Pirinen, T., Priestley, R., Stillman, N. and Thornton, J. (2000) *Warhammer: The Game of Fantasy Battles*. 6th edn. Nottingham: Games Workshop Ltd.

Cavatore, A and Priestly, R. (2012) *Bolt Action!* Oxford: Osprey Games.

Cavatore, A. and Ward, M. (2005) *The Lord of the Rings: Strategy Battle Game*. Nottingham: Games Workshop Ltd.

Chambers, A. (2016) *Dropfleet Commander*. Croydon: Hawk Wargames.

Davey, G. (2017) *Test of Honour*. [Boardgame] Nottingham: Warlord Games.

Dawson, G. and Perrotton, K. (2010) *7TV*. Lincolnshire: Crooked Dice Game Design Studio.

Haythornwaite, J. (2017) *Dracula's America: Shadows of the West*. Oxford: Osprey Games.

Hutchinson, M. (2017) *Gaslands*. Oxford: Osprey Games.

Hutchinson, M. (2024) *Hobgoblin: Brutal Fantasy Battles*. Santa Rosa, CA: Electi Studio.

Johnson, J. (1994) *Blood Bowl*. 3rd edn. [Boardgame] Nottingham: Games Workshop Ltd.

Johnson, J. (2003) *Epic Armageddon*. Nottingham: Games Workshop Ltd.

Liste, F. Rodríguez, G. and Torres, C. (2005) *Infinity N3: Core Book*. Cangas, Galicia: Corvus Belli.

Little, J. (2012) *Star Wars: X-Wing Miniatures Game*. [Board game] Roseville, MN: Fantasy Flight Games.

McCullogh, J. (2015) *Frostgrave*. Oxford: Osprey Games.

Sfiligoi, A. (2007) *Song of Blades and Heroes*. Kharkiv, Ukraine: Ganesha Games.

Warhammer 40,000 Apocalypse. (2019) Nottingham: Games Workshop Ltd.

20 Movement

Once a set of miniatures is deployed across a well-defined tabletop, we need rules defining how to move them. Systems might forgo shooting, lines of sight, close combat or victory conditions, but it is hard to imagine one that doesn't include movement. Movement is often one of the most interesting and involved elements of a game, and the mechanisms you provide to deal with it will define a lot of its gameplay interest. Every design is challenged with representing the continual, simultaneous and fluid process of movement using the asynchronous 'stop motion' mechanisms required for manageable gameplay. Abstraction and representation are inevitable, and your task as a designer is to choose where to allow the abstract and representative to be in plain sight and where they are artfully concealed. For movement, you must first decide how it will be measured and defined.

TAPE MEASURES

Probably the most usual method of defining how far a particular unit can move on the tabletop is to give it a statistic representing speed and allow players to move it that far in a chosen unit of measurement. These systems usually either offer freedom to change direction at will during movement or provide mechanisms to turn or pivot. This approach is used by a wide range of games, such as *Warhammer: The Game of Fantasy Battles* (Cavatore *et al.*, 2000), *Infinity* (Couceiro *et al.*, 2014) and *Malifaux* (Anderson *et al.*, 2013). Being widely used, it is familiar to the average tabletop miniatures gamer, and most will be unsurprised by tropes such as double-movement for marching or running and half-movement through difficult terrain. It allows for flexibility in unit design since they can have any value given for movement, which can be increased or decreased by game effects. It provides flexibility during play, as players can move models across the table in a wide range of ways.

In play, the speed statistic is translated to a distance, and that distance must be measured at the table. Flexible tape measures are overwhelmingly the most common tool deployed by gamers for this task. However, tape measures can create arguments. They are clumsy and difficult to place such that measurements can be made accurately. It is rarely possible to lay one flat on the tabletop and keep it locked in place until a miniature moves to its other end; usually, it will be hovered some distance above the heads of miniatures as they are pushed along underneath as accurately as honest players can manage. Measuring movement along an arc must be approximated or made in short straight-line sections (Figure 20.1). Should a player wish to reconsider a move, returning a model to its starting point accurately to re-attempt movement is a regular source of player disagreement. Since the tape measure is being held, bobbing above the tabletop, during movement, removed and reapplied for the reversal of choices, the accuracy of the return is even less likely than that of the initial movement (Figures 20.2 and 20.3). The result is that tape-measured movements are rarely exact, difficult to verify (relying on mutual trust

DOI: 10.1201/9781003314820-24

FIGURE 20.1 Measuring a smooth curve with a metal tape measure can be challenging. Photograph by the author.

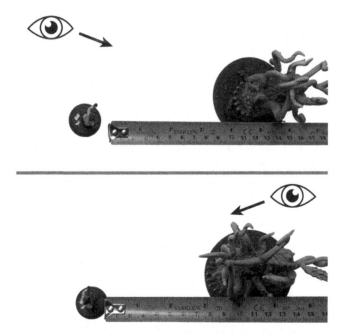

FIGURE 20.2 Same position, same measure and same models, but different perspectives give very different results. Photograph by the author.

Tape measure held low

Tape measure held high

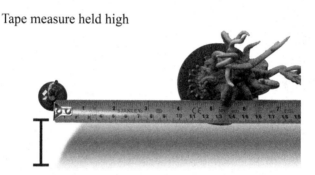

FIGURE 20.3   From a single perspective, raising and lowering the tape measure results in very different measurements. Photograph by the author.

between players) and nearly impossible to revert accurately if a player changes their mind (Figure 20.4).

For a designer looking to capture the widest audience possible, it should be noted that tape measures can put off players not already entranced with the world of non-discrete games; they suggest both a pernickety obsession with accuracy and a tendency to create inaccuracy that is bewildering to many people. The requirement to use one can also seem unexpected and alien to those used to discrete board games in which the key components for play are provided in the box.

CASE STUDY: PRE-SET DISTANCES – *SAGA*

An interesting option is to have all distances in the game based on pre-set distances, such as very short, short, medium and long. *Saga* (Buchel, 2011) does this, and the result is that players can dispense with tape measures in favour of a selection of pre-cut measuring sticks. This allows for the measuring device to be inserted between miniatures rather than floated above them for greater accuracy while still allowing non-discrete movements.

FIGURE 20.4   They're probably five inches apart, but it's hard to be certain. Photograph by the author.

MOVEMENT TEMPLATES

A less common form of defining movement is to use movement templates, such as those seen in *X-Wing: The Miniatures Game* (Little, 2012) or *Gaslands* (Hutchinson, 2017) (Figure 20.5). Mechanically, a template is laid touching part of a miniature's base, and movement is then defined by the physical shape of the template by having the miniature picked up and placed in relation to the template. This can increase the

FIGURE 20.5   Gaslands template. Photograph by the author.

barrier of entry for new players (or for the game manufacturer) versus a tape-measure system, as the game-specific templates must be either provided as part of the game product or left to the player to procure or manufacture themselves. It avoids many of the arguments that tape-measurement systems entail, since a template can remain in place or be easily returned to reverse movement.

Template-based movement systems can be more intuitive and approachable for non-gamers than general-purpose tape measures, since they can be designed both to fit neatly the needs of your game and to communicate rules information in context. The physical template provides a canvas to provide additional information or 'user-interface' for the players, summarising key rules, using iconography to high-light game effects, or using graphic elements to convey complex things (like geometry) in intuitive visual ways.

A significant advantage of templates is that they can be left on the table once placed, allowing for movements to be reset effectively if needed and potentially a temporal picture to be built up over a turn. Modelling the narrative assumption that all units on a tabletop are moving simultaneously is difficult, but laying templates across the table first and moving units later is one way this can be simulated.

Templates suffer from certain disadvantages, chiefly that they provide a finite number of movement options, potentially shared across units, removing some interesting non-discrete choices. To replace this, your design can restrict or open up the range of templates available to units based on factors such as inherent manoeuvrability (such as in *X-Wing: The Miniatures Game*) or current speed (such as in *Gaslands*). The discrete nature of movement templates requires that altered movement rates, such as when marching or moving through difficult terrain, have novel mechanics created to represent them and this can afford less intuitive or familiar options than the mechanics of 'tape measure-based' systems. The fixed size and shape of a movement template can prove awkward in play when compared to the flexibility of a tape measure. When attempting to navigate a dense play space, particularly during small or partial movements, the inflexibility of the movement template may introduce frustration with requirements to hold the template over models where it would normally be put flat on the tabletop or to slide the template under intervening models and terrain, introducing opportunities for inaccuracies and nudging of game elements.

Should a unit stop partially along a template, you will need to ensure your rules conclusively define that moment, possibly requiring complex definitions (see the 'Final Position' rules in *Gaslands*). Tape measures have clear gradations; their partial measurements are part of widespread convention; templates generally do not. If templates are required to be placed in a regimented fashion in relation to a unit, units may be required to have flat-edged bases to facilitate this, having aesthetic and accessibility bearings on the game. If they can be placed freely around a unit, curved or shaped templates become significantly more difficult to make meaningful.

GRIDDED MOVEMENT

A direct alternative to measuring device movement is to use a gridded system, typically either with square or hexagonal spaces, as displayed in *Warhammer Underworlds: Shadespire* (Sanders, 2017) and *BattleTech* (Brown, Leeper and

Weisman, 1984), which can use many of the same mechanics of a measuring device system by simply replacing units of measurement with spaces. In fact, many measuring device systems can be transferred instantly to a gridded system with a simple conversion, and games such as *Dust 1947* (Parente and Zamfirescu, 2016) provide parallel rule sets for use with gridded or non-gridded movement. Gridded movement provides a good deal of freedom of movement while significantly reducing disagreements; however, it can create a potentially large barrier to entry since even entry-level play requires a custom-printed playing surface.

Many systems choose to restrict players from pre-measuring their moves in order to keep play fast-paced. Some do so as a simulationist concern, since in the real world, commanders and combatants have begun charges that ended in exhaustion before battle was joined due to misjudging distances. A gridded play area removes the opportunity to make judgement of distances a meaningful gameplay element.

ZONED MOVEMENT

An alternative to the fully discrete option of gridded movement is zoned movement, in which the play area is divided into 'zones' (possibly delineated by terrain such as forests or buildings), and a model may move with complete freedom within one 'zone' but is limited in the number of 'zone boundaries' they may cross in a single movement. Within a zone, their specific placement may be meaningful for lines of sight or engagement. Zoned movement allows for the removal of measuring devices while maintaining a degree of non-discrete figure positioning that is unique to these games (as opposed to gridded movement, where the position of the miniature within a grid cell is abstracted). *Rogue Planet* (Spivey, 2015) requires no tape measures; instead, units may move any distance in a straight line until they come into contact with an obstacle or enemy, cross into another type of terrain or an enemy unit expends a resource to intercept them.

Zoned movement is not yet common to players. It has the advantage of reducing the requirement for measuring movement but the disadvantage of increasing the specific requirements on the play area, which must be constructed in such a way as to clearly demark zones and be mindful of large contiguous zones that permit surprising rapid transit across the table.

DEGREES OF FREEDOM OF MOVEMENT

Within measurement-based systems, movement tends to be defined as one of three grades of freedom, roughly attributable to individuals, squads or blocks.

Individual-based movement systems focus on how a single person moves, allowing free pivoting and movement in any direction with little or no penalty, freely moving around or over obstacles. One opportunity to differentiate movement in these systems is having rules for climbing, jumping, falling and other sorts of adventurous or dramatic manoeuvres, as can be seen in narrative skirmish systems such as *Freebooter's Fate* (Klocke, 2010) or *Carnevale: Second Edition* (Thorpe and Clarke, 2019).

Squad movement focuses on groups of loosely associated individuals trained to work together but moving quite freely. These will tend to include additional coherency rules such that no individual is permitted to stray beyond a certain distance from the rest of their squad, requiring that some movement be curtailed to allow stragglers to catch up. This sort of system is prevalent in games simulating modern combat from World War Two onwards and games inspired by that kind of warfare, such as *Warhammer 40,000* (Chambers *et al.*, 1998) or smaller historical skirmish-based encounters such as *Saga* or *Lion Rampant* (Mersey, 2014).

Block movement requires the unit to move as a single object on the tabletop, with freedom of movement restricted and mechanisms such as wheeling used to introduce inertia to changing direction. The unit might be a single vehicle or a group of combatants formed into strict ranks and files. Obstacles in such systems can be serious impediments, and games will tend to revolve much more around positioning and placement, which can be amplified if the design places high importance on the vulnerability of flanks and rears.

It is possible for a game to combine two or more of these categories, such as *Man O War* (Jones, King and Stillman, 1993), which allows sailing ships to be grouped into squads with coherency rules but where each individual ship has block movement, or use different styles for different unit types, for example, *Warhammer: The Game of Fantasy Battles*, which uses squad movement for light skirmishing infantry but block movement for ranked units.

STEPS OF MOVEMENT

When designing a game, you might isolate movement into its own phase if you want to place a focus on it or allow all units to reposition before combat is resolved. If you have chosen an alternating activation system for your game, you might force models to move before they take any other action or provide freedom to move and take other actions in any order. You might choose to go further, such as in *Warhammer: The Game of Fantasy Battles*, where different classes of movement (charges, regular moves and forced moves) are broken into separate sub-phases, forcing them to be resolved in a specific sequence.

Charges are movements that end with a unit engaged in combat; they are often required to take place before other movements and may have special conditions. When games wish to use performative uncertainty to raise interest and tension, it can be created by declaring a charge without being able to measure whether it can be completed. Should players be able to measure and move other units first, this would be heavily compromised. Being able to achieve a charge, or stop your opponent from achieving one, can be important to the tactics of such games. One of the main ways of doing so can be to use the position of an opponent's own units against them. If those units can march clear before charges take place, it can be impossible to leverage this potentially interesting tactical choice. If standard movement is performed 'casually', forcing charges to be declared and moved separately provides both an intensity around the decision-making and forces procedural preciseness with which to better ensure accuracy of measurement and sequence where such movements would have out-sized impacts on the outcome of the battle, thus lowering the risk of bad feelings between players.

Forced movement is that which takes place outside of the control of its own-ing player (which is looked at in more detail in Chapter 24), for example, due to a rule simulating a unit running in fear. Breaking out the resolution of forced move-ment into an isolated sub-phase has the advantage of ring-fencing complex rules and exceptions, increasing the likelihood that the rules will be observed correctly. Such movement can often be unpredictable and outside of the player's control, so isolating its resolution can provide an opportunity for tactical reflection after its resolution, as opposed to requiring a player to resolve forced movement in the midst of their other decision-making. It has the added advantage that by stepping back from the tactical engagement, players can more easily build emergent narratives from what occurs.

RATES AND OPTIONS

There are established standards for movement rates in non-discrete games. Units will have a standard movement rate or action, often referred to as a 'walk', allow-ing them to move up to their listed movement statistic in the specified unit of mea-surement across any part of the tabletop defined as open ground. There will tend to be a faster rate, known as 'march' or 'run', which will allow them to move up to double their listed movement. Faster movements may come with costs, such as ruling out actions like ranged attacks or conditions such as not moving within a certain distance of enemy units. Offering a higher speed movement option both allows players tactical flexibility and speeds up potentially low-interaction parts of the game. In *Saga*, units beyond a certain distance from enemies are permitted to move repeatedly to allow them to close the distance to combat engagement, mean-ing that the element that the game is centred on, close combat, occurs more quickly and repeatedly. Finally, there will tend to be a 'charge' option, which will often be faster than walking, though not always as fast as running, and allow for combat to be joined, possibly with other advantages.

CHARGE DIFFERENTIATION

For various gameplay reasons mentioned above, charges are often separated out as a type of movement. Once designated separately, it often feels appropriate that a combatant launching with momentum into a fight will have different rules than one walking into combat or receiving a charge, in particular when attempting to re-create the tactical importance of, say, cavalry charges successfully breaking a unit at first impact. On the game design front, requiring that players seek to charge rather than be charged can create a sense of tension and a puzzle of positioning. The mechanics used to differentiate charges tend to be movement restrictions, charge advantage and charge reactions.

Charges often come with one or more movement restrictions or requirements, the most common being that movement must be made in a straight line, but that can include random movement rates or tests to be completed. It's not uncommon for charges to be declared prior to checking if these restrictions can be fulfilled, causing charges to be a sort of movement that can be 'failed', when the restrictions mean that the charging unit is unable to end its movement in combat with an enemy. It's possible to require that once a charge is declared, the charging unit must move as close to an enemy as they can and that a charging unit can do nothing else during their activation, meaning that failing a charge can leave a unit at a significant disadvantage.

Many games include an inherent charge advantage, such as increased hitting power or the ability to strike before an opponent can hit back. While there is a natural and emergent advantage for the charging unit in that it selects which units will fight, our experience has shown that if you do not provide an explicit charge advantage rule, players may be surprised or frustrated, as the trope is so widespread that players expect an additional advantage for charging.

We have heard the argument that a charge advantage is necessary to stop players from sitting back and engaging the enemy with ranged attacks, but we don't believe this to be the case. Firstly, the most certain way to get a player to charge another is to give their units swords rather than bows. Secondly, unless unit movement ranges are quite heavily asymmetrical, a player will have to risk being charged in order to be able to charge, so heavily rewarding charging can result in players simply never wishing to risk being charged and choosing to sit on what they have as loss aversion kicks in. If you are adding a charge advantage to your design, it may be better used not with the intent of making combat more attractive but instead for making decisive single-round combats more achievable and attractive. This does not necessarily mean a game that is more aggressive or action-filled, but one built around sudden and striking moments.

One of the advantages afforded by defining out charges as a distinct form of movement is that they can be allowed to trigger out-of-sequence reactions from an opponent. This can be during a formal declaration step before any models are physically moved or at the point that models become engaged and a charge is officially completed. Allowing reactions to movement provides a sense of fluidity and motion but can slow down play, so restricting it to this specific, dramatic and important form of movement can make good sense. By allowing supporting units to react to charges, players can be encouraged to tactically arrange units in realistically overlapping formations and think in a more strategic fashion, or by providing the chance to flee from a charge, the chance to intentionally lure an opponent into a failed charge arises.

We can see that these mechanics around charges offer a sequence of risks and rewards. Movement restrictions make charges uncertain, failure can leave a player at a disadvantage, while charge advantage makes it a risk worth taking and charge reactions allow trickery and interaction in encouraging an opponent to suffer failure.

ONGOING ENGAGEMENT

Once models move into close proximity to each other, they are often referred to as being 'engaged'. Many games provide a mechanism to either restrict movement while units are engaged or punish disengagement by offering free strikes. This avoids units stepping away from conflict in a manner that is both unrealistic and tactically unsatisfying.

Restriction of movement is commonly used in games with ranked units. Once a unit in *God Of Battles* (Thornton, 2012) enters combat, it cannot move away from that combat until its opponent is routed or destroyed. This is simple and effective; in ranked unit games, miniatures tend to be removed when 'killed' from the point furthest from the actual contact between units, so the point of battle is preserved no matter how long the conflict rages. In these games, the point of engagement tends to be when units are directly touching each other in 'base to base' contact.

In order to preserve a sense of dynamism, squad-based games often allow casualties to be removed, or individual troopers targeted, more freely, and so allow the movement of individuals within an engaged unit such that battle can be maintained. Some squad- and many character-based games, such as *Malifaux: Second Edition*, allow for engagement at a short but extended range, generally up to a few inches, to allow for interestingly overlapping zones of control. In order to keep these combats dynamic, characters are usually allowed to move within engagement without penalty, provided they don't leave it. With these forms of dynamic movement within combat units are generally permitted to break from combat entirely, at the cost of an opponent being able to attempt a close combat strike out of sequence, a 'free strike' or 'disengaging strike' which might either cause damage or stop the movement and activation that would have caused the disengagement. It is worth noting the difference in pressure and control these two punishments result in. Where a free strike causes damage, damage becomes a form of fungible resource for the player considering movement; their movement has a price which they can consider worth paying or not; the power is in their hands. Where a free strike ends an action or activation, disengaging is actually a higher risk for the player, failure is far more likely to be a costly problem and control is more heavily in the hands of the passive player.

INVOLUNTARY MOVEMENT

Systems may require forms of involuntary movement, which is examined in more detail in Chapter 24. Here, it is sufficient to consider that involuntary movement requires a set of rules designating how units are moved without player control. A design principle to keep in mind for such rules and for all rules designating behaviour not intended to be under player control is that they should not require player choice. Players will otherwise be left uncertain if they should make choices in their own interests or in the spirit of simulation of the movement effect being referenced, potentially creating doubt and confusion. A simple solution is to set a target point, usually the closest edge of the playing area, and demand that movement be directed towards this point, with absolute impediments leading to destruction.

OVERLAPPING AND INTERPENETRATION

Many systems will offer a range of movement options, allowing units to pass through areas that would otherwise be impassable, such as leaping or flying. Allowing units to remain in such areas can create aesthetic, physical (since it may be impossible to place the unit comfortably in the middle of miniatures representing large rocks) and rules-based problems (since a unit stranded in terrain, it was only temporarily permitted to occupy can force strange behaviour), and so it is usual for such movements to include a caveat that units not remain in a position not permitted by the standard rules of movement. Should a system include elements such as charging that preclude pre-measurement but that allow impassable elements to be ignored during movement, it should include clear and clean rules to explain how a unit is to be safely placed if its intended position is discovered to be out of reach. In writing such a rule, it should be borne in mind that referencing a unit's position prior to movement should only be made if reference is also made to marking the position prior to physically moving the unit. A safer option is to base the placement on other units and elements, such as requiring the moving unit to move directly away from the target point until it can be safely placed.

A specific form of movement allowing passage through otherwise impassable elements is interpenetration, where units are permitted to pass through one another. The most usual form of interpenetration is to allow friendly units to pass through one another, although passing through enemy units, particularly during involuntary movement, is not unheard of. Friendly interpenetration can generally be permitted under many of the same conditions as marching, which is to say, without penalty if the enemy is distant or commanders are present. Opposing interpenetration can result in disruption or even additional damage.

PRESSURE AND CONTROL

At various points above, we have noted rules which state a range at which opponents are not permitted to 'march' or closer than which enemy units cannot approach without declaring a charge. These act as passive zones of control, and through them, we can imagine the tabletop as areas of pressure, places where units can or cannot go, go safely or go without conditions. By visualising and leveraging these zones intelligently, a player can attempt to force their opponent to move how they want them to and gain an advantage which they can translate into victory. Ensuring that the puzzle for your players of what 'intelligently' means here is a satisfying one can be a critical part of the design process.

Once zones of control are established, movement types that allow units to avoid or transgress them become valuable to a skilled player. These zone-breaking abilities form another layer of tactics and are of interest to players seeking to unravel the puzzle of a system and session.

In designing movement rules, it is important to know the intent of a game and what is important to it. Imagine the cinema and choreography of your imaginary tabletop world and select movement mechanics that deliver and amplify that feeling. If the impact of charges is to be a crucial decision point for your players, then ensure that they can be baited and avoided. If you want your players to agonise over strategy rather than tactics, maybe provide a scouting mechanic to make the placement of terrain and the construction of the battlefield an active part of gameplay. If a feeling of motion and momentum is central, consider template-based movement.

SUMMARY

- Unit's movement needs to be delineated:
  - By **tape measures**, which can be awkward to use.
  - By **templates**, which will need to be supplied.
  - By **grids**, which require bespoke playing surfaces.
  - By **zones**, which restrict terrain placement.
- Movement tends to be defined by:
  - **Individuals** who have free movement and pivoting.
  - **Squads** that have contingency requirements.
  - **Blocks** that have strict controls on movement.
- Movement might be broken into phases or sub-phases, with typical examples being **Charges** or **Forced Movement**.
  - Charges will often have specific rules about how and when they can be triggered to initiate close combat.
- Movement may be restricted by being engaged in close combat, requiring **Disengaging** rules, often tests to do so.

EXPERIMENTS

If your game uses tape measures, allow units to move in straight lines until they reach an obstruction or terrain change, or force them to.

If your game uses block movement, move units as squads; if it uses squad movement, move them as blocks.

Give charging units a disadvantage. Worsen the disadvantage until players refuse to charge.

Allow units to disengage freely, then force a test to allow disengagement, then have units in base contact strike disengaging units.

REFERENCES

Anderson, M., Caroland, N., Cohen, R., Darland, A., Gibbs, J., Hanold, D., Johns, E., Martin, M. and Weber, D. (2013) *Malifaux: Second Edition*. South Korea: Wyrd Miniatures, LLC.

Brown, F., Leeper, L. R. and Weisman, J. (1984) *BattleTech*. [Board game] Chicago, IL: FASA.

Buchel, A. (2011) *Saga*. Evesham: Gripping Beast.

Cavatore, A., Pirinen, T., Priestley, R., Stillman, N. and Thornton, J. (2000) *Warhammer: The Game of Fantasy Battles*. 6th edn. Nottingham: Games Workshop Ltd.

Chambers, A., Johnson, J., Priestley, R. and Thorpe, G. (1998) *Warhammer 40,000. 3rd edn*. Nottingham: Games Workshop Ltd.

Couceiro, A., Azpeitia, F., Rodríguez, G. and Rodríguez, C. (2014). *Infinity*. Pontevedra: Corvus Belli.

Hutchinson, M. (2017) *Gaslands*. Oxford: Osprey Games.

Jones, A., King, B. and Stillman, N. (1993) *Man O' War*. [Board game] Nottingham: Games Workshop.

Klocke, W. (2010) *Freebooter's Fate*, Oberhausen: Freebooter Miniatures.

Little, J. (2012) *Star Wars: X-Wing the Miniatures Game*. [Board game] Roseville, Minnesota: Fantasy Flight Games.

Mersey, D. (2014) *Lion Rampant*. Oxford: Osprey Games.

Parente, P. and Zamfirescu, O. (2016) *Dust 1947*. California: Dust Studios.

Sanders, D. (2017) *Warhammer Underworlds: Shadespire*. [Boardgame] Nottingham: Games Workshop Ltd.

Spivey, B. (2015) *Rogue Planet*. Bombshell Games.

Thornton, J. (2012) *God of Battles*. Newark: Foundry Miniatures Ltd.

Thorpe, G. and Clarke, L. (2019) *Carnevale: Second Edition*. Indian Queens: TTCombat.

21 Close Resolution

When two units get close, we will often want to resolve a close-range interaction. In many miniature games, this means close-quarter or hand-to-hand combat, but it can just as easily be distracting, disheartening or otherwise interacting with an unwilling opponent. The purpose of close combat tends to be to disrupt an opponent's ability to achieve their goals by diminishing or eliminating a unit's function, often in a more powerful manner than at range, in order to encourage movement and engagement.

Close resolution can be far more simple than ranged resolution, which we will cover in the next chapter, because it requires movement. To put it another way, moving into the engagement range is complex and interesting, so resolving engagement can be relatively simple.

ENGAGEMENT (FORCE PROJECTION) RANGE

Units need to have some form of engagement range, the distance at which close-resolution interactions are permitted to take place. The standard minimum being 'base to base contact', where two miniatures are close enough that their supporting base is touching that of another, or as close as is practicable. Alternatively, engagement can be projected outwards, either in a 360-degree bubble (as often seen in skirmish games such as *Malifaux* (Anderson *et al.*, 2013)) or in a straight line (as often seen in block-unit games such as *Warhammer: The Game of Fantasy Battles*; Cavatore *et al.*, 2000). The difference between a projected or non-projected system in relation to the pressures that a unit can exert is significant and, as a general rule, under-explored by miniature games: most games, whether using block or squad units, or those with character or narrative combat, will tend towards base-to-base contact, leaving variable melee force projection as an interesting area for more thorough exploration by designers.

CONVERTING POTENTIAL FORCE TO AFFECTED FORCE

In simple terms, units will tend to have a potential level of effects they can cause; for example, the number of 'attacks' a unit has is the potential number of 'wounds' they can cause. Once engagement is entered, the potential level will be run through a conversion mechanic and processed into a final level of effect. How this is done is dependent on the feel that your game is trying to create, but generally, a random number will be generated and compared to a target. The target will either be static, such as 4+, with the skills of the units involved changing the randomly generated number, or the target will be based on the skills of the units with the random number left unmodified.

RESOLUTION OF AFFECTED FORCE

Once a level of effect is found, it will then be resolved. If damage is caused, then either miniatures representing troopers will be removed, or if miniatures can take a level of damage, it will be noted until the level needed to remove the miniature is

DOI: 10.1201/9781003314820-25

reached. Aside from damage, there are a wealth of other possible effects, with reducing a unit's effectiveness or level of control being the most usual.

SAVES

Which mechanics you use to simulate close engagements depends on many factors, but one that every game should consider is saves. Once a trooper has been successfully 'damaged', it can be given a chance to 'save' the damage. This generally consists of trying to roll equal to or above a target, such as a '5+ armour save' allowing damage to be avoided on a five or six. Mechanically, the effects of a save can be re-created in other ways; a '5+ armour save' has the same probability as a '3+ to wound'. However, despite the mathematical effects of my rolling to wound you or you rolling for me to not wound you being identical, many players prefer to roll the final dice that decide their trooper's fate and will miss the chance if it is not present. To put it another way, games are often a power fantasy, and having your units taken off without being able to do anything makes people feel impotent, which can make your players feel bad.

BREAKING

During actual combat, forces rarely fight to the last man; they flee or otherwise surrender. While character-based games may represent flight or capture directly, games with larger counts of combatants will tend to abstract this part to some degree. Potentially, having damage represents effects other than direct physical damage, and having damage degrades the ability to resist further damage, so destruction comes more rapidly as combat effects build, as in the fatigue system from *Saga* (Buchel, 2011), or by having a breaking mechanic.

Breaking represents the fact that a unit or even a whole force can be lost en-masse, either due to surrender or because a retreat can turn into a rout with surprising speed. As a simulationist choice, this accurately re-creates actual events as a game design choice, it means different tactical choices need to be made at the end of a session to its start. It means holding back units can have value, thus creating strategic choices and that games can come to quick, satisfying conclusions once one player has begun losing. Breaking tends to be based on force thresholds or unit resolution and is either immediate or test-based.

Force threshold breaking has a force broken once it has suffered a number of casualties, usually calculated as a percentage of the overall force. In the case of *The Lord of the Rings: Strategy Battle Game* (Cavatore and Ward, 2005), once a force has lost at least half its starting troops, it's broken, in which case every unit must test each turn; failure means they are removed from the battle.

Breaking based on unit resolution can take a similar form, except in relation to individual units, and can focus more closely on the minutiae of a particular combat or ongoing unit performance. In *Kings of War* (Cavatore, 2012), units build up damage over time, which is applied as a negative modifier to a test, which can lead to them being partially broken (Wavering in the case of *Kings of War*), meaning they can no longer charge, or totally broken in which case they 'Rout' and are removed entirely.

SPATIAL RELATIONSHIPS BETWEEN COMBATANTS

Non-discrete miniatures games are based on the spatial relationships of miniatures, and one of the ways that close-resolution engagement can be made more interesting is to include the physical relationship between miniatures. This is generally done by including flanks, rears or support ranges for units.

FLANKS AND REARS

Defining a unit's front, sides and rear can add complexity to the spatial relationship between units. In the case of individual characters, this might represent the difficulty of defending against an assault coming suddenly from behind, such as in *Warmachine* (McVey, Snoddy and Wilson, 2003), where each character has a front arc and attacks originating outside of that arc have a 'back strike' advantage. Where systems represent block units, it can represent the difficulty of a unit responding to pressure from outside of their ordered ranks. In *Kings of War*, when units engage an enemy on the flank, they double their available attacks or triple them in the rear. In the case of *Warhammer: The Game of Fantasy Battles*, flank or rear engagement directly affects breaking, as mentioned above.

With a unit formed into ranks and files, defining a flank and rear is relatively simple since they naturally form square formations with easily defined sides. Therefore, in games with block units, flanks and rears will, almost without exception, have a mechanical effect. With an individual trooper, particularly one on a non-square base, the definition can be more difficult. In the case of *Warmachine*, players are asked to draw a line through the shoulders of their miniature to define a front and back arc or mark points on the base if their miniature doesn't have shoulders (which isn't an unusual prospect in a game of ambulatory robots and monsters).

Whether with ranked-up units or individuals, if using either or both flanks and rears, it should be clearly defined what they consist of, how opponents can be permitted to engage them and what the advantage or penalty for doing so is. Leaving any of these areas vague or difficult to parse is a particularly strong area for creating arguments.

SUPPORT RANGES

Troopers can support their allies, even when they are not personally engaged in conflict. Most usually in the form of a 'buff', an advantage to an ally's rolls or statistics, or 'debuff', a disadvantage to an opponent. In the case of games where engagement has a non-base-to-base range, this can lead to complex and interesting networks of overlapping support bubbles, the correct arrangement of which can be an enjoyable puzzle for players. Even where support is offered only for base-to-base contact, moving into support positions can be an interesting question. While systems that have an engagement range have an obvious source of support ranges, it is entirely possible to give a unit without an engagement range a separate support range.

This can be created by direct and emergent effects. In *The Lord of the Rings: Strategy Battle Game*, friendly troopers in contact with the same enemy can make their attacks at the same time, rolling additional dice, for a simple and direct advantage. More emergently, in that system, defeated troopers are moved away from their attacker; those that cannot do so allow their attacker to double their attacks, such that arranging supporting models in positions to close off avenues of escape can be highly effective.

Close engagement is based directly on movement and can be the culmination of a set of interesting and complex player choices, meaning that it need not itself be complex. However, by maintaining the necessity to pay attention to the spatial relationships of units in close engagement, interest built up through your movement systems can be maintained and intensified, rather than being allowed to bleed away due to static engagement rules that lack dynamism.

SUMMARY

- Close combat resolutions have an **engagement** range and arc.
- They convert **potential** (attacks) into **affect** (wounds) via **resolution**.
  - **Saves** avoid bad feelings.
  - **Breaking** speeds up resolution and builds climactic events.
  - **Flanks** and **Rears** increase tactical interest by emphasising movement.
  - **Support** abilities allow interest to be maintained for unengaged units.

EXPERIMENTS

Make your game's engagement range base to base, 1″, then 2″.

If your game has saves, remove them; if it doesn't then put some in.

Find a way to define flanks and rears in your game, decide on the benefit of attacking an enemy's flanks or rear and use them.

Create a benefit to a unit being within a given range of a commander. Create a benefit to a trooper being in base contact with a friendly trooper.

REFERENCES

Anderson, M., Caroland, N., Cohen, R., Darland, A., Gibbs, J., Hanold, D., Johns, E., Martin, M. and Weber, D. (2013) *Malifaux: Second Edition*. South Korea: Wyrd Miniatures, LLC.

Buchel, A. (2011) *Saga*. Evesham: Gripping Beast.

Cavatore, A. (2012) *Kings of War*. Nottingham: Mantic Games.

Cavatore, A., Pirinen, T., Priestley, R., Stillman, N. and Thornton, J. (2000) *Warhammer: The Game of Fantasy Battles*. 6th edn. Nottingham: Games Workshop Ltd.

Cavatore, A. and Ward, M. (2005) *The Lord of the Rings: Strategy Battle Game*. Nottingham: Games Workshop Ltd.

McVey, M., Snoddy, B. and Wilson, M. (2003) *Warmachine*. Bellevue, WA: Privateer Press.

22 Line of Sight and Ranged Actions

In Chapter 3, we discussed the centrality of spatial relationships in non-discrete games. When designing your game's handling of spatial relationships, there are two fundamental questions to address: what is the limit of a given miniature's force projection, and under what circumstances is one miniature permitted to draw a line of interaction to another and apply its force? The force-projection limit of a given miniature is often referred to as its **Range,** based on its origins as an expression of the effective range of different firearms. The notional line of interaction is near-universally referred to as a model's **Line of Sight** (LoS), based on its origins as a determination of whether one model soldier could 'see' another model soldier across a scale-modelled battlefield.

We have a bird's-eye view of the battlefield, compared to that of the diminutive figures that we tower above. While this omniscient viewpoint inevitably means our miniatures will act with supernatural knowledge of their environment, the importance of spatial relationships to a non-discrete game's system and its cinema makes essential the need for a method to determine when one miniature can 'see' another.

However your game chooses to define LoS, it is important that you do take the time to define it clearly in your rules, as it is hugely significant to how players interact with and experience your game. It is surprisingly common to find systems in which the author fails to define what they intend the LoS rules of their game to be, leaving it to a kind of presumed folk wisdom. Do not do this. There are many ways to approach LoS in your game, but all versions lie somewhere between purely abstract and entirely based on a notional 'model's eye view'.

'MODEL'S VIEWPOINT' LINE OF SIGHT

Model's viewpoint LoS is based on the notion of what a miniature can 'actually see'. Players are encouraged to bend down level to the tabletop, line up their eyes with the back of the miniature's head and make a determination of what they might see (Figure 22.1). It is sometimes referred to as a model's eye view, true LoS, or WYSIWYG (what you see is what you get) LoS. The model's viewpoint LoS is somewhat divisive: seen by some players as an indeterminate, consensus-based nonsolution and by others as the most practical and intuitive method of dealing with the infinite variety of relationships between miniatures and their scale environments.

It should be noted that if you choose to use the model's viewpoint LoS in your game, take care not to express their rules tautologically. A statement such as 'For a model to have line of sight to another it must be able to see it' does not tell your players how you expect them to adjudicate LoS or how to resolve uncertainties during play. And one thing is certain: there will be uncertainties. Anyone who has

DOI: 10.1201/9781003314820-26

FIGURE 22.1   Drawing an LoS using the model's viewpoint. Photograph by the author.

tried to point out something at a distance to another person will know that even a very slight change in perspective can significantly alter what can be seen, meaning that any two individuals who crouch down to tabletop level will almost certainly and entirely honestly see two slightly different things. While most LoS judgements are clear-cut and won't require players to get down to eye-level, it is the ambiguous ones that two or more players will actually go to the effort of examining, and this will rarely result in unequivocal shared conclusions, instead requiring generosity by one player.

The impossibility of a shared perspective is particularly fraught in systems in which the percentage of a miniature that is visible is given meaning. Generosity when determining if any part of a model is visible to another is one thing; but asking players to honestly agree whether precisely a half (*Frostgrave,* McCullogh, 2015), a third (*Infinity,* Couceiro *et al.,* 2014) or a quarter (*Adeptus Titanicus,* 2018) of a miniature is obscured from the point of view of another is often going to result in an uncertain gut-feeling consensus. Given the centrality of spatial relationships in non-discrete games, the decision to leave the adjudication of such a critical factor as LoS or cover to gut-feeling in your own game is worthy of examination.

Oftentimes, the notionally concrete 'what you see is what you get' nature of the model's viewpoint LoS must be abstracted, or indeed abandoned, mid-game. Lines of sight are drawn from the frozen forms of the miniatures that represent the troopers, abstracting around the fact that the animated forms of such troopers would be hugging cover, crouching and peering around corners rather than standing proud with stiffly-hoisted swords throughout the proceedings. A great many systems ask players to wholly suspend the WYSIWYG nature of the model's viewpoint LoS when dealing with organic terrain, such as forests or jungles, ignoring the fact that they can see clearly through the brown oval arrayed with three spindly wire trees and counting such terrain as partially or wholly opaque (see Chapter 25). To represent the interweaving movement of squad members, some games rule that the gaps between troopers in a given unit block lines of sight. With each such exception, the model's viewpoint system is inched towards an abstracted system, blurring the lines between when a player must trust their own eyes and when they must apply a set of abstractions.

Viewed from one perspective, the model's viewpoint LoS is arguably the whole point of non-discrete gaming. Great tacticians and strategists are exactly that because they can see what others cannot; they are able to project their point of view across the field and realise what is possible from a given perspective or what the enemy will be unable to spot from their own position. The tabletop equivalent is to be able to project oneself onto the tabletop and to understand that a given model will have a protected line of fire from a particular position or a clear lane to charge down despite it appearing otherwise to another player. When using an abstracted LoS, information is more accessible, and so these moments of brilliance and discovery are far rarer. However, the omniscient player's ability to move around the table and view the action from any number of celestial viewpoints abstracts away from the notion that a given force is operating only based on what they can 'see'. The act of concealing information gained by virtue of a privileged physical perspective such that an opponent is surprised by an action they didn't know was possible may sit poorly with some players, particularly if they assumed visibility and LoS to be open information within the game. It is worth considering communicating your intentions to your players: are they to adopt the role of a ground-level general, operating with limited and imperfect information, or are they expected to act as the omniscient commander of a technologically advanced force with total visibility of the field of battle? Such an expression of intent can aid players in achieving consensus when debating lines of sight.

The model's viewpoint might well be the best choice for your game, particularly if it contains a lot of verticality or is envisioned to take place in man-made (rather than organic) environments. Furthermore, there is an argument to be made that the use of the model's viewpoint LoS is one of the main things that justifies the use of miniatures in tabletop gaming at all: with an abstracted LoS, miniatures are (functional-speaking) purely decoration atop the geometric shapes that are the units' true in-game representation, while the model's viewpoint LoS ensures the miniatures have a firm gameplay purpose.

ABSTRACTED LINE OF SIGHT

Abstracted LoS rules ask players to draw an imaginary line or lines between the seeing model and its target, or from the base of one to the other (Figure 22.2). They then place a series of specific conditions on how those lines are drawn and what those lines can and cannot cross for the target to be considered visible. Usually, this will entail agreeing on a height value for each item of terrain on the tabletop, along with a height value for each model. This results in an abstract 'hit box' for the model controlled by their footprint and their height value. This abstracted notion of a model's volume has the advantage of allowing players to create whatever model they like and the disadvantage of making models mechanically superfluous to the game since a set of blank bases would function identically.

These rules tend to take the form of something like: 'draw a line between the attacker's base and that of the target, if the line crosses no opaque terrain equal or greater in height than both attacker and target, the target can be seen'. Use of a secondary line, as well as a check for terrain of any height, can provide rules for partial LoS or cover. Once we define terrain types and include some allowances for the attacker to ignore nearby terrain, we should have a fairly robust rule set until someone decides to climb some stairs.

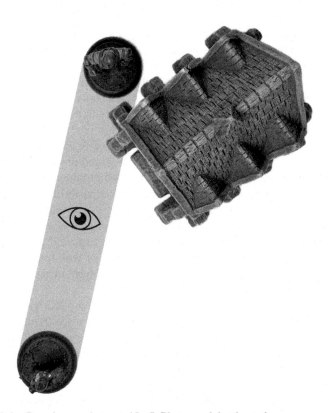

FIGURE 22.2   Drawing an abstracted LoS. Photograph by the author.

ABSTRACTING ELEVATION

The straight line we are asked to draw in an abstracted LoS system rules tends to assume two models on a two-dimensional plane. If this is not the case in your game and players are expected to trace a line between two points in three-dimensional space, it is advisable to be clear from where the lines must be drawn: from the model's base, from their head, from the tip of their weapon barrel, etc. Many successful games essentially assume a two-dimensional play area, particularly those games that centre around large block units, ground vehicles or naval engagements. However, if your game is envisaged to functionally support a three-dimensional play space, in which one model might be standing on a balcony firing down at another on the road below, you may find it challenging to write clean abstract LoS rules for this situation (Figure 22.3).

A possible solution is that LoS is only blocked by terrain the same height of the balcony plus the model or greater, but of course, a man on the ground tight to a wall fifty yards away from the model on a balcony would be comfortably obscured from his attacker in real life. So we might include a caveat that a model within a certain distance of terrain of at least its own height is not visible. Then we wonder what happens when

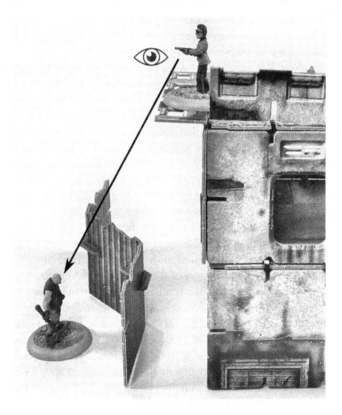

FIGURE 22.3 A character on top of a building can easily draw a line from their eyes to the character on the floor below them, but a wall larger than either character is close to the target, which would obstruct most abstract lines of sight. Photograph by the author.

that same wall is almost directly below the balcony, with the attacker peering directly down at the top of the man's head, wherein the LoS being obscured is clearly wrong.

In addition, if the abstracted line is drawn directly from the base of a model standing on the upper floor of a building, it will inevitably be blocked by the floor of the building they are standing on, resulting in the temptation to add further complexity. The second edition of *Malifaux* (Anderson *et al.*, 2013) had players measuring how far a model was from the edge of a platform and comparing the distance to the height of the model to see if they could see those below (which, despite its inelegance, doesn't even solve the issue since it ought to be dependent on a relationship between the higher model's distance from the edge and the lower model's distance from the building).

Abstracted LoS offers the promise of mechanical purity, not governed by the capricious perceptions of the fallacious eye. However, oftentimes, as soon as a model climbs a set of stairs, it's time to take a good, hard look at the model's viewpoint LoS and how you might best define its usage in your game.

FIELD OF VISION

As an additional control on a model's LoS, some systems restrict the area through which it can be traced: the model's **field of vision**.

Many squad- or character-based games allow LoSs to be traced in any direction from the model on the assumption that an individual creature is free to look and turn around as they move. It is common for games involving ranked units or lumbering war machines to restrict their units' field of vision, but controlling how LoS is generated can create spatial puzzles for players to unravel in any non-discrete game and is worth consideration as a potential source of tactical interest in your system. A restricted fixed field of vision demands that players plan ahead in order to ensure that they manoeuvre to apply force, react to threats and avoid leaving units with exploitable blind spots.

There are two common types of restricted fields of vision: **arcs** and **corridors**.

Arcs of vision restrict a trooper's LoS to only within a certain arc projected from each trooper's base. When using square bases, two imaginary lines can be projected through the corners of the base, creating a 90-degree section in front of the model within which its LoS can be traced, such as in the units of *Warhammer: The Game of Fantasy Battles* (Cavatore *et al.*, 2000). If using circular bases, a rule system will sometimes suggest drawing a line through the shoulders of the model to mark off a 180-degree arc, such as in the troopers of *Warmachine* (McVey, Snoddy and Wilson, 2003), or hovering a set square over the head of the model to mark out a 90-degree arc.

Corridors of vision restrict a trooper's LoS to a corridor created by projecting one of its edges, or sometimes the width of its base, out in a straight line. This sort of system makes most immediate sense when applied to sailing ships firing broadsides during a naval warfare game such as *Man O' War* (Jones, King and Stillman, 1993), although it can be applied to a range of vehicles with static-mounted weaponry, such as in *Gaslands* (Hutchinson, 2017). *Adeptus Titanicus* (2018) uses both arcs and corridors of vision, applying them to different weapon systems to represent the manoeuvrability of their mountings.

One common challenge with both arcs and corridors of fire, when combined with circular bases, is adjudicating the facing of a given model. You might consider instigating a convention in your game to ensure players are clear in which direction arcs are projected, avoiding surprises for players during play.

RANGE

The implementation of range is trivial in most cases (notwithstanding the discussions of measurement in Chapter 11): units can project force up to a range and may only target other units with ranged action if that target is within range, LoS and its field of vision.

That being said, we will point to a handful of interesting examples of variations on this near-ubiquitous approach. *Dropfleet Commander* (Chambers and Lewis 2016) portrays space battles between fleets of ships, and as such, there is little in the way of LoS blocking terrain. In this game, force projection ranges are not fixed but rather contextual based on the 'signature' of a potential target and the acting unit's 'scan' range. A unit's force projection range is the combined total values of their scan value and their target's signature value in inches. This range can be extended should the target perform actions that cause energy 'spikes'. This creates an interestingly dynamic and tactical range system in which the decision of which actions to take can increase or decrease your unit's vulnerability to ranged attacks. *A Billion Suns* (Hutchinson, 2021), also a spaceship game, creates interest by naming minimum as well as maximum weapon ranges. In it, particularly powerful weapons have minimum and maximum ranges, meaning that the biggest guns are vulnerable to counter-attack by smaller and weaker units that can get inside their minimum range, and players have to set up layers of supporting units and reaction fire.

RANGED ACTIONS

The main reason for wanting to know which units can see which during a game is to discover which can shoot the other (or cast spells at, shout mean things, etc.).

It should be noted that any damage-dealing ranged action can be a very low-cost, high-reward tactic, and systems that wish to include significant amounts of it should take pains to create interesting controls on arcs and lines of sight. For example, *Warhammer: The Game of Fantasy Battles* permits situations in which it is impossible to hit with a shooting attack but places no such limits on close combat. Close combat units are generally limited in the number of rounds they are actually able to spend in combat (it takes time to move to engage the enemy) and rarely deal damage without taking some in return, whereas ranged units are often able to deal damage every round without the necessity of chasing down the enemy and with no risk to themselves. As such, it is common to find ranged units with low damage outputs in a mixed-arms game. Other controls include proximity-based targeting criteria and move or fire requirements.

Proximity-based targeting criteria are the commonly-found requirement that a unit target their closest opponent when shooting, such as in *Lion Rampant* (Mersey, 2014), or at least pass some form of quality test to target more distant opponents, such as in *Dracula's America* (Haythornwaite, 2017). Enforcing proximity-based targeting has the benefit of stopping ranged units from cherry-picking any target they wish and allowing their opponent the opportunity to use clever movement and positioning to screen more fragile or important units. Some games offer lone characters the protection of proximity targeting criteria, even when larger units are not treated the same. *Warhammer 40,000* (2023) grants some character models the 'lone operative' rule, disallowing units more than 12″ away from targeting it with ranged actions.

Move or fire restrictions are common, requiring units to choose between moving or firing weapons or choosing from a reduced set of movement options when firing, restricting them from being able to both avoid incoming close-combat threats and maintain their damage output.

COVER

Rules governing the defensive effects of intervening terrain on shooting attacks are ubiquitous, but their examination must be made in the context of the broader definitional systems for terrain, so we will address **Cover** in Chapter 23.

OVERWATCH AND REACTION FIRE

Being shot should have a relatively high rate of lethality, but being removed at range has a fairly low rate of fun. Often, the most interesting thing about ranged actions is their projection of force across the table, creating zones within which an opponent must consider their movements more carefully. Alternating the active application of projected force is one option (see the discussion of activation systems in Chapter 19), but allowing the passive threat of projected force to be triggered into an active state by the actions of an opponent can be even better, creating multi-directional play.

Another way around the problem of ranged lethality is to make players not want to take the shot when it becomes available; this can be provided with 'overwatch' or 'reaction fire' rules. With reaction fire, a unit can fire when another unit enters into their LoS. Reaction fire is often a state entered into at the cost of actions, and when used, the state is generally lost. The resultant effect is that the first unit to move, which necessarily has no targets, will set up lanes of fire and enter a reaction fire state, and then have to choose to shoot at the next target to present itself in return for being unable to react to whatever happens later in the turn. Through this exchange, players can enter into a game of bluff and risk, maintaining interest in shooting without actually firing a shot.

CASE STUDY: RAISING RANGED LETHALITY – *INFINITY*

Infinity is a game that seeks to replicate the tense and urgent firefights seen in tactical first-person shooter video games. Ranged attacks have a high lethality: if a gun hits its target, there is quite commonly a greater than 50% chance of the model being killed. All units have the ability to react to enemy movement with reaction fire. Models can declare reaction fire at any point during an opponent's movement, meaning that remaining in cover throughout your whole movement is important in a way it is in a few other miniature games, which will tend to assess the situation of the model only at the end of its movement. In *Infinity*, the projection of force through ranged actions is elevated to the point that avoiding enemy fire or limiting its effectiveness becomes the central concern of the game, as one tactical slip can give your opponent a fatal opening.

CHARGING

Another way in which lines of sight are made important is by requiring that units can see a target before charging it. Charges are often a pivotal moment in games that make close combat the centre of attention, so setting up the ability to charge becomes of paramount interest. See Chapter 21 for a discussion on charge advantage.

Lines of sight, fields of vision and ranged actions are among the main methods of laying out force projection patterns on a tabletop, and restricting them ensures that those patterns create a greater range of potential tactical interactions and puzzles. By combining these LoS projections with minimum and maximum weapon ranges, move or fire options and reaction fire, a complex and compelling pattern of force can be projected onto the tabletop.

SUMMARY

- **LoS** is a continuum from the model's viewpoint to fully abstract.
  - The **model's viewpoint LoS** is vague and struggles to define partial views.
  - **Abstract LoS** is complex and struggles to handle elevations.
- LoS can be restricted to within a **Field of Vision**, for example using **Arcs** or **Corridors**.
- **Ranged actions** can represent risk-free application of force at range, and constraints should be considered.
- Reactive fire, cover and charging also make the LoS interesting.

EXPERIMENTS

If your game uses the model's viewpoint line of sight, create a set of abstracted line of sight rules for it that consist of no more than three conditions. If it uses an abstracted LoS rules, remove at least one of its conditions first, and then use the model's viewpoint LoS.

Reduce all arcs of vision in your game by 45 degrees.

Give everything in your game the power to reaction charge or overwatch fire in return for not acting during their activation.

REFERENCES

Adeptus Titanicus. (2018). Nottingham: Games Workshop Ltd.

Anderson, M., Caroland, N., Cohen, R., Darland, A., Gibbs, J., Hanold, D., Johns, E., Martin, M. and Weber, D. (2013) *Malifaux: Second Edition.* South Korea: Wyrd Miniatures, LLC.

Cavatore, A., Pirinen, T., Priestley, R., Stillman, N. and Thornton, J. (2000) *Warhammer: The Game of Fantasy Battles.* 6th edn. Nottingham: Games Workshop Ltd.

Chambers, A. and Lewis, D.J. (2016) *Dropfleet Commander.* Indian Queens: Hawk Wargames.

Couceiro, A., Azpeitia, F., Rodríguez, G. and Rodríguez, C. (2014). *Infinity: N3 Rulebook.* Pontevedra: Corvus Belli.

Haythornwaite, J. (2017) *Dracula's America: Shadows of the West.* Oxford: Osprey Games.

Hutchinson, M. (2017) *Gaslands.* Oxford: Osprey Games.

Hutchinson, M. (2021) *A Billion Suns.* Oxford: Osprey Games.

Jones, A., King, B. and Stillman, N. (1993) *Man O' War.* [Board game] Nottingham: Games Workshop.

McCullogh, J. (2015) *Frostgrave.* Oxford: Osprey Games.

McVey, M. Snoddy, B. and Wilson, M. (2003) *Warmachine.* Bellevue, WA: Privateer Press.

Mersey, D. (2014) *Lion Rampant.* Oxford: Osprey Games.

Warhammer 40,000. (2023) Nottingham: Games Workshop.

23 Terrain

The miniatures that represent our forces are the focus of our attention, but they are often only a small percentage of the stuff that adorns our tabletop, scale-modelled man-made and natural structures or terrain, often being the majority. In addition, collections of terrain are often self-made and thus can vary wildly between players. Given its centrality to the game experience and its diversity of form, players need clear mechanisms to define their terrain's impact on the game to avoid ambiguity (and arguments) during play.

Terrain has two main purposes in non-discrete miniature games. The first is to evoke the physical environment, helping with immersion and mental cinematography. The second is to provide, from a purely schematic point of view, variety and texture on the tabletop, ensuring force cannot be projected evenly in any direction and from any location on the table, forcing decisions about where to position models and by what routes to move them to achieve their objectives.

In this chapter, we will discuss the common approaches for handling the great variety of terrain types in rules terms, including how their boundaries are handled, a survey of some of the common rules for terrain and how best to guide your players to a common understanding of the terrain pieces arrayed before them.

TERRAIN COLLECTIONS

A player's terrain collection is a compromise between functionality and aesthetics. As Mel Bose writes in *Terrain Essentials: A Book About Making Wargaming Terrain* (Bose, 2020):

> Good terrain involves three key concepts: functionality, realism, and durability. …
> Wargaming terrain's functionality means things like balconies being made wide enough to hold model bases, or rooms being designed to accommodate a full squad. Your chosen ruleset might need features that allow movement through or over them, or it might require clear indications of building access points, or the boundaries of area terrain effects. A ruleset using true line of sight (TLOS) will have a considerable impact on the design constraints of your pieces, compared to a ruleset that uses a more abstract system. Ensuring buildings and ruins have plenty of windows or blast holes at the right height for the models using a TLOS system makes the difference between creating a key location to be defended and held in the game, and producing an 'unusable' piece that models move around rather than interact with.

The relationship between a player's collection of scale-modelled terrain and the game systems they play goes both ways. The game a player plans to play affects the decisions they make when designing and building terrain pieces, and the design of those terrain pieces then affects their suitability for use in subsequent game systems (and thus the barrier to trying those systems). Both because it is physically more demanding to store bulky wargaming terrain pieces and because it is the miniatures

DOI: 10.1201/9781003314820-27

that tend to be the focal point for most gamers, many players have a small set of 'workhorse' terrain pieces that will see usage across multiple game systems. Players will find it easier to adopt a new game that makes functional demands on their terrain similar to something they already play. Sympathy for the likely nature and variability of your potential players' existing terrain collections will help you design terrain rules that lower the barrier to entry for your game. Of course, requiring some amount of unique eye- or imagination-catching terrain can be a hook for your game, providing both a kickstarting of the hobby loop and a visual hook for the physical and cinematic enjoyment of your system.

CASE STUDY: UNIQUE LIMITED TERRAIN REQUIREMENTS – *MYSTIC SKIES*

Mystic Skies (Hutchinson and Sutter, 2023) is a tower-defence game in which both players are required to deploy a wizard's tower terrain piece as part of their force. This tower is central to the gameplay; a player loses if the other player destroys their tower. This terrain requirement presents a specific hobby challenge to players, providing a hook into engaging with the hobby aspect of the game and allowing players to have a large centrepiece model in what is otherwise a small-warband-size skirmish game.

TERRAIN RULES

Rules for terrain tend to encompass four key characteristics:

- Their effect on line of sight (**opacity**).
- Their effect on movement (**passability**).
- Their effect on conflict resolution (**advantage**).
- The boundaries of that terrain piece (**footprint**).

Rules can be provided beyond these baseline areas to add character and interactivity to terrain, for example, a gun emplacement that can be activated by models in proximity or a spooky tree that negatively affects morale.

OPACITY

Opacity defines to what degree the terrain piece may have lines of sight drawn across it (see Chapter 22), and it is standard to provide options for **opaque**, **obscuring** and **clear**. Opaque terrain fully blocks the line of sight; clear terrain in no way blocks it. Obscuring terrain either blocks line of sight only under certain conditions or confers some disadvantage for attempted actions sighted through it.

Some games have obscuring terrain counted as opaque at a certain depth or distance, such that a unit moving through it may pass from being visible to not. In *Flames of War* (Yates, 2019), a unit that is more than two inches from the boundary of obscuring terrain may only be seen by units that are within six inches of the unit; they count as concealed within opaque terrain for all other units. In *Malifaux: Second Edition* (Anderson *et al.*, 2013) models may see into and out of an area of obscuring terrain, but models trying to draw lines of sight through it count it as opaque.

The gameplay purpose of terrain having varied opacity types is to constrain lines of sight: forcing unit movement; balancing the power of long- and short-range units; and constraining the possible targets for any given unit at any given time, allowing players to use movement to engender favourable conflicts.

PASSABILITY

Passability defines to what degree the terrain affects movement (see Chapter 23), and it is common to provide rules for **frictionless, resistive** and **impassable** terrain, and it is possible to provide rules for **accelerating** terrain.

Impassable terrain does not permit movement onto or through it, acting as an impenetrable barrier or zone for models. Frictionless terrain, often called open, does not affect movement in any way. Resistive terrain reduces movement rates in some way or increases the cost of movement for units moving into or within. Accelerating terrain increases movement rates in some way or provides free or bonus movement for units moving into or within. In *Flames Of War* (Yates, 2019), units have their fastest movement speed reserved for movement on roads. In *Bolt Action* (Cavatore, 2016), vehicles that complete their entire move on roads double their movement speed.

The gameplay purpose of movement-affecting terrain is to channel the action on the tabletop: creating interesting zones of conflict, forcing player interaction and changing complete freedom of movement into interestingly constrained movement decisions.

Discrete pieces of resistive terrain, such as low walls, are commonly abstracted into a single discrete reduction in movement, such as reducing movement by a single point for an entire unit to cross over, rather than slowing movement throughout the action of crossing, as would be more usual for resistive terrain.

Some more narrative rule systems may require a unit to make a test to see if they can cross a piece of terrain, providing conditionally resistive or conditionally impassable terrain. If your game provides a method for units to ignore the passability impacts of terrain, for example a 'flying' rule, it is worth considering the case in which a unit's movement might end on impassable terrain (or worse, when it might end on frictionless terrain entirely surrounded by impassable, unassailable terrain, too small to allow reasonable engagement).

ADVANTAGE

The effect of terrain does not have to be limited to affecting the line of sight or movement. It is common for units within or behind terrain to gain a defensive benefit when attacked, be that a negative effect on the attacker or a positive effect on the defender. A common example is that units stationed directly behind a defensible structure, such as a low wall or rampart, will gain a combat advantage.

In *Pike & Shotte* (Morgan, 2014), units fighting from within buildings gain a bonus to their combat result, used for determining the victor of a given close-quarters combat.

More rarely, some systems grant units within or atop terrain an offensive benefit due to their protected or elevated position. For example, your game might include an advantage, with an attendant risk, to charges made from elevated positions (jumping from a saloon roof down onto a foe) or melee attacks from an elevated vantage (swash-buckling on staircases). However, in order to do so, you will need to have rules for climbing and falling damage, in the case of diving attacks, and a robust system for defining, when drawing level on a slope, the elevation ceases to be sufficient to offer an advantage.

TERRAIN FOOTPRINTS

Whereas miniature troopers tend to have regular footprints due to the uniformity of their bases, terrain models tend not to be so consistent; there are no accepted conventions for the footprint of a forest, pillbox, or river.

Terrain pieces may be mounted on bases or freestanding. It is therefore advisable to provide rules to allow players to crisply define the **footprint** of a terrain piece, such that when to apply the associated rules for that terrain piece is as unambiguous as possible. Many systems tacitly leave the definition of the boundaries of terrain pieces to the interpretation of the players, but such omission risks confusion and disagreement and can be avoided.

There are two common conventions of terrain footprints: **area** and **WYSIWYG**.

Area Terrain

Area terrain confers its rules across the whole of an area equally, regardless of any internally modelled details, and affects any unit that passes its boundary. It is common for rocky ground, woodlands and marshland to be treated as area terrain. This allows us to designate woodland as sufficiently dense to make movement extremely difficult while still having a tabletop that allows for easy movement of scale miniatures. A few conveniently spaced trees can be a near impenetrable thicket. Area terrain combines the benefits of clean boundaries between zones on the tabletop affected by a terrain's rules and zones that are not, with the practical necessities of positioning static miniatures mounted on rigid bases, potentially in large groups.

When used for terrain that has natural boundaries and a homogeneous structure, such as a cornfield or pond, area footprints can retain a simulationist feel. When applied to more complex terrain with unclear boundaries, such as ruined buildings, the use of area footprints can lead to a feeling of abstraction.

When combining the area-footprint definition of terrain with a model's viewpoint line of sight system, players can be left with uncertainty (Figure 23.1). Imagine an area of terrain classified as 'hard cover' giving a penalty against shooting through it in a model's viewpoint line of sight game: are the players supposed to apply the cover bonus to any model within the area terrain, or are they supposed to use the model's

FIGURE 23.1 Woods are often modelled as area terrain, which can cause players to assume they are supposed to apply some abstraction to the line of sight and cover. Photograph by the author.

viewpoint line of sight to assess if the model is in cover, and then apply the cover bonus of the terrain only if the model is in cover?

WHAT YOU SEE IS WHAT YOU GET

WYSIWYG (what you see is what you get) terrain confers its rules based on the physical characteristics of the scale model itself. This is commonly through the presence of specific details on the model, such as ladders or doors, which provide a rule effect only in those specific spots. If the terrain model is mounted on a base, that base is purely a practical convenience (to aid the model's stability or durability) and has no rule function; the rules of the terrain are connected only to the physically appropriate parts of the model. For some models, the distinction between the functional parts of the terrain piece and those that are not will be clear. Think of a set of pre-moulded plastic walls, glued to some card for stability. The distinction between what is a cover-providing wall and what is just the base will be obvious. For other models, the boundaries will not be so clear. Imagine a realistic and carefully modelled blending between the rotting timbers of a wooden wharf and the muddy swamp waters they are sinking into: where does the boundary of the movement-impeding swamp lie, and might it cause disagreement during play?

It is fairly common for players to freely mix elements of area and WYSIWYG footprints within a single piece of terrain: for example, treating the ground floor of a ruined building as area terrain with regards to movement, but having only the modelled ladders permit unimpeded vertical movement.

TERRAIN DEFINITION SYSTEMS

In order to apply rules to our terrain pieces, we need an application system. There are two common ways to create a system of terrain definitions in your game and organise their rules: **fixed** and **taxonomic** terrain types.

It is common for game systems to mix these approaches. For example, *Frostgrave: Second Edition* (McCullough, 2020) uses taxonomic-style keywords for movement affecting terrain and cover and fixed terrain types for scenario-specific terrain types.

Experienced gamers have likely developed the habit, through painful experience, of taking a moment before deploying miniatures to discuss and agree on both the nature of each piece of terrain in game terms and their boundaries. It is advisable, though actually not that common, to include the discussion and agreement of terrain definitions during setup. *Malifaux: Second Edition* (Anderson *et al.*, 2013, p. 60) makes the first step of game setup explicitly a terrain agreement step and provides guidance for the discussion:

> Every gaming group will have different terrain pieces available for their game table, and it's important that the players discuss the terrain they are using, and then place it on the table fairly.
>
> Some questions the players will need to answer are:
> - What are the Ht and base of the terrain?
> - What traits does the terrain have?
> - Are there special interactions with the terrain?

FIXED TERRAIN TYPES

Your game can provide a non-exhaustive set of common types of terrain that you anticipate players will use in their game sessions, and you can define those terrain types specifically. For example, a low-fantasy game might provide specific definitions for areas of woodland, rivers, wooden fences, stone walls and stone buildings, with the assumption that these will be the most common scenery items used by its players. Such an explicit and restricted definition of terrain types has the benefit of reducing ambiguity and the need for discussion. If you place a stone wall into play, we do not need to agree on its impact on this game session; its impact is pre-agreed. It also allows you to suggest to your reader the sorts of terrain you imagine they will need in your game, which is a useful channel for communicating your vision for the look and feel of your game.

An extreme example of fixed terrain types is seen in Warhammer Age of Sigmar: General's Handbook (2018), which provides explicit 'warscrolls' for each of the terrain models sold for use in that game at that time, providing complete and unambiguous rules for how each 'official' terrain piece is to operate within the game. Players placing these terrain kits into play can be confident in the designers' intentions for their effect on the game. The downside of such a system is that it is less flexible in the inclusion of terrain pieces that fall outside those you have defined explicitly. If a player provides an unanticipated terrain piece, perhaps a pool of lava in our hypothetical low-fantasy game, they must either force it to fit one of the existing types of terrain (which may not match their expectations) or improvise some 'house rules' to describe the effects of the terrain on the game. In a hobby that values 'do-it-yourself' so highly, this downside bears consideration, particularly if the game system will be offered to consumers without a line of 'official' fixed terrain models.

TAXONOMIC TERRAIN TYPES

The second common method of defining terrain is to provide a glossary of key-words, which may be applied flexibly to the items in a player's terrain collection. Each keyword can provide a modular block of rules to represent a class of terrain effect, such as 'sight blocking' or 'impassable'. You can invite your players, perhaps in a specific step during setup, to agree and assign keywords to the pieces of scenery on their tabletop. For example, players might agree that a rocky outcrop is 'sight blocking' and 'impassable', whereas the crevasse next to it is just 'impassable'. Such assignment of keywords permits a wide variety of scenery, whether purchased or scratch-built, to have unambiguous game effects within a controlled and learnable palette of generic terrain rules. The advantage of this approach is the openness of the system to accept and gamify almost any object the players might choose to place into the play area as terrain. As a downside, it can make terrain feel like a collec-tion of generic parts rather than unique and powerful narrative locations. Also, this approach requires players to go through a process of keyword assignment during setup, an onerous task for strangers meeting over an unfamiliar table but one rapidly ameliorated for regular adversaries using the same terrain pieces game after game.

A *Song of Ice & Fire: Tabletop Miniatures Game* (Lang and Shinall, 2019) invites players to agree and assign keywords to the pieces of scenery in their play area, including 'Rough' (affects passability), 'Blocks Line of Sight' (affects opacity) and 'Cover' (affects defence), as well as some that sit outside the standard types, for example, 'Inspiring' (affects morale). It is interesting that *A Song of Ice & Fire: Tabletop Miniatures Game* provides terrain in its starter boxes (as flat cardboard templates; Figure 23.2), eschewing the need for player-provided terrain but still providing a flexible taxonomic system for defining terrain types, ideal for use with player-made terrain.

FIGURE 23.2 Cardboard area terrain from *A Song of Ice & Fire: Tabletop Miniatures Game*. Photograph by the author.

COVER

Whether terrain is defined as a fixed stone wall type or built up from taxonomic terms such as 'opaque' or 'obstacle', these definitions will only ever establish *that* a piece of terrain, for example, blocks line of sight, not how, where or when. To do that and establish the relative relationship between attacker, terrain and defender, we need cover rules. Rather than agreeing at the start of the game which areas of the table are blocked by which pieces of terrain from where, that adjudication is performed at the time of a unit making a shooting attack and assessed relatively to the attacking model. To assess cover, models' viewpoint systems often use the percentage of a target that is visible to the attacker, and abstract line of sight systems often use the presence of partially occluded sight lines. Here is part of the cover rules from *Necromunda* (Chambers, Johnson and Priestley, 1995, p. 17), a model's viewpoint system:

> If the shooter can see at least half of the target's body but not the entire body, the target is said to be 'in partial cover'. The shooter suffers a -1 to hit penalty.

As we discuss in Chapter 22, this requires the players to make a tricky on-demand model's-eye adjudication. In *Malifaux: Second Edition* (Anderson *et al.*, 2013, p. 41), an abstract line-of-sight-based system, the strength of the cover is a taxonomic characteristic of the terrain piece, agreed upon at the start of the game rather than based on visible percentages, and triggered using abstracted sight lines:

> A model will gain the benefits of cover from a Projectile Attack when any LoS line between the Attacking models and the target model can be drawn through any terrain with the soft or hard cover traits that is within 1" of the target model.

This has the benefit of removing the 'percentage of model visible' adjudication, at the cost of making the effect of a given terrain piece homogenous, regardless of the relative positions and sizes of partially obscured models.

COMMON TERRAIN TYPES

There are a number of terrain types that are commonly encountered in non-discrete miniatures rule systems. When combined with impassable and opaque terrain types, they provide game effects for the majority of terrain pieces that decorate most tabletops.

ROUGH TERRAIN

Uneven ground that prevents confident movement is commonly called 'rough' or 'difficult' terrain and is the predominant form of resistive terrain encountered. The overwhelming convention for rough terrain rules is to reduce a unit's movement speed by half. Here, ubiquity doesn't equate with excellence. This convention can result in a reduction in choices and engagement. It is common for units to get mired in such terrain for several activations, leading to an unsatisfying 'miss-a-go' feeling to the terrain's impact. This, in turn, can lead to players avoiding interacting with the terrain, as it's no fun, at which point it may as well have been impassable. There are a range of options to make such resistive terrain more attractive to players: the level of movement reduction can be randomised or otherwise varied, making surprise engagement possible; effects other than movement reduction can be used, such as making the unit more vulnerable; slowing effects can be a choice with damage set as the alternative.

If movement rates are to be reduced by a fraction, it can result in some practical awkwardness, both in the measurement of fractional moves and in adjudicating when and for how long the reduction should be applied. Is a unit considered clear of the terrain when the front of their footprint leaves it, or only if the whole base is clear? Does the movement reduction apply after the first millimetre of penetration, or is it checked after each inch, or only at the start of a movement action? Clean and clear answers to these questions should be provided.

Rather than having areas of the table in which units have their movement reduced, consider imagining that units' movement rates represent them moving across rough terrain by default (e.g. the battlefield is predominantly soft or broken ground), and instead provide areas of accelerative terrain (such as roads) to increase the flow of units and extend their force projection in certain areas. Such an inversion can provide a more positive player experience, in which they are seeking areas of increased options and enjoyment rather than avoiding areas of decreased optionality.

Hard/soft Cover

The defensive benefits of cover are commonly granulated into hard and soft cover, with soft cover (materials dense enough to impede vision but not slow projectiles, such as a hedge) providing a negative to striking, and hard cover (materials dense enough to deflect or absorb projectiles as well as impede vision, such as a wall) providing both a negative to striking and to causing damage. In place of reducing the offensive ability of the attack, cover often increases the defensive abilities of the protected target, for example, by increasing their armour value.

If your game is one in which seeking cover is the norm, you might consider treating cover as assumed, instead of granting a benefit to units firing at exposed enemies. If most models in your game will be in cover most of the time, this approach moves the rules exception to the less ubiquitous case, reducing rules overhead, and also signposts to players that this is a game that assumes you are hugging cover. For example, *Gamma Wolves* (Barker, 2020) provides no negatives for targeting a mech in cover but grants a +1 to Gunnery Tests if attacking a mech in the open.

Dangerous

Terrain perilous to troopers, such as marshes and rivers, magma flows or toxic pools (Figure 23.3), may require rules to represent their potential for injury if moved through. Commonly, this will be either a set level of damage or an accumulation of damage based on the distance travelled through the terrain. The damage may be automatic or require a test of some kind. In *Warhammer Fantasy Battle* (Cavatore et al., 2000), areas of dangerous terrain are considered safe for models moving at normal speeds, but any rapid movement through them (marching, charging and fleeing) triggers tests for each model, with a roll of one resulting in a wound without saves.

FIGURE 23.3   An area of swamp terrain. Rough and possibly dangerous too. Photograph by the author.

INTERACTIVE TERRAIN TYPES

There are a number of less common terrain types that are sometimes encountered in tabletop miniatures rule systems that provide more interactivity between units and the terrain they navigate.

CLIMBABLE

If your game anticipates the use of multi-level terrain, you will likely want to provide rules for climbing and rules for which pieces of terrain are climbable. Climbing rules are an area that can hamper player enjoyment if you focus on the risks of climbing and falling rather than the positive gameplay outcomes of allowing models to traverse complex terrain. If you desire a game with dynamic movement across complex multi-level scenery, consider generosity in your climbing and falling rules.

Many rules systems require tests for vertical movement across climbable terrain, with failure possibly resulting in fall damage (generally dependent on the distance fallen). *Carnevale* (LaPorta, Thorpe and Tonkin, 2018) is a game set in the streets of 18th-century Venice which expects players to use multiple levels of terrain. To ensure models can move dynamically through the full scope of the table, general climb rules are provided: any time during a model's move it encounters a vertical surface, it may make a dexterity test to continue its move vertically, gaining bonus movement on a critical success. Failure results in the model halting its movement, and only a critical failure (approximately a 10% chance) results in the model falling, resulting in a climbing system which is quick to resolve and tempting to engage with.

If you choose to include tests for climbing, identify under what circumstances failure increases the fun of your game. Consider allowing players to spend resources (action points, order tokens, etc.) to automatically succeed in climbing, but allow them to accept the risk of a climbing test if they wish to conserve or gain resources; this can turn climbing into a tactical decision rather than a random outcome. If your game has multi-level terrain and objectives that are placed by players, you can be sure that objectives will end up on the tops of buildings. It is advised to anticipate and avoid situations in which chance results in multiple models wasting multiple turns trying and failing their climb tests to reach some critical game objective. Either warnings about objective placement or some form of climb failure mitigation should be considered to avoid this.

Consider the situation in which a model only has enough movement to climb partially up a piece of terrain. Will this be permitted? If a trooper can climb four inches in a round and wishes to scale an eight-inch-high ladder, is it simply impossible, or are players to abstractly note their position between rounds until they can complete their ascent? If desired, you can avoid the requirement to track a 'floating' model by making climbing a binary outcome: models may only start an ascent if they have the resources to complete that climb in a single round. If they don't have the available action points or movement, they'll need to wait until the next round to initiate the climb. Alternatively, to avoid accidentally unclimbable, lengthy ladders, they can be treated as escalators, and those who climb them are automatically skipped to their end.

DESTRUCTIBLE

In games with heavy vehicles, explosive weapons or fragile terrain, it may be appropriate to include rules for the destruction of terrain. In the abstract, this is a thematic and exciting inclusion, but the practicalities are important: few players will have access to terrain that has destructible features or a range of matching 'destroyed' versions of terrain pieces, so it will be necessary to carefully outline exactly how the destruction can be conveniently and immersively modelled on the tabletop during play.

The simplest implementation of destructible terrain is to remove it from play, as in *Gaslands* (Hutchinson, 2017) or *Marvel Crisis Protocol* (Pagani, Rowan and Shick, 2023). While convenient, this can result in peculiar situations where smashing a few bricks from one end of a wall can result in the whole wall vaporising entirely. If collapsible buildings are a feature, the practicality of removing or swapping pieces of terrain while retaining the position of miniatures must be considered. Some systems sidestep this issue by making buildings impassable when undamaged and only passable when destroyed; others force all miniatures out of the terrain piece (or into the dead pile) when it is destroyed.

The challenge with destructible terrain is getting players to take on the additional hassle and preparation and not just ignore the rules. For this reason, destructible terrain rules are best used where preparation can be naturally minimised. Part of the reason destructible terrain works in *Gaslands* is that the main form of destructible terrain encountered by players is that formed by the wrecks of their own vehicles, simple, discrete, terrain pieces, created during play and understandably removed by a single following impact. This leads to most players engaging with the destructible terrain rules on a first playthrough and being very comfortable with designating small terrain pieces as destructible during play.

The ability to destroy or move terrain may necessitate a measure of each terrain piece's size or mass to allow calculations of its resistance to damage, or structural endurance, again, defined during set-up along with any other functions of the terrain. *Marvel Crisis Protocol* uses a five-point scale, from 'Size 1' (being lampposts and small crates) to 'Size 5' (being buildings).

MOVEABLE

Terrain features such as crates and barrels might logically be movable, potentially creating the chance for changing cover options, barricading doors or creating dynamic, dangerous environments (moveable crates on rooftops feel like they should have some way of achieving diving attacks when nudged). In science-fiction settings, it might be imagined that walls themselves might be moveable, particularly if they are intended to represent force fields or computer projections. As with destructible terrain, moveable terrain rules should be prepared to make allowances for player terrain collections.

CASE STUDY: DYNAMIC TERRAIN – *BOARDERS AND BLACK FLAGS*

In *Boarders and Black Flags* (Ford, 2023), the terrain represents the deck of a ship at sea, including unsecured cargo and crates. As the game plays out, the sea shifts and swells, causing crates to slide across the deck and potentially disrupt or kill crew in their path. This creates a dynamic and changing environment of threats that can be manipulated for player attack or defence.

CREATABLE

Providing units with options for creating terrain during their activations and letting them change the tabletop environment can create opportunities for extremely engaging play. Wizards that can summon dangerous wandering tornadoes, troopers that can throw smoke grenades whose clouds have persistent line-of-sight effects, vehicles that remain in play even once disabled – all of these can provide dynamic and emergent ways for the play space to shift in response to player actions. In most cases, you will need to provide very specific guidance on the footprint of the created terrain; commonly, games provide pre-designed templates for these effects. In the case of effects linked to the destruction of a unit, the size of the destroyed unit can provide a guideline. You will need to consider if the created terrain is temporary or permanent within the game session.

When a titan is destroyed in *Adeptus Titanicus* (2018), players are invited to place 'a crater or pile of wreckage approximately the same size as the Titan's base … in the destroyed Titan's place', which acts as difficult and dangerous terrain. When a vehicle is wrecked in *Gaslands* (Hutchinson, 2017), it is flipped over, creating a piece of terrain as well as maintaining the location of the destroyed unit should it be repaired. In *Necromolds* (Bohaty, 2021), players construct miniatures from modelling clay for a single play session; when troopers are slain, they are mashed flat using special moulds to create terrain.

VARIABLE OR RANDOMISED

It is possible that the rules you provide for terrain result in terrain being largely avoided, and this can occur due to terrain becoming predictable. When players know for certain that they cannot cross an area in time to complete their goals, it effectively becomes a dead zone. A unit may choose to stand next to terrain that is too deep for an assault to be mounted through in a single turn, at which point the terrain may as well be a cliff face.

One way to tackle this problem is to make the effects of terrain partially or largely randomised or attach hidden information to them such that one player might consider a piece of terrain effective protection while their opponent knows otherwise. This can be done by requiring players to roll on a randomising table during set-up, publicly or privately, representing a general's privileged understanding of the battlefield. Alternatively, it can be rolled when a unit first enters the terrain, allowing for surprises or strategic scouting. A stretch of forest could hide boggy terrain, hunter's traps or useful paths. A player being able to take a gamble to move or attack through terrain is far more representative of reality and creates more interesting gameplay moments than one that knows the exact effect of all terrain at all points. However, perfect information is quick and simple to engage with, so a designer needs to consider the worth of slowing a system down and whether any resulting interest and randomness are worthwhile.

In *Warhammer Age of Sigmar: General's Handbook* (2016), the rules pertaining to terrain are designated randomly, with the fantasy setting allowing for forests to be 'damned' or hills to be 'mystical'. Coming after terrain set-up, this roll can change the nature of the battlefield and create replay value, as the same scenario can differ depending on the special terrain rules in play.

SUMMARY

- More than any other rules, terrain rules need to consider and be respectful of practicality and availability.
- Terrain rules should deal with:
  - **Opacity**, the effect on line of sight.
    - Which will be **Opaque**, **Obscuring** or **Clear**.
  - **Passability**, the effect on movement.
    - Which will be **Impassable**, **Resistive** or **Frictionless**.
  - **Advantage**, the effect on conflict resolution.
  - **Footprint**, the extent of the terrain piece.
    - Which will be **Area** or **WYSIWYG**.
- Terrain will be defined by **Fixed** or **Taxonomic** systems.
- Terrain will often result in **Cover**.

- Terrain can also be:
  - Dangerous, causing damage.
  - Climbable, including falling rules.
  - Destructible, while respecting practicality.
  - Moveable, possibly creating cover or causing damage.
  - Creatable, but clearly delineated.
  - Variable, usually randomly generated.

EXPERIMENTS

If your game has terrain that slows movement, instead have it speed movement up by the same degree.

Make all terrain in your game targetable with attacks and destructible when it suffers damage that would kill a unit of comparable size.

Create a simple, variable D6 table for each terrain type in your game.

REFERENCES

Adeptus Titanicus. (2018) Nottingham: Games Workshop Ltd.

Anderson, M., Caroland, N., Cohen, R., Darland, A., Gibbs, J., Hanold, D., Johns, E., Martin, M. and Weber, D. (2013) *Malifaux: Second Edition.* South Korea: Wyrd Miniatures, LLC.

Barker, A. (2020) *Gamma Wolves.* Oxford: Osprey Games.

Bohaty, C. (2021) *Necromolds.* [Boardgame] Minneapolis, MN: Necromolds LLC.

Bose, M. (2020) *Terrain Essentials: A Book About Making Wargaming Terrain.* Baltimore, MD: Dave Taylor Miniatures, LLC and The Terrain Tutor.

Cavatore, A. (2016) *Bolt Action.* Oxford: Osprey Games.

Cavatore, A., Pirinen, T., Priestley, R., Stillman, N. and Thornton, J. (2000) *Warhammer: The Game of Fantasy Battles.* 6th edn. Nottingham: Games Workshop Ltd.

Chambers, A., Johnson, J. and Priestley, R. (1995) *Necromunda.* Nottingham: Games Workshop Ltd.

Ford, G. (2023) *Boarders and Black Flags.* Dover: Man O' Kent Games.

Hutchinson, M. (2017) *Gaslands.* Oxford: Osprey Games.

Hutchinson, M. and Sutter, S. (2023) *Mystic Skies.* Santa Rosa, CA: Electi Studio.

LaPorta, D., Thorpe, G. and Tonkin, J. (2018) *Carnevale.* Santa Rosa, CA and Indian Queens: TTCombat.

Lang, E.M. and Shinall, M. (2019) *A Song of Ice & Fire: Tabletop Miniatures Game.* Singapore: CMON Global Limited.

McCullough, J. (2020) *Frostgrave: Second Edition.* Oxford: Osprey Games.

Morgan, S. (2014) *Pike & Shotte.* Nottingham: Warlord Games.

Pagani, W., Rowan, S. and Shick, W. (2023) *Marvel Crisis Protocol.* Roseville, MN: Atomic Mass Games.

Warhammer Age of Sigmar: General's Handbook. (2016) Nottingham: Games Workshop Ltd.

Warhammer Age of Sigmar: General's Handbook. (2018) Nottingham: Games Workshop Ltd.

Yates, P. (2019) *Flames of War.* Auckland: Battlefront Miniatures Ltd.

24 Control Removal

Players bestride the tabletop battlefield like colossi; they can see all that happens and their tiny, immobile soldiery march where they are told and will stand and die to the last man for their beloved general. If your game is concerned with the simulation of human behaviour, this is something of a problem.

Simulation of soldiers fleeing the battlefield can be abstracted by stating that damage represents mental trauma as well as physical trauma, so a miniature removed due to damage could represent one slain or who has fled the battlefield. However, depending on the scale of the game and its level of detail, such abstraction can create narrative dissonance. In many games, psychological effects are played out on the tabletop, and this is generally achieved by removing control temporarily from players.

Control removal can be used to simulate physical as well as psychological effects. In the car racing game *Gaslands* (Hutchinson, 2017), drivers sometimes lose control of their vehicles and are moved without control of the player, while in the fantasy gridiron game *Blood Bowl* (Johnson, 1994), an uncaught ball will bounce around without any player agency. Control removal commonly affects unit movement but may also be used to force actions, such as a berserker being forced to attack the nearest model, whether friend or foe, or a model shooting into a melee being forced to choose their target at random. Such forced actions, whether physical or psychological in explanation, are moments in which the situation passes from the control of the player to that of someone, or something, not under their auspices.

Control removal can increase narrative harmony in a game, with players having their units behaving recklessly or ingloriously because the rules demand it, rather than struggling with the uncomfortable ludo-narrative tension of the best gameplay choice being at odds with the narratively-congruent action of the unit.

WHO'S IN CONTROL?

The most important question with forced actions is who is in control: the game or an opponent (and it can sometimes be a little of both). When the game assumes control of a unit, a set of automated instructions can be provided, sometimes combined with random effects, which players are required to follow exactly, so it doesn't matter which player is operating them. For example, the rules for a unit fleeing from the battle could look like:

- On the turn fleeing begins, move as far as possible away from the source of the effect.
- On subsequent turns, move as far as possible towards the closest table edge.
- Move around terrain and other units by the shortest route possible.

This could be combined with movement distances or directions being randomised to further increase unpredictability and remove the ability for players to plan for and

DOI: 10.1201/9781003314820-28

thus control the outcomes of the erratic movement. The key problem with this method is that if there is any ambiguity in the instructions, it can cause disagreement, and secondly, lists of instructions to be followed to the letter can be boring and fiddly. An alternative is to have the opponent take control of the unit temporarily; this has the virtue of simplicity, is more engaging than following basic instructions and can be an entertaining interaction point as a cackling opponent runs your unit into the cruellest situation they can imagine or selects just the wrong model of yours to attack. The downside is that always having a unit do the worst possible thing can cause narrative dissonance. As is often the case, a combination of the two options is probably preferable where a set of instructions is given, but to keep them simple, an opponent chooses when unclear.

RANDOM DIRECTION

Generating a random direction in a non-discrete miniatures game bears mentioning. If custom components are available, then some form of spinner or dice with a directional arrow is a simple solution. Rolling two dice and drawing a line from the highest to the lowest result is a solution available to most dice systems (albeit needing a rule for ties). Where a game already employs D8 or D10, their pointed tops provide a simple way to generate a direction.

MORALE

Where control removal is used, units will generally have a value to represent their resistance to it. This will tend to represent a variety of values, such as exhaustion, training and the relative quality of equipment, which we will contain under the term 'morale'. As a rule, this will either represent a testing target or a threshold value.

One narrative advantage of emulating the psychological effects of conflict separately from physical harm is the perception that the two affect people in importantly different ways. People have a sense that how someone reacts to being shot is largely predictable, while how someone reacts to having the person standing next to them being shot is far less so. If so, physical damage might be designed to predictably degrade combat capacity in a linear fashion, while psychological damage might create sudden and possibly unpredictable spikes and turn-arounds. To achieve this, a unit can be given a testing target value morale, and when control removal might occur, a random number is generated and compared, with the unit suffering its effects depending on chance.

Alternatively, psychology can be seen as actually relatively predictable but distinctly different from physical damage, caused by different effects and recoverable in different ways, but just as linear. In that case, morale will generally represent a threshold value with negative effects building up over time, similarly to but separately from damage; if they exceed the value, the effects occur.

It is worth noting that one of the more universal elements of any system measuring a unit's morale is a bolstering effect generated by nearby leaders or commanders. This can take many forms, but is commonly implemented as a permanent passive aura (see Chapter 3).

ORDERS

In addition to a unit's morale simulating its ability to resist the effects of panic and shock, it may also be used to model their ability or proclivity to follow orders as directed. This can range from a willingness to perform specific actions, follow complex mission directives or even perform questionable actions when ordered, depending on the focus of your game. Order systems range significantly in complexity and specifics, depending on the intentions of the game in question, but their purpose overall is to introduce uncertainty into the operation of a player's force, asking them to consider risk mitigation strategies and plan for scenarios in which their units do as they are told and those in which they do not. Order systems can vary from simply allowing units within range of a commander to activate as a group as in *Frostgrave* (McCullogh, 2015) to requiring that units activate in a set sequence or have a set list of actions to select from as in *Torch and Shield* (Etherington, 2023) through to a test to perform specific actions as in *Lion Rampant* (Mersey, 2014). Where a test is required, units may simply be required to waste their activation, as in *Lion Rampant,* or might default to certain preset behaviours, for example, 'Instinctive Behaviours' in *Warhammer 40,000: Tyranids* (Cruddace, 2009).

Order systems can include a risk versus reward element by requiring higher target numbers for more complex orders or an increasing level of risk for additional actions, as in *Song of Blades and Heroes* (Sfiligoi, 2007). This can be combined with unit-specific target numbers to create a level of narrative as well as a tactical effect. *Adeptus Titanicus* (2018) and *Battlefleet Gothic* (1999) both feature systems in which units carry out standard activations but may choose to take a morale test to perform more contextually powerful special order activations, the risk being that once one morale test is failed, no further special orders may be issued to the force.

CASE STUDY: NARRATIVE TACTICAL ORDERS – *LION RAMPANT*

In *Lion Rampant,* units must roll over a target number on 2D6 in order to activate. The target number in question varies depending on the unit in question; archers require a six or more, while slower-loading crossbowmen require a seven, while the generally elite mounted men-at-arms have one of the worst targets for moving in the game at seven, representing the fact that they have very little interest in looking for targets outside of their immediate arc of charge. These differences between units create not only tactical interest as units must be placed where they can engage in their preferred fashion but also build a narrative as units act how one might imagine.

PANIC AND SHOCK

Probably the most usual source of control removal is that created by panic and shock. Historically, units panicking on the battlefield have turned as many, or more, combats than actual casualties. Panic can stem from many sources, such as casualties from shooting attacks or being outflanked by an enemy while already engaged. Depending on the story you're telling, it can come from particularly disturbing weapons of war (the effect of black powder weapons in the Flintlock era is often said to have been primarily psychological) or combatants (in a horror-based game, units might cause panic by their very presence). You might choose to list panic-inducing events and require a morale-based test if triggered, perhaps resulting in forced movement, some other uncontrolled action or forced state change if the test is failed.

FLEEING

A common form of forced movement is for a unit to flee. This might be simulated by having a unit move away from the source of the flight or towards a 'home point' (such as a friendly table edge) in a manner not under the control of their owner, sometimes to their maximum movement range and sometimes to a randomly decided distance. Fleeing may be a single move, or it may be an ongoing state with a unit fleeing repeatedly. If fleeing is an ongoing state, then a unit in the process of fleeing might automatically flee when attacked or be considerably easier to strike.

A standard corollary to fleeing rules is some form of rallying ability to allow the player to regain control of the unit. This might represent the unit recovering their wits autonomously or a friendly commanding unit steadying them. If fleeing is an ongoing state, then some form of rallying mechanic is a necessity to avoid flight being simply a meaningless book-keeping requirement; without it, units that begin to flee are potentially better simply removed from play.

As with much control removal, fleeing can suffer from the problem of requiring a player to go through an amount of mechanical activity without much in the way of interesting choices. Some amount of flight can provide interesting and unpredictable changes to the board state; too much can cause the game to drag into busy work. Observe your playtesters carefully to see when such uncontrolled movement ceases to add to the game's fun, as you may find players have only a low tolerance for it.

REFUSAL

Another common form of control removal is refusal, where units simply refuse to move or act. This might represent a unit shrinking from engaging a fearsome enemy unit, poorly-trained or disordered units failing to coordinate themselves in response to an order (in the case of systems where orders or activations require tests), or failures in communication or technology.

Refusal mechanics are possibly even more controversial than fleeing, because at least with fleeing, a unit will move and the game state will change; with refusal, something that could have happened simply doesn't. If refusal is to be included, consider offering players options to avoid it, as we explore below.

IMPETUOUSNESS

The inverse to refusal, impetuousness mechanics cause units to automatically take actions outside of their player's control, such as charging headlong towards the enemy, simulating bestial rage or being lured forwards. Impetuousness usually causes movement in the opposite direction to fleeing, causing the unit to move directly towards the target of the impetuousness. Impetuousness might come as a negative side effect to a positive ability, such as a berserker rage that drives them uncontrollably towards the enemy but causes them to hit harder when they arrive. This tendency to offer players a reward for taking a potentially uncontrollable unit relates to the issue of frustration that control removal can create. Again, if players have options to avoid control removal, the pain is significantly lessened.

PURSUIT

Where there are units fleeing, one could offer the ability for units pursuing. Pursuit can be a form of uncontrolled movement, potentially with the option to restrain the pursuit. This allows for the classic tactics of baiting enemies into a pursuit and pulling them out of position. Including elements such as fleeing from battle allows for lines to be broken. In massed battle games (and in massed battles), breaking the enemy line, turning and rolling up a flank is devastatingly important. Even in modern warfare, squads do not do well when under enfilading fire. In ancient warfare, it can be deadly, and forced pursuit is one of the most usual methods of achieving it. Pursuit should follow roughly the same rules as fleeing in your game; if one is random, the other should be, and it may make sense to limit how often a unit can pursue in a single round.

RECKLESS INERTIA AND CONFUSION

Some forms of control removal are relatively predictable; fleeing units will move away from the thing that made them flee, and impetuous units will move towards the enemy. Others are absolutely not, resulting in largely random movement. These forms of movement are rare; control removal generally requires quite clear and unambiguous instructions, which is difficult to achieve with random movement, but it can be highly effective if used well.

In *Warhammer* (Cavatore *et al.*, 2000), goblins will often use deadly frenzied ball and chain-wielding fanatics; these are moved by the use of a specific 'scatter' dice, a dice with an arrow marked on it to indicate a random direction. In *Gaslands*, if a vehicle gains too many hazards, it will be pivoted in a direction chosen by an opponent and may flip uncontrollably through the air depending on a die roll, and in *Gorkamorka* (Chambers, Priestley and Thorpe, 1997), vehicles that lose control are required to roll on tables that dictate their movement. In each case, the type and direction of random movement are clearly defined and carefully considered.

DEVIATION

Related to uncontrolled movement, control can also be removed from attack actions, such as those that might model inaccurate projectiles or barely controllable magical energies. Checking where every missed arrow or bullet ends up would be tiresome in the extreme for most games, as such deviation or scattering rules tend to be reserved for attacks with unusually high damage outputs, those that can affect multiple models ('area-of-effect' actions) or whose target is unpredictable (such as shots into close combat). Typically, missed attacks are given some form of random direction and sometimes a random distance to define their final target point. This allows for a moment of tension for both players as a potentially deadly shot has a chance of landing somewhere of even greater interest. This can be very useful since players being shot at during a ranged phase are often in an extremely disengaged state, and these moments can bring them back into the game. It also increases the tactical choices around potentially devastating weapons as their risk increases as battle lines meet, offering a possible catch-up option as players in a comfortable position ease off on more powerful shooting while more desperate players take possibly high reward risks.

A related mechanic arises when ranged attacks are made against combatants locked in close combat. Typically, this takes the form of requiring either that missed shots are randomly assigned to combatants other than the original target or that all shots are randomised among all combatants. This offers again a moment of tension as fate takes hold, but it also offers a form of balancing behaviour since players will be less inclined to shoot into a combat they have a chance of winning, but if their unit is certain to die whatever they do, they may as well open up with shooting.

An uncommon, but interesting, option is for repeated deviation. In *Blood Bowl*, the ball will, at some points, bounce, land and then bounce again. A D8 is rolled to generate one of eight compass directions, and if the ball is moved to a space containing a player or into the crowd, it may potentially bounce again, requiring another D8 roll. This chaotic mechanic allows loose balls to bounce in multiple directions, and any regular *Blood Bowl* player will be swift to relate an occasion where doing so won or lost a game against the flow of play. Such stories are more than reason enough to consider including such a mechanic in your game, if it makes narrative sense.

PINNING

Ranged attacks can be surprisingly difficult to add interest to (see Chapter 22): if too powerful, they can discourage movement, which is one of the central elements of interest in non-discrete miniatures games; if too weak, they can cease to be relevant options. A potential fix can be a 'pinning' effect resulting from ranged attacks. When under fire, real-life combatants can be trapped behind cover and controlled by virtue of incoming fire even without actual injury being caused, and pinning can represent this effect. In simple terms, ranged attacks that fail to cause actual injury can contribute to stopping a unit from moving, either immediately or due to a cumulative effect. When simply removing movement options, pinning can unfortunately reduce interesting choices. However, if the player is given the choice to make either attacks that pin or attacks that damage, representing the difference between a constant stream of fire designed to keep heads down and more controlled bursts actively waiting for targets to break cover, then it can add a tactical choice. Likewise, if pinned units can (for example) choose between remaining still, retreating, or breaking for better cover, it can shape and offer thematic options. Perhaps units pinned in the open suffer some additional control removal, forcing only movement towards cover rather than remaining still under fire without cover, offering unit behaviour on the table that is both more logical and more interesting.

FUN AND FRUSTRATION

Players like to be in control. A game is a series of interesting choices, and the removal of control means the removal of choices. The use of control removal mechanics must be carefully balanced with maintaining player agency and engagement. If used, the mechanics are best if resolved quickly and kept to exceptional circumstances or units rather than being commonplace throughout the game.

One of the most effective ways of leavening the frustration provided by control removal is to include choices and intentions before and after the uncontrolled actions. Perhaps the unit is permitted to take wounds or expend some other in-game resource to avoid the control loss, or perhaps it only suffers control removal if the player chooses to move the unit away from some command locus. Consider requiring an intentional choice by one player to inflict the control removal effect on the other player rather than having it be a natural side-effect. Contrast the game-feel of a shooting attack that causes damage and *also* causes movement-limiting pinning effects, as opposed to the aggressor choosing to eschew damage in favour of movement-removal effects.

With most control removal mechanics, it is best to seek systems that provide a sense of active tactical play and a reward for smart planning around the risk of uncontrolled actions.

SUMMARY

Control removal:

- Creates narrative moments.
- Requires clear rules for how control is applied.
- Is often based on a specific statistic test.

It may model:

- Orders – command ranges allowing greater control.
- Panic and shock – including casualties, multiple engagements, shocking weapons or terrifying opponents.
- Fleeing, rallying and pursuit – as panicking units flee, try to rally and are chased by opponents.
- Impetuousness – reckless troops may uncontrollably charge towards the enemy.
- Inertia – units may move uncontrollably based on previous movements.
- Deviation – shooting can result in shots landing elsewhere than intended.
- Pinning – units under fire can have their ability to move and react removed.

EXPERIMENTS

Require units to take a test to perform any actions each turn; if a test is failed, play passes to the opponent. Then:

- Allow units to take any number of activations and players to retain initiative if it is not passed. Increase the difficulty of the test for each action a unit takes.
- Make the test harder for certain actions.
- Allow the test to be re-rolled within range of a commander.

Have units take tests to see if they panic and flee:

- Only when shot at by two or more different units. Then only if those units are between them and different table edges.
- Only when reduced to 25% or 50% of the starting unit strength.
- Only when charged by an outnumbering unit.

Have fleeing units:

- Automatically rally if they are not pursued.
- Run towards random table edges.
- Fight normally if charged.

REFERENCES

Adeptus Titanicus. (2018) Nottingham: Games Workshop Ltd.
Cavatore, A., Pirinen, T., Priestley, R., Stillman, N. and Thornton, J. (2000) *Warhammer: The Game of Fantasy Battles.* 6th edn. Nottingham: Games Workshop Ltd.
Chambers, A., Johnson, J. and Thorpe, G. (1999) *Battlefleet Gothic.* Nottingham: Games Workshop Ltd.
Chambers, A., Priestley, R. and Thorpe, G. (1997) *Gorkamorka.* Nottingham: Games Workshop Ltd.
Cruddace, R. (2009) *Warhammer 40,000: Tyranids.* Nottingham: Games Workshop Ltd.
Etherington, D. (2023) *Torch and Shield* Australia: Grimskald.
Hutchinson, M. (2017) *Gaslands.* Oxford: Osprey Games.
Johnson, J. (1994) *Blood Bowl.* 3rd edn. [Boardgame] Nottingham: Games Workshop Ltd.
McCullogh, J. (2015) *Frostgrave.* Oxford: Osprey Games.
Mersey, D. (2014) *Lion Rampant.* Oxford: Osprey Games.
Sfiligoi, A. (2007) *Song of Blades and Heroes.* Kharkiv, Ukraine: Ganesha Games.

25 Damage

When we play games based around combat, there will be damage, and where there is damage, there will be death and destruction, which we will need to model on the tabletop in some form or another.

DAMAGE AND PROGRESSION

In Chapter 4, we discussed the concept of 'zeroing in' during a non-discrete miniatures game being greatly more common than 'laddering'; players can generally do less on their last turn than their first, but what they can do will have a clearer aim and intention and likely a greater impact. Players discover the shape of the play session together, building their story and the accompanying tactical puzzle emergently through their actions. To achieve this, units need to be removed; diffuse action at the end of a game is, in this framework, a bad thing. We want players to be able to do fewer, more impactful things; their shared focus should be on a few vital spots. Furthermore, we want a sense that this impactful moment is rushing up on us at speed, providing urgency and interest to decision-making. At the same time though, players want to play, so swift wholesale destruction of a force is something we wish to avoid. There are a few things that can be done to pace the destruction of units, providing momentum towards an exciting conclusion while keeping the game fun and interesting to all involved.

PLOT ARMOUR

Characters, commanders and even special weapons within units can have rules that make them the last to die. These range from allowing players to remove the miniature of their choice from a unit when it is damaged to requiring that command duties be passed around the unit, sometimes with attendant penalties. This has the effect of concentrating power as games go on, often with more basic troopers providing little more than ablative armour to their leaders. This is both cinematically appropriate and gives a sense of progression.

CASE STUDY: PLOT ARMOUR AS PLOT POINT – *THE LORD OF THE RINGS: STRATEGY BATTLE GAME*

The Lord of the Rings: Strategy Battle Game (Cavatore and Ward, 2005) is based on the books and movies of the same game, where it would be entirely inappropriate for a leading hero such as Aragorn to be slain during a minor encounter. As such, named characters have 'fate' points, which can be spent to avoid a fatal wound on a roll of four or more, and 'might' points, which can be used to adjust a roll of the player's choice. Aragorn having three points of each

---

DOI: 10.1201/9781003314820-29

is literally unkillable to the first fatal blow he suffers. An excellent touch is that the character Boromir, who dies to bow fire in the story, has a high might score of 6, making him near unbeatable in close combat, but a fate of only 1, meaning that he can be killed easily by ranged attacks. The mechanics created to project plot concepts have been used to create them.

Removal Timing

Many systems will allow a unit to operate at full, or close to full, capacity until removal. Since units often reach the point of removal around the same time, this can create a sense of a sudden rush of removals and a quick gathering of focus. This effect can be built on depending on when removal occurs, either as soon as the damage happens or during a removal phase.

Removal within a round means that as soon as a unit or trooper suffers damage sufficient to destroy it, it is removed from play. The biggest issue with this system is that units can be removed before acting, often before significantly affecting the game state. If one force has more capacity to effect damage at range, then this can mean that to balance forces, one side has to include units who have little purpose other than to die. When units are represented by multiple expensive miniatures requiring hours of preparation, this can be disheartening for players and result in a barrier to entry. The primary advantages to removal as soon as damage is applied is that it is intuitive; when someone gets shot, they die, and it requires minimal book-keeping since damage does not always need to be noted until a removal phase.

Alternatively, a removal phase is a specific phase, generally at the end of a round, during which all damage takes effect and units are removed. Such that every unit has at least a chance to engage with the game, but it can require additional book-keeping since damage has to be noted until the phase occurs. Arguably, although less intuitive, this is more realistic. Games are turn-based attempts to re-create simultaneous action, so removal within a round can mean that two units that should be moving and attacking simultaneously can see one removed before they so much as raise their weapons in response.

Weakness

As units take damage, they may degrade in performance. A simple example being as a squad loses troopers, the unit is able to make fewer attacks. In *Bolt Action* (Cavatore, 2016), damage against vehicles requires a roll on a table that can result in stunning the crew, immobilising the vehicle or causing morale effects. This can be a difficult balance to get right; degradation is interesting and realistic, but a unit able to do less is potentially less fun to operate. There are two risks: one is that the performance of the unit is reduced to the point at which it can no longer have a meaningful impact on the game, at which point activating it becomes little more than an administrative chore, and it would likely have been better for it to have just been removed. For this reason, degradation is rarely a central mechanic in a system, but if used, degraded units should not require more administration than active ones, and they should maintain a level of control, particularly in relation to movement and basic operations. Units which move normally have tactical worth to players as distractions, speed bumps or objective claimers, even if their combat effectiveness is close to nil, while those that suffer movement penalties quickly become little more than irritations. The second risk with degraded units is that loss of abilities means the removal of choices and a reduction of interest; instead, it is worth considering degradation, which results in increased unpredictability as units or vehicles lose control. This has the advantage of possibly resulting in increased rates of damage to the unit itself, speeding the end of the game.

Providing the players with choices is, as ever, a key route to interesting game play. In *Man O' War* (Jones, King and Stillman, 1993), an aggressor has the option of 'aiming high', which increases the chance of damaging their target's sails and slowing them down, or 'aiming low', which increases the chance of building up attritional damage towards sinking the vessel, but without any attendant degradation in performance.

It should be said that degradation can provide drama. When a desperate task needs to be completed to save the day, the fact that the individual given the job of achieving it has to drag themselves to the vital point can be highly dramatic. A barely surviving combatant crawling to a detonator as the enemy rushes towards their position is a moment so repeated as to be nearly cliche. If it is possible for a player to be excited to activate a largely degraded unit, a game has achieved something very special, but since injuries and objectives will arise unpredictably, this is extremely difficult to orchestrate with any level of reliability.

RECOVERY

As miniatures games tend to utilise a zeroing structure, allowing units to recover or be introduced can divert a game from its dramatic goal and, worse, give players the sense that they are repeating the same sequence of events without advancing the game state. However, there are some ways of interestingly allowing the recovery of combat effectiveness if such a narrative arc is suitable for the game.

HEALING AND REPAIRING

Units can have the ability to heal or repair themselves or other partially damaged units. This can be via a repeatable action or a limited resource. If based on repeatable actions, this amounts to increasing the wounds of more highly valued units, particularly if the action to heal replaces the chance to perform other actions, at which point the question becomes, why take a healer rather than more of the healed unit? If a game has a good range of battlefield roles, the answer is that healers provide flexibility, essentially becoming extra copies of whichever unit turns out to be most important in a given session. Healing based on limited resources inherently creates choices of management and application of those resources, but it also increases book-keeping and a potential sense of loss aversion to create bad feelings for players. It is worth considering whether you will allow such healing or repair effects to fully restore (or even add to) a unit's starting wounds. Allowing healing, but never fully, allows for player decision-making about whether to apply a scarce resource, but without providing a mechanism to fully revert changes in the game state, which can feel frustrating to players and, in worse cases, elongate a game significantly as the zeroing in is reset for a given unit.

SUMMONING

Units can have the ability to summon others, often explained by magical powers in fantasy-based games (summoning is an expected trope of undead forces), but easily explained by calling in dynamically deployed troops in other settings. Summoning can be a difficult ability to balance, particularly in a game with alternating activations where activation advantage can make summons extremely tactically powerful. Furthermore, summon abilities change in value as the game progresses, as fewer remaining turns provide less time for the summoned troops to make their presence felt. For these reasons, summon abilities should be tightly controlled, in particular in relation to the victory condition value of any summoned troops, usually specifying that they have no inherent victory point value and sometimes that they cannot affect other victory conditions.

REINFORCEMENTS

Summon abilities create additional troops not purchased during force creation; reinforcements are purchased during force creation but are introduced to the table outside of the initial set-up. Since reinforcements are bought during normal force selection, they can leave the force that makes them underpowered in the early stages of play, which means the advantage of late arrival must be significant if this is to be a selected ability. Reinforcements that are simply late arrivals to the standard deployment zone should be considered a disadvantage, although they can interestingly alter the game tempo.

Both summoning and reinforcement mechanisms represent 'laddering' mechanisms that are uncommon to these games and thus can feel surprising and novel at best, but can potentially feel counter-intuitive or even unfair if implemented unsuccessfully.

GAME TEMPO

We have mentioned the speed with which a game approaches its climax, the rhythm of actions and abilities and the narrowing and widening of options. These all create a game's tempo, places where the choices speed up with player familiarity or increased simplicity and then slow down as goals become clarified and focus narrows. Rates of attrition are one of the major contributing factors to the tempo of a game, and forms of reinforcement are ways of refining that tempo. With healing, it becomes more efficient to attack and remove units with sudden, powerful strikes, creating a tempo that jumps in steps. Summoning creates a situation where forces may increase in early turns but more quickly dwindle in later ones, causing an accelerated sense of late-game momentum. Reinforcements can cause a more level, stretched-out tempo as forces are added a little at a time, or when used to surround an enemy and attack from a superior position, a sense of slower, quieter turns of manoeuvring followed by sudden ambushes and sprung traps.

None of these are right or wrong, better or worse than another; they are choices, only truly meaningful in relation to what you want your game to achieve. Select and understand your tempo, the rhythm of your game, and then commit to it. Slow moments of building tension, sudden assault, ongoing pressure and desperate struggles for life are all valid dramatic choices; all that really matters is to choose.

SUMMARY

Games use **Damage** to create **Progression** but can result in **Disengagement.** This can be avoided by using:

- **Plot Armour** – protecting significant units.
- **Removal Timing** – taking units away only after they've had a chance to act.
- **Weakness** – degrading the performance of units rather than removing them.

Games can use **Recovery** to subvert expectations and provide flexibility using:

- Healing – can cause stagnation by reversing player actions.
- Summoning – can be tough to balance throughout a game.
- Reinforcements – alter tempo rather than balance.

EXPERIMENTS

Give each player three chances each turn to cancel a given action's wounds. Allow them to use it on any unit, then only on characters, then only on their force's leader.

Take off casualties as soon as they are caused, then take them off only at the end of the round.

Give each force a healer, which once each round can restore a unit to one fewer wound than it started the round with, then have them restore all wounds, but only up to twice per game.

Split each force into two parts; have one part arrive halfway through the game from a deployment zone at least three moves away from the original deployment zone.

REFERENCES

Cavatore, A. (2016) *Bolt Action*. Oxford: Osprey.
Cavatore, A. and Ward, M. (2005) *The Lord of the Rings: Strategy Battle Game*. Nottingham: Games Workshop Ltd.
Jones, A., King, B. and Stillman, N. (1993) *Man O' War*. [Board game] Nottingham: Games Workshop.

26 Victory Conditions

All good things come to an end, including games. Your game will need to designate how it ends and, potentially, who wins.

GAME LENGTH AND ENDING

The length of a session and the manner of its ending are vital in setting the tempo of a game. Tension is maintained by players feeling the pressure of having less time than they need to achieve all their goals. This tension can be created in various ways.

PRESET

The simplest and most common approach is to set a number of rounds the game will last for and end the game at the end of the last round. By examining the average speed, range and damage output of a unit in your game, along with their starting distance from the enemy, you can estimate the number of rounds it takes for engagement to begin and resolve. Take that number and subtract one, and it's a safe bet you've got a good game length.

The strengths of this system are significant: it's easily understood by even inexperienced players and is easy to plan a strategy around. It's simple to calculate and balance to give a solid, consistent game experience. The downsides are that it's artificial and can lead to artificial behaviour. There's no diegetic reason for the battle to end after six rounds. Why do the armies decide to cease hostilities at exactly that point? No-one knows. A set number of turns can encourage odd behaviour since players know exactly when a game will end, what their troops can and can't achieve and when objectives will be scored. It's not unusual to see units at the end of preset session-length games turning their backs on the enemy and running over to empty table quarters or unassuming hills.

SEMI-RANDOM

One method of solving the player behaviour problem of a preset game length while maintaining its strengths is to make the game end conditions semi-random. A totally random game length would make designing a consistent game experience near impossible. But if, for example, a session would generally last six rounds, players can instead roll a D6 at the end of each round and add the round number to the result, ending the game on a ten or more. Before round 9, players cannot be certain that the game will end after the current round, but games would remain a practical length. The ending would remain arbitrary, but artificial behaviour may be reduced by the uncertain tactical rationale of rushing over to the aforementioned

DOI: 10.1201/9781003314820-30

hill when there may still be battles to be fought. The solution you choose will need to take into account the variability in game length you believe your players will tolerate and the average round length of your game. For example, if each of your game turns is 30 minutes, the D6 solution above can vary the game length by up to three hours.

EVENT TRIGGERED

It is common for combat-centric games to include at least one form of event-triggered game end condition: if only one player remains with units in play, the game ends ('last player standing'). If a game's victory conditions are such that one player can obtain victory during a session, the game should end at that point, avoiding players mechanically operating the game beyond the point at which its outcome is decided.

It is also possible to detach the game-end conditions from the victory conditions, which can create strategic decisions such as players choosing to end the game quickly once leading. These end conditions can be based on diegetic effects (such as 'once the castle wall is breached, the game continues for three further rounds and then ends') or non-diegetic effects (such as 'once a player has spent their last command token, the current round becomes the final round').

CASE STUDY: NON-DIEGETIC PLAYER-CONTROLLED GAME END – *7TV*

In *7TV* (Dawson and Perrotton, 2010), a session of play ends when a deck of cards known as the 'cliffhanger' deck runs out. At the start of each turn, a card is flipped from the deck, giving a temporary rule affecting the game. Players who wish to speed towards the end of the game can elect to flip two cards in return for all players gaining activations.

An interesting feature of the *7TV* deck is that the number of cards in it depends on the size of the playing area. While unusual, this ensures there is always time for the game to be resolved before it ends.

It is important to note that putting the triggering of the game end entirely in the hands of players can mean that by wilfulness, incompetence or incapacity, they may create a session that is problematically long or short, damaging their or their opponent's enjoyment of your game. A sound principle is to include both player-controlled and preset end conditions. For example, in *7TV*, players can speed or delay the coming of the game's end, but it will always occur eventually. A good mix is to have a game end after a certain number of rounds, when a player is wiped out, or when an event occurs, and then drive the game towards that event occurring. A common formulation of this principle is to state (for example): 'the game ends when one player has three victory points, or when only one player has units in play, or at the end of round five, whichever is sooner'.

VICTORY CONDITIONS

Before beginning a session, players usually need to know how they are going to win, and once a session is finished, players will usually want to know who won. The conditions and rules for selecting a winner are the **victory conditions**. We explored the role of the victory condition in games more generally in Chapter 8. There are a range of options for their implementation, though points removal and objective-based are the most common.

As we said before, even if your game crowns only a single winner, the design of your victory conditions can ensure multiple players feel like they *almost* won. If your victory conditions permit scoring, consider having scoring occur at regular intervals or continuously. If scoring is only checked at the end of the game, the losers just lose, but if scoring occurs at multiple points in your game, an ultimate loser can still potentially have the fun of having been the winner for a stretch.

POINTS REMOVAL

Units tend to have point values attached for army building purposes, as we discuss in Chapter 30. Conveniently, this puts a value on the casualties a player causes during a game, which can be used to define victory: count up the point values of the units each player removed, and the most removed wins. This is easy to comprehend since players familiarise themselves with point values before a game in the process of list building, and removing more of an opponent's troops than they remove of yours is easily grasped. It also builds in basic tactical exchanges and possible surprises, as small elite forces can have fewer troopers removed but still lose.

However, this method has some potential issues. Firstly, it lacks the chance for interesting reversals; once a unit is removed, it tends to stay removed, so sudden changes in the dynamic are unlikely. Secondly, there really is only one story points removal scoring can tell: that of a direct war of attrition. It contains only the most basic concepts of a larger strategy and says little about the motivation or relationships of the combatants. Thirdly, many army list-building systems allow for a good deal of customisation of the player's forces across many units; this can result in the process of counting casualties being non-trivial. Often, to keep resolution, snappy units will be worth no points if more than half of their troopers remain or half points if some remain, making the last members of the unit strangely precious. Fourthly, victory conditions are a method of guiding player behaviour to make a game more interesting and enjoyable. Not only will players seek to destroy their opponent no matter the victory conditions, but all victory conditions become easier when an opponent has fewer units. Therefore, victory conditions based on removing opposing units don't really guide player behaviour and can be a wasted opportunity.

The key consideration with points removal is its tendency to snowball. Consider a game in which the player who has removed the greatest number of their opponent's in-play wounds (or list-building points) at the end of the game is the winner. This game has players risking what are essentially their victory points (in the form of their troopers) to gain victory points (by killing the opponent's troopers). This means that the player who is ahead in victory points has more of the means to gain more victory points, and the game is a single-track, zero-sum process (one player's gain is equivalent to the opponent's loss). This might be exactly what a game wants; it is focused and zeros in swiftly and inexorably on a winner. However, it creates a snowballing effect where an early lead makes winning easier, which can feel unsatisfying. Alternatively, we can design a game in which victory points are decoupled from wounds, allowing for situations in which a player has to choose between spending their activations to remove an opponent's ability to activate (by killing their troopers), gain victory points (by completing objectives) or become more capable in future attempts (by gaining resources that facilitate actions). In this game, the player who is winning in victory points can be the one with the least chance to pick up more since they have spent activations without reducing their opponent's resources. This is why objective-based games often feel more satisfactory from a game-play perspective.

INTERACTIVE OBJECTIVES

A more narrative approach is to give units the ability to perform actions in relation to objectives. Players could be asked to deploy markers at the start of a session that could be activated, searched or moved, with points being scored throughout or at the end of the session for markers being in the right state at the right time. Markers can be affected by both sides, changed and reversed and can score more points in later turns than earlier ones, allowing players to catch up. They can allow for a range of complex stories and subtle guidance for players while being simple to calculate with few objectives, creating complex and dynamic stories. However, depending on the subject matter of the game, such objectives can require rules not inherent to the basic process of the game in the way that removal tends to be, requiring players to engage with extra rules and potentially complex tactics. This additional complexity can be a double-edged sword, depending on whether the difficulty of engaging it outweighs the interest.

POSITIONAL OBJECTIVES

A potential middle point is to have players score due to the position of units on the tabletop, potentially taking into account the points values of the respective units. For example, the player with the most troops in a given quarter of the table, at a high point or within a set distance of a certain point could win, or score, on a given turn. Units can move in and out of position, providing dynamism; the required positions can tell interesting stories; and the system remains relatively simple to engage with.

DIFFERENT AND HIDDEN

Objective-based victory systems provide the opportunity to give different players different objectives and, furthermore, to potentially keep those objectives hidden from opponents. This can add both narrative and gameplay tension, as well as further verisimilitude, since a commander will rarely know exactly what their opposite number intends. In *Malifaux* (Anderson *et al.*, 2013), for example, players generate a pool of available objectives from which they secretly choose a certain number to attempt during play. While such hidden, uneven objective generation systems can create highly dynamic games of bluff and counter-bluff as players feign interest in one area while secretly coveting another, they can result in two players that simply have entirely separate goals and so fail to have reason to interact directly. Ensuring that whatever combination of objectives are generated, players are driven to interact with each other is vital.

An interesting option for uneven objectives is to design them to be in direct opposition. For example, one player could be trying to stop a building from being occupied while another is attempting to occupy it. These sorts of asymmetrical objectives are often seen in set-piece scenarios, such as siege games or last stands, but there is no reason that they should not be generated like any other form of objective with 'attacker' and 'defender' being randomly assigned.

Fundamentally, as discussed in Chapter 8, victory conditions are a game designer's best tool for showing players what they are 'meant' to be doing and what they should be focused on. It is best to try to make this the most interesting and enjoyable part of the game. It is unfortunately common to find rule systems whose play experiences and design goals are undermined by ill-considered victory condition design or otherwise fine games that use a 'simplified' method of determining victory in the first or 'tutorial' game, which leads to a disappointing or unthematic first-touch experience for new players. Strong victory conditions with clear criteria, points of interaction and narrative threads are essential to strong games and thus worth spending considerable time and effort on.

SUMMARY

- A session's length defines its **Tempo** and **Tension**. It can be:
  - **Preset** – easily understood, but can create unusual unit behaviour.
  - **Semi Random** – restricts non-simulationist behaviour but can be hard to judge and control.
  - **Event Triggered** – at least when one force is eradicated, the game should end. Can lead to endless games if used alone.
- Players should know how they will win before play and have it quickly resolved after, usually using **Victory Conditions**:
  - **Points Removal** – if units have a value, it can be used to calculate victory, simple but without narrative range and suffers from in-built snowballing.
  - **Interactive Objectives** – highly narrative but can require additional complexity to define, interact with and score.
  - **Positional Objectives** – simple to interact with and fairly flexible.
    - This can all be **Asymmetrical** and **Hidden** from one player to another.

EXPERIMENTS

End your game two turns before it would usually end, then two turns after. End it after any turn after the second when a coin flip comes up heads. End it when one player loses half their force or moves their last unit across the centreline of the table.

Have a player win if they end the game having removed one more unit than their opponent, or two, or three. Have a player win if they have a unit on a designated terrain feature for two full turns.

REFERENCES

Anderson, M., Caroland, N., Cohen, R., Darland, A., Gibbs, J., Hanold, D., Johns, E., Martin, M. and Weber, D. (2013) *Malifaux: Second Edition*. South Korea: Wyrd Miniatures, LLC.

Dawson, G. and Perrotton, K. (2010) *7TV*. Lincolnshire: Crooked Dice Game Design Studio.

27 Special Abilities

It is vital that players stick to the rules while playing your game. However, a couple of powerful motivators in playing are the twin desires to feel smart and powerful, and few things give those feelings more than 'breaking' the rules of the game. As such, most games include rule-breaking abilities or powers, which we will refer to as 'special abilities': that go directly against the established rules of the game, allowing players to step outside the normal boundaries and do something unusual and potentially spectacular. This can be done with a special abilities sub-phase as well as by including special abilities to trigger within other phases of the game.

In general terms, the strength of special abilities is to provide wholly new tactical and strategic options and to potentially limit those options from being evenly distributed among players, creating tactical asymmetry and the chance for players to act in 'uniquely' clever-looking and cinematic ways. Ideally, special abilities do not simply increase existing numbers (five goes to six), but offer access to otherwise impossible actions or options (flying in a game in which most things walk on the ground).

SPECIAL ABILITIES SUB-PHASE

One of the significant advantages of special abilities is that they allow for additional story and a sense of personality to be added to the game or the forces. For example, how a game names its special abilities sub-phase, if it has one, is highly indicative. If it's called the 'magic phase' we generally know we're playing a fantasy game, 'psychic powers' most likely indicate science fiction, 'special plays' a sports theme, 'hacking' cyberpunk, with the same going for a range of other terms and genres. These sub-phases are largely functionally similar; special rules will be employed, and everyone can be prepared for some fireworks.

Boxing out special abilities into their own phase has strengths and weaknesses. On the plus side, by sectioning off rule-breaking powers, it is relatively easy to limit the disruption they can cause to the rest of your rules. In addition, it reduces the chances of a player feeling bad because a rule-breaking ability created a 'gotcha' moment, since there is at least a phase to expect 'gotcha' moments in. On the downside, creating a separate phase for rule-breaking moments can reduce their impact, and it can limit the design space for what can be done with them. However, there's no inherent reason a system can't have both forms of special rules.

Special abilities phases tend to take a set pattern, namely, each player will have a selection of available abilities, quite often emanating from a powerful or important single character (affording the capability to perform special abilities is one of the quickest ways of identifying a character as powerful or important to players and provides another reason to include special abilities in your game). A player will select an ability, possibly perform some form of test or check; if successful, their opponent

 DOI: 10.1201/9781003314820-31

may have the chance to stop or respond to the activation of the ability, and then the ability will be applied.

THE MENU

The abilities offered in a special abilities phase tend to come with players being offered a menu of choices, such as a spell list in a fantasy game. This allows players more choice and for each ability to be focused and situational to limit their game-breaking powers while still being attractive due to their being a selection available. Often, there will be an even broader set of options that a player will take, one or another of a subsection of choices from which they can select during the special abilities phase. These can be linked intrinsically to the faction a player selects, such as in *Saga* (Buchel, 2011), where each faction comes with a 'battle board' of special abilities that can be selected by dice placement during the 'orders phase'. Alternatively, there can be a choice, such as in *Warhammer: The Game of Fantasy Battles (sixth edition)* (Cavatore *et al.*, 2000), where a wizard can select from a range of 'magic lores', each of which comes with a selection of spells to use.

THE TEST

Once an ability is chosen, there may be a randomised result required to trigger the ability in question. This can be done by expending a limited resource and taking it before or after choosing the ability. In *Saga*, 'Saga dice' are rolled during the order phase and then applied to special powers, so the random event takes place before the abilities are chosen. In *Warhammer*, a spell is chosen, and then a wizard needs to assign and roll limited 'power dice' against a target number to see if their casting is successful. This means players get to engage with choosing how to assign limited resources and that these powerful abilities are limited and potentially unpredictable, stopping players from relying on them too heavily.

THE RESPONSE

Since special abilities can be quite powerful, it is sometimes beneficial to give opponents a chance to respond to them or negate them. In the case of *Warhammer*, players have 'dispel dice'; if they can beat the total rolled in casting, then the spell does not take place.

The decision to include a test to trigger an ability and the possibility to respond or cancel it is one that will go some way towards defining the feel of your game. If special abilities can fail or be cancelled, there is a risk that what players were promised as a fireworks factory can turn out to be a damp squib. Thinking you are going to trigger something that will make you feel smart and powerful and having it taken away can cause a moment of disappointment for the player. On the other hand, being powerless to respond to an opponent repeatedly triggering awesome game-breaking effects can create its own moments of player frustration. A game may want to allow players to feel powerful when they are active in return for a lack of control while passive, and ask them to understand that they take their lumps in return for being allowed to get their licks in when it's their shot. Alternatively, a game may prefer players to feel as though they always have a chance to respond to everything as it happens and that they can protect themselves against their opponent's vicissitudes.

The Effect

The effects of special abilities should, to some degree or another, break the standard rules of your game. It can be as simple as an attack that doesn't need to test to hit, through to passing control of a unit to their opponent. A good rule of thumb is to approach each of the game's rule areas and create a set of abilities that break them in interesting ways. This will give you the raw materials from which to create interesting and synergistic clusters of special abilities into faction-specific or 'magic lore' style menus.

TRIGGERED ABILITIES

In addition to boxing-out specific abilities into their own phase, they can be triggered within other phases of the game and originate as part of a unit's capabilities. Allowing players to take an action that their opponent doesn't have access to right in the middle of play can make them feel powerful. The downside can be that, if there are a lot of potential special abilities that players have access to, they may be less likely to know the details of their opponent's options, potentially increasing the possibility of players feeling as though they were surprised by a rules interaction that was open information but which they missed due to overwhelming complexity.

Options

Unit-bound special rules will tend to either be inherent to a given unit or bought prior to playing. In *Malifaux: Second Edition* (Anderson *et al.*, 2013), units have a list of inherent special abilities which are pre-set. Players need to find the combination of units that offers the set of special abilities required to achieve their goals. The advantage of offering special abilities in this way is that it is relatively easy to control players' access to them since there will generally be controls already in place limiting which units a player has access to. The downside is that it is possible for the concept of exceptional unit capabilities to lose much of its meaning (when every unit has multiple special rules, they start to just be the rules) and for the cognitive load placed on the players to increase significantly.

In a game with a lot of units and factions, such as *Warhammer* or *Malifaux*, similar unit capabilities may be folded into a central list of standardised special abilities that are then given to multiple units, and rules that have similar or complementary effects are named in a manner that connects them together. In both cases, the objective is to manage the growth of complexity and permit players to more easily recall rules elements that are used less regularly than the core rules of the system. With special rules, a disciplined approach to limiting the total number of special abilities and repeating terminology wherever possible will significantly ease the pressure on players.

Alternatively, units can be offered the chance to purchase special rules as upgrades. *Gaslands* (Hutchinson, 2017) takes this option by offering players the chance to purchase special abilities for their units, called 'perks', in combinations that they choose from sets of options. This can allow players to decide on the level of complexity that works for their own playstyle, although closing out powerful combinations and loopholes while providing a range of viable options can require careful testing and design. *Gaslands* only allows any given player access to two menus of six perks at a time, significantly curtailing the chance of unforeseen combinations.

BUFFS AND DEBUFFS

Two standard classes of special abilities are those that give a unit positive modifiers, or 'buffs', or an opponent negative modifiers, or 'debuffs'. It is important to create clear rules on how buffs and debuffs interact or 'stack', that is, if they can be repeatedly used to increase the level of effect. For example, if a buff increases a dice roll by one, should having five of them on one unit make all six-sided dice results successful? Allowing stacking or not is a design choice. Games that allow the stacking of buffs can result in powerful combinations, which, in turn, can require players to engage with them to remain competitive. A useful alternative to consider is to allow stacking, but not if effects come from the same source. This allows control over which alternative sources players have access to and can force diversity of interaction. However you choose to deal with stacking, it is a good idea to ensure that the choice is applied consistently. Allowing some effects to be stacked but not others can lead to overly powerful edge-case combinations and moments of frustrated surprise in play. While buff options tend to increase the tactical interest or effectiveness of a unit, the design of debuffs can be more thorny. Debuff options can range from reducing the affected units options (allowing them to hit just as hard, but potentially reducing the unit's tactical interest), making them less effective (keeping their tactical options open, but potentially reducing their controller's power fantasy), or making them more susceptible to enemy actions (potentially building a 'correct' way of combing units, creating options that will be ignored in favour of direct damage or increasing their opponent's power fantasy without directly decreasing their controller's).

PASSIVE AND ACTIVE

Special abilities can be passive, meaning that they are in play once attached to a unit irrespective of what else happens, or active, meaning that they need to be triggered by expending resources, such as actions.

Keeping track of passive abilities can be tricky for players since they are always in play and they don't need to be engaged with actively. However, there are often effects that only make sense if they take place during the activation of other units or players. Additionally, active abilities generally require they be triggered rather than doing something else, meaning more subtle effects will need to be offered passively since players will be unlikely to ever trigger them otherwise. To help players keep track of passive abilities, it can be a good idea to trigger their effects somewhat consistently so that players know to check their passive abilities at a certain range, when an opposing model activates, or when an opposing model attacks, rather than trying to remember to check for every possible in-game action or state change.

Passive abilities require triggering conditions, either when the attached unit performs a certain action or when something occurs within a set distance of the attached unit. Active abilities are triggered directly, making them easier to integrate into the standard play loops of the game, although they can sometimes require additional bookkeeping to track how often they can be triggered.

AURAS, PULSES AND TARGETS

Special abilities that affect other units will need to make clear exactly which other units they affect. This will tend to be based on either all units within a certain range, often referred to as 'aura' effects (or sometimes 'pulses' if temporary), or selecting a single specific target. Targeted, active abilities create questions of resource management; aura abilities create a tabletop more focused on areas of pressure, creating fields of effects through carefully managed movement. Careful use and combination of these types can shape the feel of your game. Restricting targeting to only friendly or only enemy models or forcing the ability to affect all models within range each provide different feelings and tactical challenges.

AESTHETICS AND LORE

Players can be motivated to play and collect a game from a range of interests. Aside from purely mechanical gameplay concerns, the look of a particular miniature, either if supplied directly or suggested by art and background, or the lore that attaches to a unit, can be a strong drive. Special abilities can be an excellent tool for allowing a miniature's capabilities within the game to match up to their appearance or background; they can allow you to ensure that a unit performs in the manner that your narrative text promised it would. By considering and integrating these disparate elements, you can ensure immersion in your game.

For example, a given character could be stated in its background to be the greatest sniper in your universe. You could simply give them a higher accuracy statistic, but this often leads to the sense that they are just on a sliding scale, more capable than other combatants, but in a manner that is reachable and achievable. If, instead, you give them the ability to make multiple shots in a single action or automatically hit in certain situations, they become unique and powerful in a manner that no other unit can match.

Special abilities can allow players to feel smart and powerful. They can not only let players feel as though they are playing a unique force, but one that matches your background and plays the way you promised it would. They can also lead to confusion, frustration at unexpected rules interactions and disappointment if they do not deliver on their promises. Keep them consistent and logical in their effects; they should result in a player targeted by them celebrating just as hard as the player who triggered them because just the right cool thing happened in just the right way.

SUMMARY

Special Ability Sub-phases allow players to feel powerful and clever while reducing frustration. Special abilities tend to consist of:

- **A Menu:** Choosing a set of abilities can theme a force or unit.
- **A Test:** Before or after triggering the ability.
- **A Response:** To allow opponents a sense of agency.

Special abilities can be **Triggered** within play. They can then be:

- **Options:** Limiting access to abilities can control their interactions.
- **Buffs** and **Debuffs:** Buffs increase abilities, debuffs decrease them.
- **Passive** and **Active:** Passive abilities are constantly in play, active ones require specific triggers.
- **Auras, Pulses** or **Targeted:** Auras affect troopers within a set range in all directions constantly; pulses do so in a single action. Targeted abilities select a single individual.

EXPERIMENTS

Place all special abilities in your game into a single, shared, sub-phase, then spread them throughout the game.

Require special abilities to have a test passed to trigger, then simply trigger them by expending a resource. Allow targets to respond to cancel abilities, to trigger an ability of their own or to have no response at all.

Have buff abilities freely stackable, then allow no stacking at all, then only stacking of non-identical abilities.

Have debuffs reduce a unit's action options, then their statistics, then make them more susceptible to other abilities and attacks.

REFERENCES

Anderson, M., Caroland, N., Cohen, R., Darland, A., Gibbs, J., Hanold, D., Johns, E., Martin, M. and Weber, D. (2013) *Malifaux: Second Edition*. South Korea: Wyrd Miniatures, LLC.

Buchel, A. (2011) *Saga*. Evesham: Gripping Beast.

Cavatore, A., Pirinen, T., Priestley, R., Stillman, N. and Thornton, J. (2000) *Warhammer: The Game of Fantasy Battles*. 6th edn. Nottingham: Games Workshop Ltd.

Hutchinson, M. (2017) *Gaslands*. Oxford: Osprey Games.

28 Scenarios

While a system can, and should, have a strong set of satisfying mechanics and play loops, even the best of them can become predictable when each session shares the exact same parameters. In order to allow for play to stay fresh both tactically and narratively, games often provide sets of special rules to be applied to a single play session. These rules are generally called 'scenarios', and in this chapter, we will enumerate the most common reasons for creating them and the standard elements they tend to contain.

VARIED META-GAME

When players repeatedly engage with a game, it is possible for play to become predictable. If your game has a focus on list-building, over time, play can become more about predicting which forces your opponent will likely field rather than skill at the tabletop. By offering a range of scenarios, it can be made much more difficult to come to the tabletop with a pre-set plan of play based on the force being used, increasing at the tabletop engagement. *Malifaux: Second Edition* (Anderson *et al.*, 2013) asks players to generate a scenario by randomly selecting from one of four set-up conditions, one of five 'strategies' and five of a possible 19 'schemes', creating a head-spinning range of possible combinations which presses players to adjust to the game at hand and creates a dynamic and replayable game.

NARRATIVE OR HISTORICAL EMULATION

While the core rules of a game can create a strong narrative and players are free to spring off from them in a range of directions, they offer a single starting point with a single perspective. Offering scenarios that have distinct narrative rules and stories attached can provide a range of jumping-off points. For example, *The Lord of the Rings: Strategy Battle Game* (Cavatore and Ward, 2005) includes scenarios such as 'Balin's Tomb', which allows players to both directly re-create one of the most dramatic combat scenes from the movie trilogy the game was based on and then alter the scene to tell new versions of the story.

FIRST TOUCH OR HOBBY PROJECT

Scenarios are interesting in relation to the idea of your game as a hobby, in that they often sit at the extreme ends of being part of a fast-pick-up game or dedicated hobby project. Making a decision on which sort of engagement your scenarios want to engender is vital for them to be effective.

PICK-UP GAMES

If a scenario is intended to provide a competitive challenge and perhaps be played between relative strangers without pre-planning, you should consider that it will then often be first encountered at the table. Whenever a player arrives at a game, there

DOI: 10.1201/9781003314820-32

can be a lot to take in: setting out terrain, organising armies, understanding an opponent's list and possibly meeting a new person. A scenario introduced in this situation needs to be quickly and easily comprehensible, particularly its victory conditions, which need to be clear and any special rules simple. A good principle is to put a lot of the scenario's elements into its set-up conditions. This is because the set-up of a scenario is done publicly, with both players co-operating and the rules under shared scrutiny. Furthermore, set-up is generally engaged with once and then finished. The victory conditions should be exceptionally clear, partly because this type of play is more often directly driven by victory and partly because victory conditions are rarely discussed and examined publicly, with players preferring to plan their strategy for victory secretly.

HOBBY PROJECTS

Scenarios make excellent hobby projects. Offering a scenario that requires specific terrain models, strange non-player-controlled creatures or special characters gives players the chance to indulge in extra hobby activities leading up to playing a scenario. In this case, players will organise to play a scenario before meeting up to play, at which point it's reasonable to assume that all players will familiarise themselves with the scenario. In turn, if players have spent hours creating special terrain or miniatures, they will expect those pieces to have an interesting and significant effect on the game. Essentially, a virtuous hobby circle is created. Players want to create interesting miniatures, which your scenario gives them the chance to do, and their creation of the miniature makes them more invested in its special rules, which allows you to let loose in creating them. It is worth mentioning that the aim is to offer the chance to engage in extra hobby projects, not to demand them. Allowing and inspiring players to build an entire bespoke tabletop is an excellent hobby motivator; requiring it will drive people away from your game.

PROCEDURAL SCENARIOS

Scenarios are generally built from a set of rules, such as set-up, special rules, ending and scoring. As such, it is possible to set out tables of options for each and have players randomly generate the various elements to create a scenario procedurally. This has the advantage of quickly offering a huge range of varied scenarios. *Malifaux* has a system which spans just eight pages and offers over 9,000 possible different scenario combinations. If your objective is to throw off competitive players who wish to practice every possible combination, this has obvious advantages. Such systems can also throw up fascinating emergent narratives. *A Billion Suns* (Hutchinson, 2021) generates its scenarios procedurally by asking players to combine three mission options from a possible 12, each containing a small three-act structure which can interact in surprising ways to produce rich genre narratives. The greatest strength of such a system is its greatest weakness, in that while each of the parts of the scenarios can be tested and examined, testing each of even a hundred possible combinations is a huge task, so problematic combinations will almost certainly find their way through.

PRE-WRITTEN SCENARIOS

A more controlled set of options can be created by writing out a set of rules and presenting them as a pre-built scenario. This is an approach found in many systems, as it gives the players a stable, predictable way to play which can easily be agreed upon in advance and prepared for. They can be playtested much more thoroughly than a procedural system. If a specific narrative is to be created, such as *The Lord of the Rings: Strategy Battle Game*, recreating specific scenes from a series of movies, this is the only realistic option. Possibly the biggest disadvantage of set scenarios is that players have a tendency to default to the perceived 'standard' scenario, which will tend to be the one that invites players to line up and beat each other senseless with whatever comes to hand. How much of a disadvantage this is depends on whether you're aiming for engendering familiarity or avoiding staleness, and how well the core experience of your game is represented by whatever constitutes its standard scenario. With a procedural scenario system, it is easier to suggest that there is no default option, so players naturally mix things up every time they play.

STANDARD SCENARIO FORMAT

Scenarios can potentially offer special rules for any part of a game, but they tend to do so in four distinct sections: set-up, special rules, game end and victory conditions.

SET-UP

A scenario's set-up rules might include rules for the forces to be taken, how they are to be deployed and how the rest of the tabletop should be set-up. Providing restrictions on forces means players will need to prepare for the scenario ahead of time. They are commonly reserved for narrative or campaign play but can introduce both theme and strategy by requiring that players use forces with a story attached and/or unequal or complementary capabilities.

When including terrain rules, you should be mindful of both the terrain your players are likely to have access to and what you might be requiring them to prepare ahead of time specifically for this scenario. Terrain pieces can have rules in the main body of your game, with the scenario simply requiring them in specific positions and amounts.

Probably the most regularly altered scenario set-up condition is that of the player's deployment zones; any of the range of options presented in Chapter 18 that are not part of the standard rules can be used instead to create the effects explained there.

SPECIAL RULES

Scenarios may attach special rules to terrain, areas of the tabletop or units. Scenario terrain special rules tend to be more extreme than their standard rules, possibly being unbalanced or problematic if they were standard rules, such as forests of carnivorous plants or minefields. Rules can even be attached to areas of the tabletop as a sort of an abstracted version of terrain rules, representing narrative events such as extreme weather or darkness. The biggest issue to be aware of with these rules is that, unlike those pertaining to set-up or victory, they will be triggered or referenced during ongoing play, making them more likely to be forgotten in the heat of play. There are a couple of ways to lessen this problem:

- Trigger events from a state change. If your rules have a unit attacked by a carnivorous forest, make the attack occur whenever the unit moves into the forest; the movement triggers the standard checking of terrain rules and so the special rules.
- Trigger at set times in the round. If an effect can't be tied to a specific state change, it should at least be regularly checked at the same point in the round.

GAME END

A simple way of mixing up the standard version of play is to change how the trigger to end the game happens. It's reasonably standard to have a session end when a certain number of rounds have passed. Simply reducing or increasing the number can mix things up, as can making the number of rounds random by asking players to roll a dice, and add one to the result for each round, with the game ending if the result is, for example, an eight. Alternatively, the ending conditions could be events players can trigger rather than simply waiting for, such as when a certain unit dies or an objective is held for a set number of rounds. Player-triggered ending conditions are exciting and tactically interesting, but you must be sure that they will not result in unsatisfyingly short or excessively long play sessions. It can be useful to have secondary ending conditions in these instances, such as a limit to the number of rounds.

VICTORY CONDITIONS

Probably the most common special rule is to include a new scoring objective or change the standard objective scoring if your game already includes one; any of the versions of scoring outlined in Chapter 26 not otherwise present in your game would work effectively.

In short, scenarios are a method of taking your normal game and mixing it up, either to keep players tactically on their toes or tell a new story. A good rule of thumb is to design them by taking your normal play experience and asking players to start differently and end as usual, start as usual and end differently, or start and end as usual but have something unusual in between.

SUMMARY

Scenarios are a set of special rules applied to a single game session. They can:

- Keep competitive play fresh by offering unpredictable challenges.
- Provide narrative by re-creating specific events.
- Create hobby projects for players.

They can be:

- **Procedural** – sets of options generating multiple scenarios.
  - Procedural scenarios are extremely challenging to playtest fully.
- **Pre-written** – each scenario being specifically written.
  - Pre-written scenarios can lead players to default to a standard choice.

Scenarios tend to consist of:

- Set-up conditions – designating how forces should be selected, terrain placed and forces deployed.
- Special rules – adding new effects to terrain or objectives.
- Game end conditions – making the game longer or shorter.
- Victory conditions – including new objectives.

EXPERIMENTS

If your game uses procedural scenarios, create some pre-written ones; if it includes pre-written ones, create a procedural method for creating scenarios for it. If it has neither, make both.

REFERENCES

Anderson, M., Caroland, N., Cohen, R., Darland, A., Gibbs, J., Hanold, D., Johns, E., Martin, M. and Weber, D. (2013) *Malifaux: Second Edition*. South Korea: Wyrd Miniatures, LLC.
Cavatore, A. and Ward, M. (2005) *The Lord of the Rings: Strategy Battle Game*. Nottingham: Games Workshop Ltd.
Hutchinson, M. (2021) *A Billion Suns*. Oxford: Osprey Games.

29 Campaigns

While playing a self-contained session is satisfying, it can be rewarding to connect a series of sessions together with an overarching meta-system that provides a framework for them to fit into. These linking frameworks are generally contained under the umbrella term 'campaigns' although they can more properly be divided out into **meta-scoring systems**, which allow results to be compared across games, **structuring systems**, which connect games and their results together and **progression systems**, which allow players' forces to change and grow as they play more games. A system can combine any or all of these frameworks or offer a range of options that can be played separately.

HOBBY MOTIVATION

One of the benefits of an overarching linking framework is that it offers players ongoing hobby motivation. Either in the creation and alteration of their forces or in the preparation of the materials needed for a scenario, progression systems can ask players to add to their forces or even alter the appearance of individual models, while campaigns can ask players to use specific forces or units depending on the events they portray. Campaigns can inspire players to invest time in special terrain or non-player-controlled miniatures, encouraging them to step out of their creative comfort zone.

REWARDS

Linking frameworks provide a number of natural methods for motivating and rewarding players. These rules may be some variation or combination of:

- **Overall victory:** A player can win or lose a campaign just as they can a single session.
- **Narratives:** Sessions can be influenced by the results of previous ones, allowing for a linked narrative to unfold across games and for setup and objectives to be coherently connected to that narrative, rewarding both winner and loser.
- **Gameplay:** Players can be given additional force-building options or new abilities for their units from one session to the next, experimenting with which can increase enjoyment and gameplay depth over the campaign.

THE DROP-OUT PROBLEM

The common issue with linking frameworks in multiplayer environments is that they often don't get played to a mutually satisfying conclusion. Where they give advantages to victorious players, or simply cumulative scores, losing players may start to

DOI: 10.1201/9781003314820-33

lag behind, making victory more difficult, and they may choose to drop out before the conclusion, feeling that they can no longer compete effectively. It's one thing to expect a player to engage with an additional half an hour of play once they know, or strongly suspect, that they've lost when it follows a previous hour of close-fought and compelling gaming. It's quite another to expect a player to engage in organising to go to a play session, set-up and play through ninety minutes knowing that they've lost the war no matter what they do, particularly when they have days or weeks to think about it. Additionally, these frameworks can be a long-term and continual commitment that not everyone is willing to follow through with; committing to playing the same game again and again over multiple sessions may seem initially attractive to players who then lack motivation to see it through to the end. As such, how to prevent losing players from disengaging and how to control the length of the framework are both of primary concern to the designer of a campaign system.

META SCORING SYSTEMS

The very simplest linking framework is a system to record and rank results from one session to the next to find an overall winner. The most usual being a tournament or league system. Simple knock-out tournaments are the most robust overall since any player still in the tournament has a chance of winning it, and those not in it can get on with their own thing. However, tournaments require a pool of players that most groups struggle to corral and are so simple as to require little in your rules other than a suggestion that they could be a suitable option. Tournament points can be awarded in place of knock-out systems, and by escalating the available points over the course of the campaign, it can be possible to make early losses less impactful on the overall result, keeping players feeling they are in the game for longer.

League systems are possibly the worst of the available options, since they add little in the way of gameplay or narrative while creating a situation where players at the bottom of the league facing those at the top may feel they have lost before they begin. It takes a committed and self-sacrificing mindset to finish out a league when losing, and they will often peter out before their conclusion as bottom-table players go looking for a battle they can win. Again, most people can design their own league system perfectly well, so it requires little writing. If such a system is included, a few useful tips are to pre-set the number of games to be played and include a climactic scenario for the top-placed players to decide an overall winner and finish on a bang. Such a scenario can even include secondary roles for lower-placed competitors.

STRUCTURING SYSTEMS

A structuring system is a method of linking together a series of game sessions into an overall narrative. They can include overall winners and losers or progression but do not need to. Their usual purpose is to add further scope and motivation to playing. However mighty two armies might be, it is hard to imagine that the fate of entire nations would ever hang on a single isolated battle, so creating a linking framework can add an epic scope to a session. A series of linking games showing what's at stake and what is risked or won can provide diegetic motivation to keep people coming back to play when players might otherwise switch off. Campaigns do this by offering a narrative to connect results together, usually in the form of sequential narratives or map-based systems.

SEQUENTIAL NARRATIVE

A sequential narrative campaign offers different scenario elements after each session, depending on who won or lost. For example, where one player is attempting to ambush a relief force on their way to a castle under siege, if the ambusher is successful, the next scenario could require the besieged player to make a desperate sally forth to avoid starvation; if not, it could have the besieger caught between fresh arriving troops and those within the castle surging forth. These can be branching or contained. With branching campaigns, each result offers entirely separate possible scenarios; however, the number of required scenarios increases exponentially with the campaign's length (Figure 29.1). With contained results, each scenario has a range of options that the results of the previous game select between rather than entirely separate scenarios, keeping the number of scenarios required far lower and easier to follow, but possibly creating an unsatisfying situation where a player who wins every game concludes the campaign with the same result as one who only won the last one or two (Figure 29.2). A combination of the two methods can help each with their failings, such as converging a branching campaign such that winning or losing the same number of games has the same result, whatever the order of results

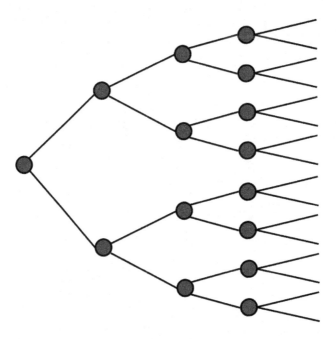

FIGURE 29.1   Fully branching campaigns require exponential numbers of unique scenarios.

FIGURE 29.2   A contained campaign can lack variation for replay value.

(Figure 29.3), or allowing sprouting branches during a contained campaign so that players who win significant pivot games in the campaign take different paths or reach different concluding scenarios (Figure 29.4). Two useful resources for further study are Chapter 17 of *The Art of Game Design* (Schell, 2020) and Appendix 1 of the sixth edition of *Warhammer: The Game of Fantasy Battles* (Cavatore *et al.*, 2000), both of which explore various approaches to branching and contained sequential narratives.

MAPS AND NODE SYSTEMS

The campaign can be set on a map, with victories claiming areas or unlocking routes to new areas. These can be constructed with a tiled system, such as in *Mighty Empires* (Priestly and Stillman, 1990), or an abstract network of connected nodes (Figure 29.5). This makes victory easy to envision, as the player holding the most locations can be ruled the final winner. It has the advantage of adding a framework in a multiplayer campaign for which players will have the chance to face which players. Where battles occur on the map, they can give an emergent set of conditions for scenarios; players can even be given the chance to improve the locations they hold

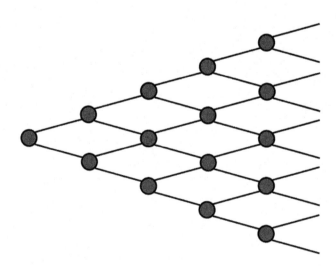

FIGURE 29.3   By converging results, the number of new scenarios can be reduced, but the breadth of options can be kept.

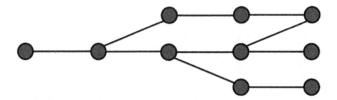

FIGURE 29.4 By sprouting secondary, tertiary and other options and allowing players to switch back and forth, scenario complexity can be reduced, but satisfaction can be provided.

with fortifications to change later scenarios that take place there. Map campaigns tend not to be amenable to narrative rewards since they are inherently quite emergent, but they give strong gameplay rewards as players can engage on the tabletop and the campaign map. Further approaches to map and node campaigns may be found in *Wargaming Campaigns* (Hyde, 2022) and *Warhammer: Lustria* (Hoare and McNeil, 2004).

The primary issue to be aware of in map campaigns is to ensure that skills within the meta-game of developing locations and controlling the map should not overrule the skills at the tabletop. Maintaining the availability of armies and troops while allowing map engagement to only shape which players face each other and the scenario conditions they experience can avoid this.

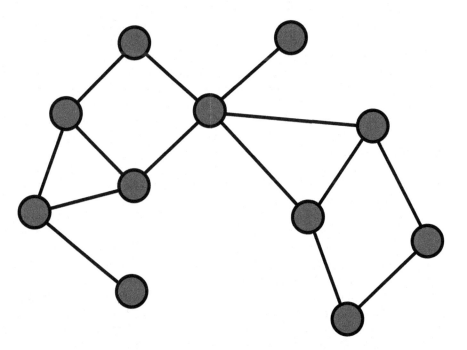

FIGURE 29.5 Node campaigns can provide an abstract campaign structure that implies a living world of cities and roads.

PROGRESSION SYSTEMS

The story behind scenarios is often that of gaining great wealth and power, and as such, a system that reflects that power and allows players to spend their wealth makes diegetic sense. In a progression system, troops can open up additional powers and abilities depending on what occurs during a campaign. This allows the system to include a potentially satisfying laddering system, where players can do more at the end of a campaign than when they began. It is also common for such systems to include negative resources in the form of injuries.

When people play games, they inevitably create stories about their troops, improbable escapes and impossible odds. A progression system with changes based on specific events can allow players to entrench these moments and their stories into rules, making them an 'official' part of the system of the game.

SNOWBALLING

Progression systems that reward the winner with more resources than the loser are common. The counterintuitive fact is that this is a poor way to design a progression system. If we assume that, on average, the better player wins, then rewarding the winner results in the better player now being both the better player and having a resource advantage. The weaker player is now at an additional disadvantage and more likely to lose the next game, creating a 'snowballing' issue. There are a few possible fixes for this, although it always remains a concern.

A popular fix is to include a 'headwind' mechanic to slow the leader. This means a system where the more powerful a player becomes, the harder it is to acquire further power. One common approach is to escalate the cost of purchasable advantages: the first advantage costs a small amount of resources, the next advantage costs incrementally more and so on. Another approach is to introduce a maintenance cost for forces, such that a player with a larger or more powerful force is 'taxed' relatively more of their earned resources to maintain their larger force. Both of these options mitigate the issue to a degree and provide in-built catch-up mechanisms. However, headwinds slow the problem down rather than fixing it (which can be enough if the campaign is short).

Another option is to detach winning from progress and even reverse the relationship between the two. That is to say, winning the campaign can be based on one measure, while becoming more powerful is based on another. For example, if players are part of a larger force fighting an overall series of battles, it could be that winning a battle gains recognition from the overall commanders, possibly advancing towards victory in the campaign but not necessarily resources for advancement. Resources could come separately based on actions during the session or could be reversed since the overall command sends more resources to problem areas, so losing players get more resources while winning players advance to victory. However, this can feel like punishing winners, particularly as losing players might get to have more fun with new interesting units or mechanics while winners just get to win.

Alternatively, advancement can simply offer more, or different, choices. If your game is balanced with something like a points system, as discussed in the next chapter, then access to higher points cost, powerful units need not result in a more powerful force; starting forces can have more limited options that broaden as the campaign goes on, so winners earn choices rather than direct power. Unfortunately, this can result in winners wanting to stick with a winning formula and losers feeling trapped in a losing one, so nothing really changes across the campaign.

NEGATIVE PROGRESSION

Progression systems may contain negative resources, most commonly injuries. Injuries add a sense of importance to in-game unit removal and create additional tension around decision-making. A player may be less eager to risk a trooper to claim an extra victory point if they are risking the availability of that trooper in subsequent sessions.

There are a few considerations around negative resources in progression systems. The first is that they risk doubling the snowball effect: if a player who loses receives fewer positive rewards and suffers negative rewards as well, they are punished twice. The second is that injury systems in particular quite commonly produce narrative dissonance if 'dead' models can be determined as 'not dead'. Imagine a trooper being struck by a powerful weapon – a shot which the mechanics tell us could have killed them five times over. The players frame the moment between themselves as the poor trooper being rendered into little more than a red mist, but come to the end of the game, the injury roll announces that they have made a full and miraculous recovery and will be seen, hale and hearty, for the next game. When designing a game intended for connected campaign play, be aware that the potentially hyperbolic descriptions of deaths and their sheer frequency from stand-alone games will need to be treated more carefully when forces are expected to return for further actions.

LOCKING UP THE SWEETSHOP

Many games have a standard mode where players have access to all options straight away. A number of campaign-centric games instead offer a limited set of starting options, and the majority of the in-game options (weapons, spells, abilities, etc.) must be discovered at random or unlocked across the campaign. To some players, this can feel unedifying, as much of the game's content and gameplay options are placed behind a 'play-wall' something, which, for want of a better term, we refer to as 'locking up the sweetshop'.

This style of progression system teases players with things they might want but may have to play for a long time to get, if they ever do. This is common in video games, but it can be combined with the delight of discovery, and the player may never learn what they missed out on. In a game presented as a rulebook or a set of cards, the player can trivially examine the content that is restricted to them.

The problem can be lessened by creating a system where players can target their efforts to gain specific rewards. Marrying advancements to narrative moments can help. If a character gets, say, a 'duellist' special ability for killing opposing named characters in single combat or a 'parkour' special ability for repeatedly successfully climbing or jumping, diegetic and non-diegetic rewards can be aligned.

Some of the most popular campaign progression systems, such as *Mordheim* (Cavatore, Pirinen and Priestly, 1999) and *Frostgrave* (McCullogh, 2015), have random tables for many elements of progression. That is to say, not only is the proverbial sweet-shop locked, but gaining access to it is made random and outside of player control, and many players enjoy this. It makes use of the powerful 'variable reward' effect (Nir Eyal, 2014) that drives the effectiveness of slot-machines and video-game loot boxes.

Arguably, players who choose to engage with a progression system-based gameplay mode self-select as those who appreciate following the story of the progress of their troopers from lowly nobody to mighty hero. For them, delaying access to upgrades is no more 'locking up the sweetshop' than starting a whodunnit with the name and modus operandi of the murderer, which is rather missing the point. This should not be taken as an excuse to ignore the needs of gamers who want to both tell a story and not have their power fantasy too heavily gated behind things outside of their control, but it does indicate that there is an attraction to never getting what you want in a campaign.

SUMMARY

Linking Frameworks provide rewards and can incentivise hobbies, but suffer from a drop-out problem. They come in three forms:

1. **Meta-scoring systems**, which allow results to be compared across games and are simple to design.
2. **Structuring systems**, which connect games together narratively sequentially, or using nodes or maps.
3. **Progression systems**, which allow players' forces to change and grow as they play more games, but which potentially suffer from snowballing and issues around locked options.

EXPERIMENTS

Create a sequential narrative campaign consisting of no more than six scenarios that is:

• Branching – no scenario may be repeated or reached by more than one set of results.
• Contained – every scenario must be played to reach the end of the campaign.
• Converging – exactly four scenarios should be played, whatever the results of each scenario is.
• Sprouting – at least four different narrative endings to the campaign should be provided.

Create a progression system, then create two forces and pass them through three games within the system where one force loses each game and the other wins. Ensure that a new player would be happy to take either force.

REFERENCES

Cavatore, A., Pirinen, T., Priestley, R., Stillman, N. and Thornton, J. (2000) *Warhammer: The Game of Fantasy Battles*. 6th edn. Nottingham: Games Workshop Ltd.

Cavatore, A., Pirinen, T. and Priestly, R. (1999) *Mordheim*. [Boardgame] Nottingham: Games Workshop Ltd.

Hoare, A. and McNeil, G. (2004) *Lustria*. Nottingham: Games Workshop Ltd.

Hyde, H. (2021) *Wargaming Campaigns*. Barnsley: Pen and Sword Military.

McCullogh, J. (2015) *Frostgrave*. Oxford: Osprey Games.

Nir Eyal, N. (2014) *Hooked: How to Build Habit-Forming Products*. New York, NY: Portfolio Penguin.

Priestly, R. and Stillman, N. (1990) *Mighty Empires*. [Boardgame] Nottingham: Games Workshop Ltd.

Schell, J. (2020) *The Art of Game Design: A Book of Lens*. Boca Raton, LF: CRC Press.

30 Forces and List Building

Few tabletop miniature games offer purely symmetrical forces to their players, and all provide a range of units with different capabilities. This is for good reason: having units with a range of asymmetrical capabilities provides opportunities to ask questions about the best use of those varied resources. Allowing players access to those units asymmetrically can provide methods to evoke specific historical elements or genre tropes.

STATISTICS

It is common practice to describe units with some set of statistics (usually numbers) that are used to both distinguish between the relative strengths and weaknesses of various units in the game and drive the game mechanics. These statistics might be attached to a unit, a weapon or an item, and their meanings transposed or combined with a unit thus equipped. These will vary by system but tend to fall into types.

PHYSICAL QUANTITIES

Regularly used with movement statistics, this type of statistic relates directly to a real-world physical property. For example, a movement statistic might be listed as four and thus allow its unit to move four inches across the tabletop.

INTANGIBLE QUANTITIES

This type of statistic states how much of a certain in-game resource a unit has access to, the most usual being the number of wounds they can take before being removed as a casualty, but it can also refer to the number of actions a unit can take when activated. While often controlling resources that refresh periodically during the game, these types of statistics can also be used for resources that do not refresh during the game, such as an ammunition limit.

TARGET NUMBERS

Statistics can list target numbers – the minimum number that needs to be rolled on a dice for a roll to be considered a success. For example, an armour save statistic might be given as five or '5+', indicating that the unit will need to roll a five or more to save a wound. The key advantage of presenting unit statistics as target numbers is that the player can look at the unit's statistics and understand exactly what they need to roll without further rules reference. This simplicity does bring a couple of disadvantages. Assuming higher numbers are better in your game, this system does mean that the lower statistic is more effective, which can be counter-intuitive for players.

 DOI: 10.1201/9781003314820-34

INDIRECT STATISTICS

Statistics can be used to indirectly generate target numbers via a simple mathematical formula (e.g. 'subtract the attack statistic from seven to find the target number') or look-up tables (such as is found in the weapon skill-driven to hit table of *Warhammer: The Game of Fantasy Battles*; Cavatore *et al.*, 2000).When compared with target number-style statistics, the advantages and disadvantages of indirect statistics are reversed. The fact that the statistic is abstracted one layer from the resolution mechanics provides flexibility and design space but at the cost of requiring the players to perform a mental calculation or to look-up a chart.

An instructive, if extreme, example of an indirect statistic is found in *Battlefleet Gothic* (Chambers, Johnson and Thorpe, 1999), in which the firepower statistic of a ship is compared indirectly with both the class of the target vessel and its relative aspect to the attacking ship. These are looked up on the gunnery table to produce a number of dice to be rolled. These dice are then rolled in direct comparison to the armour statistic, which acts as a target number statistic.

MODIFIERS

A simple method of avoiding look-up tables while keeping 'higher numbers are better' is to use statistics as modifiers to dice rolls that would otherwise have a static target number. For example, most actions in *This Is Not A Test* (McGuire, 2014) require the player to roll a D10 and add the relevant statistic with the hope of meeting or exceeding a target number.

DICE-TYPE STATISTICS

Statistics can be stated as one or another dice type, such as D4, D6, D8 and so on. Whenever the given statistic is to be used, the chosen dice is rolled. Commonly, in non-opposed tests, a static target number is provided by the game, and in opposed tests, the dice might simply be rolled against each other. This allows for modifiers to the rolled value of a dice and also for a dice to be shifted up or down a type, from a D6 to a D8, for example. *Burrows and Badgers* (Lovejoy, 2016) uses this system while including critical hits, based on a dice rolling its highest value, which always wins an opposed roll-off. Since D4s roll their highest number far more often than D12s, this creates an interesting underdog dynamic. These systems have an attractive elegance of not requiring tables to be looked up, but they do require players to own a range of unusual polygonal dice. On the other hand, since this system means massed dice rolling requires a significant investment from players and dice combinations can be difficult for players to calculate, it is best avoided in games with a scope that might require multiple combatants or a theme that would suffer from unpredictable swings of fate.

COMPARATIVE STATISTICS

It is possible to include a statistic whose only purpose is to act as a comparison with those of other units in the game. In *Inquisitor* (Thorpe, 2001), characters are sometimes called on to make tests against their speed and initiative statistics, but much more commonly, they are simply comparing those statistics passively to see who acts first in the round (characters act in speed order, with those of equal speed acting in initiative order).

Cost

The final sort of standard statistic is a cost or 'points value'. In order to make sure that players can be sure of a fair game, whether they are taking elite or untrained units, each profile will have a points value attached, and games will suggest a standard points limit for an average game. Units that are less able or resilient will cost fewer points, while those with more in-game utility will cost more, so players can select whatever they like so long as their total point values do not exceed the agreed limit. The process of selecting units with a total given value is commonly known as 'list building'.

LIST BUILDING

Many non-discrete games have the mixed blessing of rulebooks that are too long and complex for a player to learn without both study and experimentation at the table. The advantage of a game that takes a significant amount of effort to learn is that while many boxed games can suffer from a largely wasted first 'learning' game session, the common complexity of non-discrete games results in players who are more likely to arrive having actively studied and learned the rules. Since players are often studying the game alone prior to playing anyway, there is the chance to gamify that experience by allowing players to select units of asymmetrical abilities that suit varied playstyles and aims and begin making strategic decisions long before reaching the gaming tabletop. This process has the added advantage that solitary gaming time, which can be stretched over days or weeks of found moments in a very elastic fashion, can be used to get greater value from the more controlled and possibly rare group play session, not to mention being enjoyable and engaging in and of itself.

Not all games that offer list-building use 'point values', although most do. Points provide a relatively easy method of balancing units that most regular non-discrete gamers have a good understanding of and expect to encounter. However, they can be off-putting to newcomers to these sorts of games, and if a system doesn't intend to offer a fairly wide variety of options across a few factions, a points system can unnecessarily complicate manners.

The primary alternative is to allow players to select from a limited set of menus; for example, in the Path to Glory system from *Warhammer Age of Sigmar: General's Handbook* (2016), players select a leader who comes with an automatically generated set of units. These menus can consist of sets of troopers, units or even entirely pre-constructed forces. If a system intends to target more casual players, these more pre-set systems may well be more suitable, and offering pre-set lists for starting players can be a good idea even when a full points system is available.

BALANCING

At first, it can seem that balancing point values for forces should be a relatively simple mathematical problem. In theory, if each statistic is given a points value, then each trooper should simply be a total of the value of all their statistics, with some extra points for any special abilities.

In practice, this is not the case. Firstly, statistics are valued on more of a relative curve than a straight line. For example, if each point an attacker's strength is greater than a defender's toughness modifies a roll by plus one, then the seventh point of excess strength is useless. If success only needs four or more, then the fourth is useless, or the third if one always fail. As such, if most troopers in the game have a toughness of three, strength four is very valuable, but the value of strength six is dependent on the prevalence of toughness four. This means statistics used in opposed tests can never be said to be worth a set number of points. Secondly, units synergise within an army; a single shooting unit in a close combat force could reasonably cost less than a similar unit within a force where its abilities were tactically central. Lastly, abilities need, as far as is possible, to consider the psychology of someone using a given force. In the instance of the close combat force mentioned above, the player who would gravitate to such an army is unlikely to want to stay at range, wear an opponent down or let the enemy come to them. They are most likely concerned with finding the right devastating charge to win the game, as such ranged abilities will need to make themselves more tempting to be featured in their plans, although never so much that a player looking for a close-up army finds that they should be playing it as ranged.

The counterintuitive truth is that perfect balance is not necessarily a desirable goal. If all options are exactly as good as all other options, there is no advantage to or meaning in a player's choices; they would do just as well to flip a coin as make a decision. Poorer options allow players to make good choices. They also allow innovators to approach a problem in a novel fashion, taking a 'bad' choice and orchestrating its use to offset its weaknesses.

Setting and Balancing Points

Wildly unbalanced games have no real choices, and totally balanced ones also have no real choices, so you need to get in the area of balance but probably don't need to over-refine it. The first thing to get in the ballpark is to set some starting values. There's not really a secret to this; you need to start with an arbitrary number attached to what you suspect is going to be your average unit. If you suspect they're going to be a small particle of the game, such as a minion in a warband who might have a couple of pieces of equipment, then ten is most likely the right number to start with. If they're going to have more variation, such as a basic squad that might have more members, commands or other elements, start from 100. Bear in mind that these were arbitrary numbers; don't fall into the trap later in your design of thinking they hold some absolute truth. If you're struggling to break out the points for smaller options, you can double all values to provide more design space. Then you just need to go through some methods for balancing other prices around this one.

CALCULATIONS

A good starting point is to run the numbers and calculate relative values based on things like damage output or the ability to achieve objectives. By this point, you should have all the elements in place to calculate how much average damage a given unit will be able to do to your average unit over the course of a game, which should provide a simple point ratio. So, if an elite unit can kill two of your 100-point average units over the course of a game, the elite unit can have its point cost set at 200 points.

To put this in slightly more detail, if we have a ranged unit with a 24" range that wounds on four or more of a D6 and our average unit moves six inches a turn and has one wound, we can conclude that our ranged unit will tend to have four chances to cause a wound on a 50% chance of success. This will usually result in two wounds. Assuming our average unit will wound the ranged unit at a reasonably high rate in close contact, we can conclude that the ranged unit should cost double whatever we priced our average unit at. Gameplay reality will mean this is never entirely accurate, but it should provide a solid starting point from which to playtest.

OVER AND UNDER

Playtesting will be a process of iteration on your calculated values; the aim is to get the greatest possible accuracy at the minimum possible level of iteration. A good way to reduce iterations is to intentionally overshoot on value for the player during playtesting. That is to say, if you have a unit and it appears too expensive at 100 points, such that you suspect it might be worth 90 points, it's a better idea to price it at 80 points rather than 90 for the next round of playtesting. This is for three reasons. Firstly, if the unit is still too expensive at 90 points, then you've gone from knowing that the value should be less than 100 to knowing that it should be less than 90, which isn't really all that much advancement; 90 potential numbers are still quite a lot. If, instead, the unit is too cheap at 80 points, you've drastically reduced your range, and if it's too expensive at 80, you've saved yourself a step of iteration. Secondly, if you want your changes to get tested, making a choice more tempting to your playtesters will mean that it gets looked at more than if you made it closer to a balanced level. Lastly, you want to know if a choice is fun for your players as much as anything else. If a given option isn't fun for the person using it when it's overpowered, it's unlikely to be fun when it's well-balanced.

MASSED GUESSING

Many guesses are generally better than fewer, and enough guesses can actually begin to be extremely accurate. When you set a value for a unit during playtesting, you're making a single guess and then offering it to multiple people. You can instead have playtesters offer their guesses at the value of units, which can be done in a couple of ways:

- You can ask for direct ratings of units of a value from 1 to 5. These can then be averaged out to offer an alternative value multiplier from that created by flat calculations.

- You can ask players to select two opposing fair forces to a given point value, given a set value for your average unit, without them knowing which force they will be using.

With a sufficient range of these guesses, particularly from experienced playtesters, highly accurate point ranges can be arrived at.

FACTIONS

The asymmetrical selections of units that players are given access to are generally formed into 'factions', grouped sets of units described with joined backgrounds and abilities that both allow them to play in the fashion described and to synergise with other units from their faction. In addition, factions may well have special rules that apply to all units from that faction.

For example, in *Warhammer: The Game of Fantasy Battles*, players could choose to take a force consisting of undead creatures led by a powerful vampire from the 'Vampire Counts' faction. This faction has a set of special rules, such as causing fear in enemies and never fleeing from battle, and a range of upgrades available to make fear more effective during play. The faction is described as consisting of reanimated corpses controlled by necromantic magic; the available unit choices and faction-wide rules reinforce that narrative idea and, in addition, provide players with options that can be inventively deployed to build powerful synergies in the army.

For a game designer, factions have a range of uses. Players will tend to have preferences for a play style, and while they will be willing to branch out and experiment with other styles once comfortable with a game, playing in a style they are familiar with allows them to get to that point of comfort. By setting out factions, players can more easily and quickly find the play style that suits them. In addition, if all units are offered to all players, it can quickly become obvious after a few plays which units, or combinations of units, are superior. By asymmetrically limiting a player's unit choices, factions allow for a greater range of competitive armies and for armies that are weak against some factions but strong against others, keeping army selection interesting for players seeking to remain competitive.

FORCE ORGANISATION

With or without factions, many systems make use of selection limitations to create tensions and interest in list building. Typically, these will take the form of limitations on the numbers and grades of troops.

Limitations on numbers tend to take the form of requiring that a force have at least X many units, or units of a certain type, within it and sometimes no more than Y, stopping players from creating excessively elite forces or repeatedly taking certain choices. Many otherwise effective systems might break down if a player either puts all their eggs in one basket or pushes the principle of excessive numbers to its extreme conclusion.

Limitations on grades of troops: define certain groups of units as being of a given type, such as ranged, melee, vanguard, light, heavy, core, special or rare; the specific terms vary from system to system; then place requirements and limitations on those grades. *The Lord of the Rings: Strategy Battle Game* (Cavatore and Ward, 2005) limits armies to having no more than a third of their points spent on ranged troops. *Warhammer: The Game of Fantasy Battles* requires minimum numbers of units designated 'core' while setting maximums on those considered 'special' or 'rare'. These systems can create interesting puzzles, as limited slots need to be assigned to what are often a range of tempting choices. It also allows for options where certain characters or powers change what limitations are on a given force, allowing for specialised and narrative forces.

CASE STUDY: MULTIPLE CONTROLS – *WARMACHINE*

In *Warmachine* (McVey, Snoddy and Wilson, 2003), players select a force totalling a given number of points; certain units have a field allowance limiting how many duplicates can be taken; and units are organised into battlegroups, with characters having limitations on how they interact with units not in their battlegroup. In addition, it uses themed forces with tiered lists of options; if units matching the list are taken, players are given additional points, extended field allowances or additional abilities. These combine to create a list-building system that is both competitively challenging and intricate while being highly narrative.

Aside from controlling the units that can be taken by a player, systems will generally control how many troopers are permitted in a given unit. Many will also permit units to take on a range of upgrades, representing different armaments, ranks of leaders, banners and other items. Aside from costing points, these upgrades tend to present choices where the troopers of a unit can have a single set of equipment and be led by an individual of a single level of proficiency. Once again, these are layers of strategy and complexity for players to engage with.

It should be considered that while list-building restrictions are an effective tool for requiring mixed forces, they are an extrinsically imposed one, and it may be of interest to consider if our game designs can motivate the same player choices in a way that is more emergent from the rules mechanics or the game's victory conditions.

DESIGNING LIST BUILDING SYSTEMS

What a list-building system needs, as with most parts of a game, is dependent on what your design needs from it. If a game seeks to be on the more casual side, a very balanced system has distinct advantages since it doesn't ask players to learn too much or spend too long crafting the perfect force list to be competitive. If you want your players to spend some time crafting their lists, winning or losing and returning to their lists to fine-tune and adjust them into an engine of terrible magnificence, then there are some things you might want to consider trying to create in your force selection system.

Synergy

Synergy is the process whereby a final product becomes more than the sum of its parts. As an example in faction design, imagine a system that has a rule for troopers being on fire and that there is a character who can set targets on fire for an action or make people who are on fire easier to hit for an action. Those are beneficial abilities; fire is no doubt inconvenient to the enemy, so setting them on fire is bound to be good, and once the character has set them on fire with one action, they can make them easier to hit with another so other troopers could finish them off. If, however, there is a basic trooper who can set targets on fire, they and this character each become better than they would be on their own when put together. Now the fire trooper can set a few targets on fire, and the character can make them easier to hit to allow other normal troopers to take them down. The fire abilities synergise to make the fire-giving troopers more valuable than they would be on their own, making a list that includes them along with the character more points efficient. That is to say, each skill is fairly priced on its own, so when they are bought together, the synergistic effect is an essentially free bonus ability that is given to a player as a reward for spotting the combination. Their skill in list building makes them better at the tabletop. Players who return to the game repeatedly will spot and hone these combinations, developing specific heuristics and experiencing the satisfying process of learning and improving.

A key advantage of synergistic force designs is that they encourage players to act in a certain way without forcing them to. In the example above, players using the pyromaniac character want to set things on fire and want to bring more troopers who can do so. The character can be described in pyroclastic terms in the background, and sessions will play out as described, leading players to find a sense of immersion and a connection to the story behind the game, providing both narrative and game-play rewards simultaneously. Also, as a designer, you should be aware of which parts of your game are most enjoyable to engage with. Synergistic force design can direct players to engage with systems that are satisfying to manipulate and use during play, increasing playtime centred on parts you want to show off.

Intentional Design of an Evolving 'Meta'

Players will engage with your game and play it; someone will win and someone will lose, and hopefully, they will all want to play the game again. At which point, the losing player will have a choice to make. They might decide that they lost because of mistakes made while playing and use the same list again, with the intention to play it more effectively next time. Likely, they will decide that their list could use some form of improvement. How they decide to modify their list in the search for excellence is one of the ways in which your game can develop a 'meta' within a given gaming group (or an entire community if the game's popularity justifies it).

There are, in general terms, two ways a player can react to having been beaten by their regular opponent; they can decide to find a route around what their opponent did, or they can copy it. It is one of the small joys of having a game in wider circulation that this process will take place in many isolated pockets with various people heading in various directions while believing their version of events is what the game *is*. However, irrespective of what will or won't happen, it is your job as a designer to try and ensure that both paths remain interesting for the players that take them.

The easiest path to make interesting is one of evolutionary competition, where one player finds option A, leading to their opponent responding with choice B, leading to plan C and so on. Players are inventive, and the human mind can find a massive range of options and plans. All a game designer needs to do is show once or twice that there are solutions within the system to a range of lists. Once players have seen that the tools to respond to powerful options exist, they will have the trust that it's worth searching for those tools even when they are not instantly obvious. The process of play leading to force list development is a 'play loop' that players want to engage with. The cardinal sin is to create learned helplessness by causing players to feel that there is no response to an early or obvious strategy. As a game is tested, which is to say, run with players, certain initial strategies should become obvious; laying in a first layer of responses to those strategies is generally sufficient to show players that it is worth seeking solutions.

Somewhat tougher is when players adopt an 'if you can't beat them, join them' position where, once beaten, they attempt to do exactly what their opponent did. Non-discrete games can't force asymmetry on players in the manner that boxed games can. Creating mirror lists of an opponent is within the rules. There are two ways of making this path interesting. The first is to have a core system that is interesting to operate. Identical forces will put increased pressure on whichever part of the system they exploit, but they have the advantage (in game design terms) of removing the advantage of asymmetry, resulting in a play session that becomes about engaging with the core system, which is a good thing for a fun and robust system. The second method is to realise that even when a player chooses to copy their opponent, they will seek to improve on them to a small degree, usually by maximising the strengths of their strategy. It should be ensured that this sort of maximisation creates a fragile list. If each unit has a rock, paper, scissors effect and both players choose to maximise their rock units until that's all they have, it shouldn't be too long until someone brings an all-paper army.

LIST BUILDING AT THE TABLE

As mentioned above, list building is valuable in that it can extend engagement with your game away from the table. However, it can also result in lists so finely tuned that the action on the tabletop becomes all but superfluous. One response to this can be seen in *Malifaux* (Anderson *et al.*, 2013) and *A Billion Suns* (Hutchinson, 2021), which require players to build their list immediately before or even during the play session. In these systems, the objectives of a given play session are generated, and then players are asked to create their lists, offering a significant advantage to the player who can adjust to the emergent tactical situation just generated.

One potential disadvantage of a 'build at the table' system is that the game loses the ability to engage players away from the tabletop in a gamified fashion. Another is that it requires that play sessions include time for selecting a list or reduce playtime. In addition, when a system comes with its own range of miniatures, it demands players to own a greater section of that range to have the widest possible set of options to be competitive. For many games, the primary claim they have to strategy is that within list building, by making list building a more tactical decision, that claim is largely lost. However, for a very tight, competitive system, it can push the most capable players to the heights of tactical play.

BURIED TREASURE AND BREADCRUMBS

When creating a faction system, we need to ensure that what is put into the game is there for the player, not for the designer. It should be a series of breadcrumbs along a path that creates an enjoyable journey, rather than a process of burying the treasure. If there is a wonderful, synergistic build available in an army list, then hiding that among a series of units and upgrades will simply mean that some players never get to experience the fun of running that engine. You've locked away some of your sweetest and tastiest moments behind an excellence-based barrier to entry. Rather, your game should lay out some clear signposts to a few parts of the engine: abilities that clearly reference each other, elements that become cheaper when bought together or parts that directly name other units. A well-crafted army selection system can be a process of exploration and discovery, an Easter egg hunt between designer and player. As long as players can see a path to a response, their engagement with the process of list building and re-building will quickly become a self-sustaining, virtuous circle.

WEAK IS ACCEPTABLE, FORGETTABLE IS NOT

Tabletop gaming is replete with fascinating and entirely useless options; weak choices are not bad game design; forgettable choices are. It is far more interesting and beneficial to put in a piece of an engine that doesn't work but that looks like it could than another cog that does exactly the same job as five other perfectly good cogs you also put in.

SUMMARY

- Units have **statistics**, which can be:
  - **Physical**, referring to a real-world element such as movement distance.
  - **Intangible**, referring to in-game resources such as action points.
  - **Target numbers**, such as a saving throw.
  - **Indirect**, which are used to reference formulae or look-up tables.
  - **Modifiers**, added to dice for tests.
  - **Dice types**, showing which dice should be rolled when using the relevant statistic.
  - **Comparative**, used in comparison to another unit's statistics.
  - **Cost**, the price in the game's currency to take the unit, is central to the balancing of asymmetrical forces.
- Asymmetrical **Factions** offer players the chance for self-expression while giving guidance.
  - **Force organisation** systems allow for tighter control of player choices and further list-building guidance.

EXPERIMENTS

Identify what you consider to be the most important statistic in your design, make each of the types of statistic one after another and test it out. Make it a different statistic type for each unit, and then play.

Give all players access to all units in your game freely. Allow them to use only three units, but they may choose which three. Decide exactly which units they can use in their lists.

REFERENCES

Anderson, M., Caroland, N., Cohen, R., Darland, A., Gibbs, J., Hanold, D., Johns, E., Martin, M. and Weber, D. (2013) *Malifaux: Second Edition*. South Korea: Wyrd Miniatures, LLC.

Cavatore, A., Pirinen, T., Priestley, R., Stillman, N. and Thornton, J. (2000) *Warhammer: The Game of Fantasy Battles*. 6th edn. Nottingham: Games Workshop Ltd.

Cavatore, A. and Ward, M. (2005) *The Lord of the Rings: Strategy Battle Game*. Nottingham: Games Workshop Ltd.

Chambers, A., Johnson, J. and Thorpe, G. (1999) *Battlefleet Gothic*. Nottingham: Games Workshop Ltd.

Hutchinson, M. (2021) *A Billion Suns*. Oxford: Osprey Games.

Lovejoy, M. (2016) *Burrows and Badgers: A Skirmish Game of Anthropomorphic Animals*. Oxford: Osprey Games.

McGuire, J. (2014) *This Is Not a Test*. Gambrills: World's End Publishing.

McVey, M., Snoddy, B. and Wilson, M. (2003) *Warmachine*. Bellevue, WA: Privateer Press.

Thorpe, G. (2001) *Inquisitor*. Nottingham: Games Workshop Ltd.

Warhammer Age of Sigmar: General's Handbook. (2016) Nottingham: Games Workshop Ltd.

31 Conclusion

Game over! Time to count up your victory points.

The journey to this point began with the question, 'what *are* these games that we make?' It was the topic of the first episode of our podcast, and it took us more than 200 episodes (and hundred-thousand words of this book) to get confident with our answer.

There is a magic in the freedom that pushing miniatures around on an unfettered tabletop provides, and it has always captivated us. Figuring out what creates that magic could have led to it being dispelled, but, for both of us, our fascination with these games has only grown through this project.

We have dissected as much as we had space to in this book, but left a great deal unsaid. Our opinions, convictions and mental models have shifted across the preparation of this book and no doubt will shift again as we experiment more, discuss more and design more. Take what is written here as a first attempt at a holistic definition of the design space of these games, but neither a complete nor conclusive one. We are excited to hear from you and understand what you see differently or what you feel we have missed that is critical to your design approach or your enjoyment as a player. Come and find us through our Rule of Carnage podcast and design community, and we'll continue the discussion there!

We have two hopes for this book. Firstly, if you find the terminology proposed and defined useful and valuable, adopt the parts that suit you and adapt the parts that don't, and through this terminology, we are able to communicate more fluently as a design community. Our other hope is that you will be inspired to look beyond these games' roots and conventions and push them into exciting and novel places. We hope you find ways to tell new stories, provide new experiences and (yikes!) even make miniatures games that aren't about killing each other.

Thanks,
Glenn & Mike

DOI: 10.1201/9781003314820-35

Appendix 1: Tabletop Miniatures Game Prototyping Toolkit

We have examined a wide body of non-discrete miniatures game systems, analysed and itemised the common features shared by most tabletop miniatures game rules systems and identified the prevailing design conventions used by designers in implementing those features. We have discussed the hypothetical implementations of these features at length, comparing the strengths and weaknesses of various approaches and drawing on examples from published games to illustrate the patterns apparent to us.

Moving from the hypothetical to the concrete, and as a companion to this book, we have created a tabletop miniatures game prototyping toolkit as an online tool. This toolkit contains generic implementations of many of the rules features discussed in this book and provides a small array of options for each in order to illustrate some of the possible approaches.

You can generate a new miniatures game in moments by using our online tool: https://planetsmashergames.com/fundamentals/prototyping-toolkit.

The toolkit is provided partly as a rapid prototyping tool, allowing you to generate the skeleton of a tabletop miniatures game in moments. It also exists to make the point that if a design simply reorganises common mechanical tropes into a new order, it is unlikely to be an effective design. Effective game design tightly integrates its core ideas with mechanics to shape the players' experiences. This toolkit doesn't create interesting games; it creates functional ones. It can be used as a starting point or as an inspiration.

PUBLIC DOMAIN

The toolkit and its outputs are offered in the public domain via CC0 1.0 Universal. We waive all of our rights to the work worldwide under copyright law, including all related and neighbouring rights, to the extent allowed by law. You can copy, modify, distribute and perform either the output or the code of this toolkit, even for commercial purposes, with no permission or attribution required.

Index

3D printing, 10
7TV, 61, 89, 117, 135, 199

A

A Billion Suns, 23, 92, 102, 114, 125, 131, 167, 211, 232
Activation, 95, 102, 116, 117, 133, 135–141, 168
  activation advantage, 139, 196
  activation points, 116–119, 141
  activation system, 135–137
  alternating activation, 135
  full force, 135
  partial force, 135
  simultaneous, 141
  single unit, 135, 137, 139, 140
Adeptus Titanicus, 7, 15, 162, 166, 182, 187
Agency, 62, 79, 109, 191
Asymmetrical deployment, 130
Attacks, 15, 88
  deviation, 189
  eanged, 167, 168
  pinning, 190
  and terrain, 174
Aura, 13, 208

B

Background, 108, 208, 229, 231
Bag Pull, 95
Balance, 227, 228
Base sizes, 30, 71
Battlefleet Gothic, 15, 187, 225
BattleTech, 12, 111, 148
Blood Bowl, 113, 114, 136, 185, 190
Bluffing, 79, 103, 105
Bolt Action, 75, 95, 138, 173, 194
Breaking, 158
Britains, 9
Buff, 159, 207
Burrows and Badgers, 77, 92, 225

C

Campaign, 215–221
  branching, 217
  and hobby, 41, 215
  map, 218
  node, 218
  progression, 32, 49, 220, 221
Cards, 24, 30, 79, 82, 99, 100–105, 118, 134, 138, 142

Carnevale, 88, 149, 180
Chainmail, 6, 10
Charge, 140, 150–152
  advantage, 152
  differentiation, 151
  line of Sight, 163, 169
  reaction, 151, 152
  uncertainty, 78, 150
Chess, 9, 80
Climbing, 149, 174, 180
Close combat, 15, 157, 167
  forced, 14
Command range, 138
Competence, 82, 99
Complexity
  and abilities, 206
  and downtime, 96
  tolerance, 18
  and uncertainty, 78, 80
Components, 24, 31, 138, 142
  legacy, 81
Concealed information, 79, 82
Conceit, 52, 53, 108, 113
Conflict, 53
Control removal, 112, 185–191
Cover, 164, 168, 174–179, 182
Criticals, 91, 92, 180, 225

D

Damage, 86, 116, 153, 157, 158, 167, 186, 193–195, 228
Debuff, 159, 207
Deck, 82, 101, 104, 138
Deployment zones, 126, 128–131, 212
  unanchored, 131
Detail, 63, 76
Deviation, 189
Dexterity, 9, 95, 96, 104, 105, 142
  and uncertainty, 78
Dice, 84–97, 137, 205
  and cards, 105
  and uncertainty, 81
  custom, 85, 93
  pools, 87, 88
  statistics, 225
Diegetic, 39–43, 58, 62, 199, 217, 220, 221
Disengagement, 152
Donald Featherstone, 10, 126
Downtime, 96, 133, 136, 137
Dracula's America, 134, 167

Printed in the United States
by Baker & Taylor Publisher Services